RECONSTRUCTING NATURE

One of the main features of contemporary environmental crisis is that no-one has a clear picture of what is taking place. Environmental problems are real enough but they bring home the inadequacy of our knowledge. How does the natural world relate to the social world? Why do we continue to have such a poor understanding? How can ecological knowledge be made to relate to our understanding of human society?

The book argues that the division of labour is a key but neglected factor underlying people's inability to adequately understand and relate to the natural world. The argument extends Marx's theory of alienation to account for inadequate knowledge and therefore inadequate concern for nature. Using recent developments in 'critical realist' philosophy, the book aims to find ways of reorganising knowledge in the light of ecological consciousness. It also corrects the emphasis of much environmental literature by focusing on production rather than consumption.

Peter Dickens is Reader in Sociology at the University of Sussex.

INTERNATIONAL LIBRARY OF SOCIOLOGY
Founded by Karl Mannheim
Editor: John Urry
Lancaster University

RECONSTRUCTING NATURE

Alienation, emancipation and the division of labour

Peter Dickens

London and New York

First published 1996
by Routledge
11 New Fetter Lane, London EC4P 4EE

Simultaneously published in the USA and Canada
by Routledge
29 West 35th Street, New York, NY 10001

Routledge is an International Thomson Publishing company I T P

Typeset in Garamond by Routledge
Printed and bound in Great Britain by
Clays Ltd, St Ives PLC

British Library Cataloguing in Publication Data
A catalogue record for this book is available from the British Library

Library of Congress Cataloguing in Publication Data
Dickens, Peter, 1940–
Reconstructing nature: alienation, emancipation, and the
division of labour / Peter Dickens.
Includes bibliographical references and index.
1. Human ecology – Philosophy. 2. Division of labor.
3. Marxian school of sociology. I. Title.
GF21.D49 1996
304.2' 01–dc20

ISBN 0–415–08921–2 (hbk)
ISBN 0–415–08922–0 (pbk)

To Tristram and Aldous with affection

The idea of one basis for life and another for science is from the very outset a lie . . . . Natural science will in time subsume the science of man, just as the science of man will subsume natural science: there will be *one* science.

K. Marx (1844), *Economic and Philosophical Manuscripts*

As a consequence of a more advanced division of labour, each mind finds itself directed towards a different point on the horizon, reflects a different aspect of the world and as a result the content of men's minds differ from one subject to another. One is thus proceeding to a state of affairs, now almost attained, in which the members of a single group no longer have anything in common other than their humanity.

E. Durkheim (1898),
'Individualism and the intellectuals', *La Revue Blanche*

CONTENTS

CONTENTS

ILLUSTRATIONS

FIGURES

TABLES

ACKNOWLEDGEMENTS

Special thanks to Tim Hayward and Andrew Sayer. They read through the whole manuscript in detail and made a number of invaluable comments. Thanks too for suggestions from Janet Collett, Caroline New, Jenneth Parker, John Parry, Graham Sharp, Neil Stammers and Bron Szerszynski. Ted Benton, Luke Martell and Kate Soper have, over the years, provided particular kinds of assistance. The staff of Sussex University's unique Mass-Observation Archive have been especially helpful. John Urry waited patiently for the manuscript and made a number of very useful suggestions when it finally arrived. David Cocks kept body and soul together. Finally, many thanks to Anna for all kinds of support and encouragement.

The University of Sussex has been a continuous source of assistance. It provided me with a term's leave to work on this book. Furthermore, it has long been an excellent setting for interdisciplinary research and teaching. This book has largely stemmed from an undergraduate course in the School of Social Sciences called 'Health, Food and Nature'.

The Mass-Observation extracts are reproduced with the permission of the Trustees of the Mass-Observation Archive, University of Sussex, reproduced by permission of Curtis Brown Group Ltd, London. Fig. 1.1 is reproduced with permission of the Causeway Press Ltd and Fig. 2.1 with the permission of Routledge.

Longer-term debts will become clear in the book. Suffice to say here that these acknowledgements were written on the centenary of the day Engels's ashes were scattered over the sea at Beachy Head, near where I live.

Peter Dickens
Lewes, 11 August 1995

INTRODUCTION

This book proposes a new view of the relations between society and nature. It focuses on the way human societies work on nature to produce the things they need. In particular, it is concerned with the technical division of labour in the workplace and the broader division of labour within society at large. Such divisions have obviously brought great benefits and must be a central element of any future modern society. On the other hand, they have fragmented our understanding of how societies relate to nature. They have been used to marginalise lay knowledge of nature. Furthermore, they have been used to neglect certain people's tacit understandings. This latter refers to the skills and judgements which people create for themselves in all kinds of work. Information and instructions associated with explicit knowledge can be quite easily formulated, copied, stored and communicated. But this is not the case with tacit knowledge, where the skills cannot be encoded, formulated, contained and stored in the form of words and symbols. The neglect, marginalisation and decay of these lay and tacit forms of knowledge results not only in a misunderstanding and misuse of the environment but in people's misunderstanding of their own organic nature.

Divisions of labour, divisions of knowledge and the consequent mistreatment of nature are therefore the key themes. But how can the necessarily complex knowledges and divisions of labour in a future society be made compatible with an improved understanding? How can such an understanding lead not only to human emancipation but to a recognition of natural limits and the needs of other species? By considerably extending and developing Marx's theory of alienation, this book tries to open up these difficult questions for debate and further research.

A MESSAGE FROM THE KOGI

In 1989 the historian and television producer Alan Ereira visited the Kogi, an archaic civilisation in Colombia that has deliberately kept itself in isolation from the rest of the modern world. Still ruled by a priesthood and still living a culture and philosophy which has remained largely untouched by the advances

1

of modernity, they sent the message out to Ereira that they had a message for 'the Younger Brother', all the people who lived outside (Ereira 1990).

Their message was that modern society is ruining the world through environmental destruction. The Kogi did not know when, or even if, there would be a calamitous collapse but they did know that very large-scale changes were being made to the environment and that these were threatening human and non-human life. Their knowledge was, and still is, based on a minute observation of the world: the details of plant and animal life, for example. It is also based on their knowledge of the most sacred area of the Sierra Nevada, the snowpeaks near where they live. Ereira visited this area and found it dried up. The snow that usually covered the area year after year had almost completely gone. Like many ancient civilisations, the Kogi believe the earth to be alive. It is a mother offering sustenance. And yet, they say,

> The Mother is suffering.
> They have broken her teeth
> and taken out her eyes and ears.
> She vomits,
> she has diarrhoea,
> she is ill.

There are several points to this story. Perhaps the most important is that the Kogi *know* what is happening. They do not have access to modern science and knowledge. But they appreciate on the basis of their everyday knowledge and the culture handed down to them through thousands of years that something profound was occurring. Indeed, it is precisely *because* they had no access to modern ways of thinking that they were most aware of what was happening. Modernity, 'the Younger Brother', knows a great deal, they say, but this is disqualifying him from actually understanding. Modern societies decry such knowledge. Worse than this, modern knowledge is being used destructively.

> Younger Brother thinks
> 'Yes! Here I am! I know much about the universe!'
> But this knowing is learning to destroy the world,
> to destroy everything,
> all humanity.

The Kogi are reminding the Younger Brother that we have, for all the advances made by modern science and modern social science, very little understanding of our relations to nature. Our knowledge of the environment and of our relations to nature are characterised by considerable ignorance. This is the price to be paid for what are sometimes called the 'reflexive modernity' and 'detraditionalisation' associated with the modernisation of society (Lash 1994, Giddens 1991). Modernity seems to be characterised by people critically reflecting on the rules and knowledges handed down to them. They are taking their lives into their own hands, making their biographies without the benefits of generations of handed-down wisdom and demanding that traditions continue justifying their existence. Such features of modernity are, of course, emancipatory in many ways. Increased scientific understanding of nature and of ourselves has, for example, brought clear and great benefits. At the same time, and most paradoxically, the simultaneous creation and marginalisation of 'lay' understanding and tacit knowledge have in key respects made modern people more ignorant of themselves and their relations with the environment.

Such failure to understand has provided a field-day for competing ideologies. According to many in the environmental movement, we are confronting imminent and large-scale catastrophe. On the other hand, according to an increasingly influential group of pro-market New Right scientists, politicians, economists and journalists' we can relax. There is no problem. No imminent or large-scale collapse has been proved by any kind of science. There have been, for example, large-scale changes in the earth's temperature over millions of years. There is no need to assume that the current changes are anything other than part of a naturally recurring cycle.

Furthermore, these commentators argue that the environmental crisis is being cooked up by socialists. Having lost the battle against capitalism the Left, in conjunction with others such as feminists, is making a comeback. This time they are inventing a new scare to frighten people and get them all marching under a red/green banner (Beckerman 1995, North 1995, Ridley 1995). Furthermore, the neo-liberals and others who argue that all is still for the best in the best of all possible worlds, argue that even if there is a problem it would certainly be unwise to take large-scale and costly measures. In the light of our ignorance, they suggest, such strategies could well turn out to be disastrously wrong in the longer run. We are all bright and intelligent people, the argument goes. Insofar as policy is needed, the best is an incremental one whereby the environment and rare species are costed and individuals and companies pay for any environmental damage they are causing. Capitalism and the market are the solution to environmental problems, not the problem.

These arguments were prefigured with the so-called 'Tragedy of the Commons' thesis. This suggests that resources which are available to all only encourage environmental degradation, as each individual person uses them as much as possible. The benefit to the individual of such use greatly outweighs his or her costs in terms of the slight decline in the quality of life spread over the population as a whole. This 'free rider problem' eventually ends up, it is argued, in such resources being rapidly exhausted and everyone finishing up with nothing. The answer, it is suggested, is well-defined property rights. On this basis the resources will not disappear since there are now owners who have an interest in ensuring that this does not happen. The argument is, however, wrong on a number of grounds. For one thing history shows private property is no guarantee that environmental degradation will not ensue. As often happens, neo-liberals seem to be assuming an (imagined) eighteenth century world of small businesses. As Sayer (1995: 157) puts it:

> A smallholder might have an interest in sustainable exploitation, though market conditions might prevent them achieving this, but an international logging company has little interest in conserving trees in particular areas even if it owns the land on which they grow.

The position of this book within these arguments must be declared. Coming from a broadly 'green socialist' position, its author belongs firmly to that camp of people which, according to the New Right at least, is trying to manipulate and subvert the thoughts of passive populations throughout the entire world. (So far, it must be said, with rather little success.) As will become clear later, I feel extremely critical about contemporary capitalist society, its social structures, institutions and the ways it is treating the environment. On the other hand, to concentrate the attack on capitalism alone may be to miss a central problem, that of the advanced division of labour under modernity. Furthermore, it surely is the case that the free-market economists, politicians and others who insist that we do not know very much have a very serious point. All this again leads this book to the conclusion that the core problem is the division of labour and the associated divisions between knowledges. Szerszynski (1996), writing of pre-modern relations between society and nature, puts the matter as follows:

> Once, it seems, we knew what to do. Until the early modern period, knowing who we were, and in what practice we were engaged, told us all we needed to know about what we ought to do.

Try as one might, it is actually very difficult to find a consensus over, for example, global warming, famine and resource crisis. As the Kogi have insisted, our great advances in knowledge have not resulted in our achieving a greater understanding. Furthermore, conventional Marxism and socialism by no means have a necessary monopoly of wisdom and insight into these matters. How, for example, do they account for extensive widespread destruction in the old socialist or 'communist' societies? This must lead us to a departure from conventional Marxism, or at least a considerable extension of what was just a small part of his work.

The purpose of this book, therefore, is to set out on a journey towards a greater understanding. This is of course an impossibly ambitious task within one book. It is rendered even more difficult by being aware of the undoubted intellectual and material achievements made by modern society (something which the anti-green movement is better at emphasising than the Left, albeit in a highly Panglossian way) while remaining cautious and critical of these same achievements. This study is just one step along the way towards an eventual wholesale reorganisation of knowledge in the light of ecological consciousness and potential environmental crisis.

This book is partly about the physical reconstruction of nature by soci But it is also about the reconstruction of our knowledge *of* nature and o relations with it. The current organisation of knowledge about these relations (or, more accurately, its chaotic disorganisation) is a key theme. Such fragmentation obviously brings a large number of benefits. Again, few would want to reject outright the advances made by modern societies in understanding the physical, natural and human worlds. And the more that we work on nature to produce the things wanted by human beings, the more we enable human beings to develop their own capacities for innovation and creativeness. But divisions of labour are at the same time seriously disabling. They mean severe failures to communicate between different areas of knowledge.

One of the main reasons why an archaic society such as the Kogi feel confident about their relations with their environment and know what to do in relation to it is that they have a radically different understanding of it. Anthropological work on such peoples shows that they usually do not use the category 'nature' to understand themselves and their relationships with the rest of the world (Ingold 1990). As Figure I.1 shows, for them there is only one world: one inhabited by other humans, by non-human entities such as plants and by inanimate entities such as rocks, water and air. In modern societies, by contrast, a radical division takes place in how people understand their relationships with the environment. On the one hand, humans are seen in relation to a society constituted by other human beings. This is normally the province of the social sciences. On the other hand, there also exists a sphere of life called 'nature', one usually only studied by the natural and physical sciences. Human beings in modern societies consider themselves to be both social or cultural persons (a product, that is, of society) and biological or natural beings. In this latter sense they have close similarities with other beings.

The book therefore particularly focuses on the division of labour. This is the key difference between this study and others linking human societies to the natural and physical environment. Other recent work (for example, Benton 1993, Hayward 1995, Soper 1995) has very successfully linked political economy and other branches of social theory such as feminism to the environmental question. This book is firmly in line with these new directions. But at the same time it seeks to develop them with reference to the division of labour. This is one of the most central and yet most neglected features of modern society. And yet it rarely figures in discussions about our relations with nature.

The division of labour refers to the system of work specialisation that characterises all human societies. As a result of such specialisation people become dependent on one another (Sayer 1995). The division of labour is perhaps best known as a concept used for understanding relationships between people in places of paid work. This is clearly important, but the concept also applies to the relations between people and households with respect to domestic work. Race and age, as well as class and gender also form bases for

Pre-modern societies

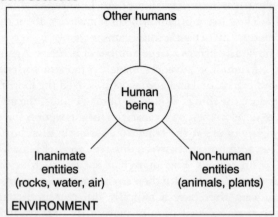

Human beings in pre-modern societies do not usually distinguish between 'society' and 'nature'. For them there is only one world, containing humans, inanimate entities and non-human entities. Knowledge of that world is gained through dwelling in it and interacting with it.

Modern societies

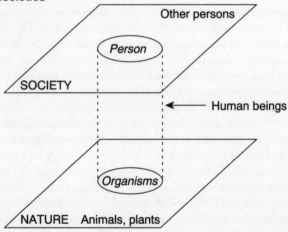

Human beings in modern societies typically distinguish between *two* worlds: human society on the one hand and 'nature' on the other. Yet in practice people are, as *human organisms*, part of both these worlds. In modern societies humans depend less on knowledge gained through direct interaction with the environment and much more on abstract knowledge gained through stepping out of the environment.

Figure I.1 Concepts of people and environment (after Ingold 1990)

6

the division of labour. As Sayer and Walker (1992) argue, the division of labour is founded on the work that a society conducts in transforming nature into its needs. It is:

> an irreducible technical foundation in the nature of the work to be done to produce a desired result from materials provided by nature and by history. Every labor process contains a series of ordered tasks as well as particular tools and knowledge. Where these exceed the capacity of an individual worker, who cannot master more than a finite number of tasks, a division of labor will eventuate. As jobs diverge in significant ways, owing to the nature of the specific materials, tools, or products involved, so will the skills and the ways of working of those holding different jobs.
>
> (p.16)

Ancient civilisations such as the Kogi in Colombia are characterised by relatively simple ways of transforming nature into the things they need. They are usually involved in exchanging goods between families, tribes and settlements, but they are not engaged in anything resembling the mass-production of commodities for cash. As a result, the technical division of labour in the production process is comparatively simple. So too is the social division of labour, the division between enterprises or between different units within society at large. And, by the same token, such division simultaneously implies comparatively little social interdependence. Relations within particular small-scale societies may of course be intense. But such interdependency is comparatively uncomplicated seen in relation to today's globalised interconnections between specialised workers of many kinds. Archaic societies such as the Kogi are also founded on an overlapping of land, production and consumption. In an important sense they know where they stand in relation to their environment. This is partly because their everyday lives, unlike those of us in modern societies, are bound up with it. And it is largely because of this that they 'know' when things are going wrong.

The spatial expression of such divisions is an important but subordinate theme and we will discuss these in more detail later. Our main focus here is on the social and technical divisions of labour more generally. The labour processes and social relations of production within a society such as the Kogi are, and were, fairly straightforward and comprehensible to those involved. In modern societies, however, they are far more complex. And the argument here is that the complex divisions of labour and the processes involved in working on nature in modern societies are not simply a product of capitalism. They are a product of modernity. Our particular focus here is on the labour process. Some kind of overarching control and coordination needs to be exercised over the technical division of labour; the very complex processes by which nature is converted into the things people need and buy. Some degree of management will be needed, some kind of supervisory process by which modern production processes are coordinated. But again, this is not to say that such supervision has to be done by the people who own, control and profit by the machines that are used. There could be other divisions of labour and other ways of managing complex production processes besides those which have evolved under either capitalism or state socialism. As Marx put it with reference to capitalism,

> a musical conductor need in no way be the owner of the instruments in his orchestra, nor does it form part of his function as a conductor that he should have any part in paying the 'wages' of the other musicians.
>
> (1981, p. 511)

The division of labour in modern society is therefore a key but neglected factor lying behind the inability of people in modern societies to adequately understand and relate to the natural world. Paradoxically, the more sophisticated have modern societies become in shaping nature, the less have they an overall understanding of that same nature.

As will become clear, such conversion of nature into things also includes the work which takes place outside workplaces, particularly that in the home. Much of this is, of course, carried out by women and children and not the industrial worker who was the focus of Marx's concerns. As in the case of paid employment, such work is of course a product of power relations, especially those between men on the one hand and women and children on the other. On the other hand, they are also partly a product of the division of labour itself. The social division of labour within society at large is to some extent also a product of the fact that not everyone can carry out all the types of task which an advanced society needs carrying out. It combines, again in complex ways, with the power relations between different groups, especially of course between men and women. It is caught up with, but is not reducible to, either the struggles between genders over work in the home or the relations between workers in places of employment.

The division of labour therefore has a dynamic of its own, one that is partly independent of the particular kind of society in which it is located. Furthermore the division of labour implies some kind of social hierarchy, all large-scale labour processes needing direction. In practice, of course, it is very difficult to disentangle the power relations actually involved in any real-world division of labour from the degree of control necessitated by the complexity of a modern production process. In any actual, real, society the division of labour is exacerbated by people trying to monopolise and defend particular skills and parts of the labour process.

But again, few people (including few environmentalists) would seriously want to return to the world of the Kogi. The dominance of a priesthood and the subordinate position of women and young people are surely wholly unacceptable to most people in modern societies. Yet modernity, and especially modernity with its green tinge, wants to have its cake and eat it, to gain from the many benefits of modernity and yet dispense with the disbenefits.

As suggested earlier, this book attempts to locate environmental issues within political economy. But the division of labour is the core theme running through the whole text. And in different ways this recurs throughout. This emphasis acts as a corrective and a supplement to the environmental literature. First, much of this work remains in the sphere of consumption, or what I later call 'civil society'. Many of the problems, however, start in the sphere of industrial production. But this latter sphere, it might be argued, is also now well recognised as the cause of environmental crises. This is true, but the particular way in which production is recognised remains insufficient. This book gives particular attention to the relationships and processes within production. These, it is argued, are the central cause of people in modern society misunderstanding their relationships with nature. It is in the conversion of nature into the commodities we need that many of the problems start.

Moreover, the issue is not simply that of how capitalism converts nature into the things we need. There is now a growing literature within radical political economy which suggests that environmental crisis is a product of capitalism's rapaciousness towards resources and other species. There is again much to recommend this argument. But it is insufficient insofar as it again does not recognise the alienation of nature which seems a central, and possibly even permanent, feature of modern society. To put this another way, it is just about possible to envisage a sustainable capitalist society, one which has adapted itself to the environmental limits within which it is operating. But the relationships and processes within modern society, involving greater or lesser degrees of local, national or international public intervention, will still leave people misunderstanding and alienated from the natural world. One chapter of this book, drawing on lay accounts of the relations between people and nature, attempts to illustrate this type of alienation. Again, all this is largely because the types of knowledge which are available for such understanding remain fragmented. The division of labour which is necessary for a modern society to progress socially and economically operates against the understanding that members of such a society need to understand their relations to their environment. In particular it militates against an understanding which links people's lay and tacit knowledges with more abstract theories and understandings.

The first three chapters of this book are linked. They sketch out, with the aid of realist epistemology, what is entailed if we are to gain a better understanding of our relations with nature. **Chapter 1** pursues the notion that modern society has largely disabled itself from understanding its relations to nature through the way in which knowledge has been constructed. Humans have remarkably advanced creative capacities for developing concepts and making things on the basis of these pre-formed ideas. As Marx in particular argued in his early writings, they definitely gain and develop themselves as human beings through constructing nature in ways that they have thought through and found emotionally satisfying. Such thinking and creative action can even be on behalf of other species. But, despite this, the way in which humans have divided

9

their thinking and their process of transforming nature manages to deny many of the advantages which they hold over other species.

The division of labour also includes the many divisions between different types of abstract knowledge – between the natural, physical and social sciences in particular. Sayer and Walker (1992:1) rightly say that 'the division of labor is one of the most neglected categories in contemporary political economy and social theory'. This despite the fact that it was a central theme for political economy from the eighteenth century onwards and for sociology up to the early twentieth century. Adam Smith and Emile Durkheim are of course key figures in this regard.

But even Sayer and Walker do not fully draw out the important effects of fragmentations between different types of mental labour. Such academic disciplines as physics, chemistry, politics and sociology have clearly made immense strides on their own. Their models and concepts dominate our understanding and displace lay and tacit knowledges because they can be stored, copied, transferred and more easily sold as commodities than people's more practical understandings. The danger now is not only that they no longer connect to everyday knowledge but that such abstract sciences are talking past each other. This, despite the fact that they are in reality intimately connected with one another. The mechanisms of the natural world are rooted in the laws of physics. The mechanisms of the social world are rooted in the laws of biology. Furthermore, human societies are, it seems, having increasingly deleterious 'feedback' effects on the precise ways in which physical and biological mechanisms are working out in practice. And yet the division of labour results in our ignoring these connections.

A further division of knowledge, that between abstract and concrete, is examined in **Chapter 2**. This chapter explores this division, examining the dimensions and extents of people's estrangement from nature. Realist philosophy, or 'critical realism', again offers ways of reorganising knowledge. It envisages knowledge as stratified. On the one hand there are relatively enduring generative structures and causal mechanisms in both the human social and the natural worlds. These enable us to conceptualise links between the different strata of nature on the one hand and society on the other. Entities such as humans, other organisms and those of inorganic nature are seen as having latent powers or ways of acting. These combine with one another. On the other hand, and most importantly, they also combine in complex ways with contingent circumstances and other tendencies to produce what is actually experienced or observed. In other words, contingent factors are centrally important in affecting how generative structures and mechanisms work out in practice. Indeed, they may be so important that such underlying mechanisms and causal powers are not observed or experienced at all.

The central benefit of this type of epistemology and ontology is that explanation of concrete events proceeds through recognising and combining both abstract laws and theories as well as information of a less abstract form.

Realism certainly does not on its own ensure that the abstract laws and theories we use are actually right. It is just as possible for scientists and social scientists using a realist framework to make 'howlers' as those using any other kind of framework. But it at least gives some sense of overview and a sense of the kinds of theories that are needed if we are to connect different types of knowledge. It can be used, for example, to begin sketching in how sciences such as physics, the natural sciences and the social sciences relate to one another. But as Chapter 2 suggests, it indicates the forms in which such sciences need to be constructed to be compatible with one another. Living organisms, for example, need to be seen as carriers of potentials and capacities which may or may not be realised. This is in contrast to, for example, the more fashionable view of organisms as 'survival machines' whose underlying purpose is to replicate genes into future generations (Dawkins 1976). Later chapters show, for example, some recent developments in the life sciences which are realist in outlook and constitute a very marked improvement on an approach which sees organisms as mere gene-replicators.

There is no suggestion here that biologists should become sociologists, or even vice versa. The important thing is to link different areas of intellectual work and share similar perspectives on the ways in which organisms (including the human organism) are organised and how their powers and capacities relate dialectically to their environments. The idea of creating 'One Science' is utopian and not necessarily desirable. Chapter 2 indicates how different types of abstract knowledge can be combined with other information to build up theoretically well-informed understandings of concrete events. It suggests that when Marxists, feminists and others talk of alienation from nature they need to explore the multiple and combined forms in which such alienation takes place. Such combinations, I argue, lie behind many contemporary forms of 'green politics'. The argument is developed with the aid of two case studies. One is concerned with indigenous peoples' relations with nature and the other with factory farming.

A central debate within contemporary environmental studies is between those who believe in the possibility of realism and those who would dismiss this type of understanding. The latter group of people, sometimes referred to as 'social constructionists', argue that all knowledge is a social construction . . . full stop. In other words, there can be no question of underlying causal mechanisms and powers. According to this line of argument, theory is only a product of language and power-play. There are no particularly privileged knowledges. There is no reality over and above that described by language and discourse. 'Strong' social constructionism of this kind is in part a result of the very division of labour of which this book complains. It is, in part at least, a product of the social sciences' asserting that they have a total understanding of the world, natural and human alike. **Chapter 3** attempts to take stock of these arguments. It also attempts, with the aid of some illustrations, to show how these perspectives relate to, and are indeed dependent on, each other. One of the main conclusions drawn from this chapter is that a distinction needs to be made between, on the one hand, theoretically informed accounts of the concrete (as particularly proposed by academics) and, on the other, the lay and tacit knowledges gained in the course of everyday life. These three forms of knowledge are often conflated and it is important to separate them if we are to develop a satisfactory general understanding of people's alienation from nature and from their own being. But the main theme of this chapter is that, while all forms of knowledge are socially constituted, this should not be used to deny the possibility that there exist real causal mechanisms which are generating the concrete events we can observe, feel and communicate about. Furthermore, the large-scale intellectual industry currently surrounding 'strong social constructionism' is making a great fuss of a routine part of social life. Social constructionists of the 'strong' variety are really elaborating on the self-evident fact that people use language to describe how the world works and that this language is socially constructed. The fact that language is caught up in power relations is an important consideration. But it need not be treated as a wholly new revelation and one worth concentrating on at the expense of discovering the mechanisms in the natural and social worlds affecting how the material world actually works.

The complexity of lay knowledge is the main theme of **Chapter** 4. This is a case study of attitudes towards scientific understandings of relations between society and nature. It uses material from a special survey undertaken by the Mass-Observation Archive at the University of Sussex. It is an attempt to show what might be actually meant when we say people are alienated from nature. Rather little is known about the kinds of knowledge which lay people actually have. This study first shows not only complex but often contradictory attitudes towards science. A number of leading sociologists argue that modernity is characterised by increasing reflexivity. As regards relations to the environment this is supposed to imply systematic and wholesale criticism of modern science by the population at large. But this turns out to be only partly true. Most people do indeed see science as an evolving and vulnerable enterprise, but they combine this with a view which continues to place considerable faith in science as indeed reflecting how the real world works. Thus the contributors to the Archive have, like academics and everyone else, a socially constructed knowledge of their relation with the environment. But from a theoretical viewpoint it is not well informed. They have taken on board much of the understanding offered by scientists but, despite this, they remain very unclear as regards their relations with the environment. This leads to a (somewhat tentative!) proposal that the languages people use to understand nature and their relationships with it may be a product of people's innate causal powers to make sense of their circumstances. The ways in which they try to make sense of their experience is through the transposing of the familiar on to the non-familiar. Nature, for example, has in the past often been conceived as a female entity, one which is caring but which is subject to retribution if used exploitatively (Merchant

1980). Few people (or at least few people in modern Western society) construct nature in such a way now. But they are prone to transfer their experience in the human social world on to their understanding of nature. This helps people to gain a sense of being, of connection with the world. And arguably it is the product of powers within the human psyche itself.

Having developed a general understanding of alienation, one based largely on the largely necessary division of labour in modern society and the separation of abstract from lay and tacit forms of knowledge, the remaining chapters are intended to develop such an understanding with reference to the main areas of contemporary social life. Given the emphasis of this book on the division of labour, it should come as no surprise that industrial production is given special attention. This accounts for the early prominence of **Chapter 5**, a section of the book giving special attention to genetic engineering and the emergent reproductive technologies. Here the raw materials being incorporated into the production process are not inert. In this case the inputted materials are living beings and their causal powers for growth and development. Modern industry characteristically disassembles elements of nature as a prelude to their reconstruction. In these particular industries the parts given such attention by the scientists and their subordinates in the production process are elements such as the gene and parts of the human body. Their separation and manipulation to produce new combinations of living things bring about potential gains to human and other species which often go unrecognised by the environmental movement. These include the mass-production of food and the curing of certain types of illness.

But while recognising their potential for good, this chapter also recognises their 'down-sides'. Does the solution to mass-hunger lie less in technical fixes and more in political strategies to end what Susan George (1986) calls the 'planned scarcity' of food? If so, where does this leave the technology? Such reconstructions of nature bring simultaneous disadvantages. These include the possibility of disastrous unintended consequences through genetic engineering. One of the best-known unintended consequences is the case of the so-called 'Beltsville Pigs'. They had their growth boosted by cow genes. But they went lame with arthritis at an early age and had heart problems and bulging eyeballs. Similarly, an additional gene (one suspected of being linked to cancer) was introduced into another group of pigs. This made them excellent as commodities, their hams and shoulders growing big and meaty. But by the time they were three months old their legs were unable to support them (Ryan 1995). Similarly, sheep in Australia have been injected with hormones bioengineered to cause wool-shedding. These so-called 'self-shearing' sheep suffered from sunburn and the effects of excessive heat. Bizarrely, they are now wrapped in large nets to hold the wool close to the sheep's bodies. Similar problems, all deriving from attempts to enhance the value of animals or to make them produce commercially valuable substances, have been experienced by cows and chickens (O'Brien 1995a,b).

In other words, for all the disassembly and reassembly of such organisms, the underlying powers and limits of organisms and of organism–environment relations remain intact. The causal mechanisms have not been changed. Indeed bioengineering depends on these mechanisms. But they are distorted as a result of human interventions with unsatisfactory and incomplete knowledge. In these instances the limits of nature have been met, though they are of course experienced by the animals involved and not by the humans that caused them.

Furthermore, environmentalists in particular point to the possible unintended consequences of manipulating small parts of ecosystems on such systems as a whole. Again, most us have a feeling something is likely to go wrong, but no-one seems to really know what the consequences might be. At all events, it is in the silent and under-publicised sphere of production that the humanisation of nature is, with all its gains and losses, truly occurring. And it is again here that such humanisation is paradoxically resulting in the human species having little understanding of the 'nature' which they themselves are creating.

All this contrasts considerably with civil society, the subject of **Chapter 6**. Here a new element is added to the general argument. The division of labour has a spatial and temporal element. To an increasing extent industrial production is organised at a global scale. This means that people, whose lives are inevitably restricted to small-scale localities, are dependent on processes and relationships of which they have precious little knowledge. Furthermore, local nature becomes just an input into this globally oriented production system. The nearest we get to the labour process involved in converting nature into food is the check-out at the hypermarket.

Such a perspective is helpful when we turn to civil society. This is a sphere of social life in which commodities are bought and sold. It is also the sphere of social life in which the potentially anarchic division of labour is to some extent regulated. If production processes typically fragment and globalise, the consumption and exchange of commodities are characterised by some kind of coordinating process. It is here that the making of commodities is coordinated with their selling. The coordinating function of the market can, however, be overestimated. The first part of this chapter gives special attention to how these arguments link to the relations between civil society and nature. Carving up the environment into market commodities is problematic in many ways, not least because it provides little insight into how our relations with the causal processes of nature actually work. But it is the way things are increasingly done, and the problems of not valuing the environment via the market certainly need to be recognised. Furthermore, green consumerism may be important in consciousness raising, in perhaps prefiguring new kinds of relation between society and nature of which we are yet only dimly aware.

Civil society is also the sphere in which social relations and cultures are reproduced. Chapter 6 builds on Chapter 3 by looking at the relationships between, on the one hand, how human beings both use and are constrained by the structures and causal powers of nature and, on the other hand, the various forms of social construction made by environmentalists and academics associated with theories of postmodernity. Using and extending the work of Raymond Williams, the chapter argues that the discourses and social constructions offered by these authors are a product of the crisis of understanding what is 'human' and what is 'natural' in a time when both are being increasingly made to interpenetrate each other. Finally, the chapter raises the issue of green politics, especially those forms of politics which remain largely located within civil society. This refers to the brand of green thinking which emphasises an 'alternative' consciousness, often based on non-Western cultures. This part of Chapter 6 argues that it would be too easy to dismiss such thinking as superficial since it avoids a radical critique of modernity. There is certainly something in such an argument, but these movements may be developing important new (or indeed very old) insights into the causal powers and capacities of human beings. Furthermore, they may also be important in formulating alternative futures, in presaging new kinds of society in which people better understand the relations between external and their own, internal, nature.

How does the above discussion relate to green politics and state power? This is the question addressed in **Chapter 7**. States have a major role to play in the administration of knowledge and, in particular, with the promotion of more general knowledge. This is a result of their role in the management of social systems. However, the knowledge recognised and promoted by states, and more particularly by their bureaucracies, cannot accommodate the many detailed practical and tacit knowledges of people in local areas. Such knowledges can be partly recognised by local and regional states, but there will always be tensions between, on the one hand, such local understandings and politics and, on the other hand, those promoted by central governments and quasi-state international institutions. The chapter pursues the relation between state power, bureaucracy and knowledge. It argues that the fragmentation of knowledge, which is exacerbated by the spatial division of labour, tends to de-legitimate the institutions associated with state authority. The so-called 'New Social Movements' have an important role in this process of exposing the contradictions surrounding national states. More generally, the chapter concludes by suggesting that these emergent struggles are a product of alienation, of people's simply not understanding themselves and the links between their knowledge and that advanced by the forms of abstract science advanced by governments.

It is easier to oppose than to propose, and **Chapter 8** undertakes the more difficult task of specifying ways forward towards emancipation. The chapter examines some contemporary green utopias. These are in many ways helpful, not least because some of them (and in particular those explored in Chapter 8) do at least recognise human social relations and the division of labour as an important cause of many environmental problems. But in other ways they are unhelpful. 'Community' is often advanced as a serious way forward but the chapter argues (much as is argued above in relation to the Kogi communities) that 'community' should not be seen as such a panacea. The different forms of knowledge that can be gained in small-scale localities can certainly be a basis for recovering an improved form of environmental awareness and possibly changed actions 'on the ground'. But community is not, on its own, adequate. If the central problem is that of alienation in its many forms, it is this that needs addressing. National, even international, agencies still have a major role to play, though this would be in an enabling capacity. They would be charged, that is, with supporting and networking local and regionally based initiatives. Difficulties, however, remain. These include the division of labour between enterprises and the problem of people gaining an understanding of their connectedness in this regard. Some forms of alienation from nature, and separation of people from their own species, will be extraordinarily difficult to overcome.

A similar point is made in Chapter 8 about the new forms of communications technologies which are allowing the mass-transfer of knowledge and information of all kinds. This is sometimes seen as 'a virtual community', one inaugurating a new era of citizenship and democracy as increasing numbers of people have access to information. Chapter 8 remains very doubtful about these claims but does suggest that these new technologies could be used or subverted for genuinely emancipatory ends. Finally, the chapter introduces political work by trade unions, groups in civil society, government and education. These are addressing some of the problems of the division of labour and the problems of knowledge addressed earlier in this book. Markets and divisions of labour of course persist, but their form is shifted in favour of the less powerful. A strategy of the kind developed here combines environmental politics with questions of power and social justice. The two are intimately combined in the real social and political world. But this is often forgotten by elements of the environmental movement.

This book is 'Marxist' in the sense that it builds on insights of Marx, some of which are no more than passing comments. The hope, however, is to build on Marx's edifice, to construct something appropriate for a time when concerns have shifted elsewhere, particularly of course to the internal and external limits to social development. There are four aspects of Marx's earlier and later work that are especially inspirational for our own time. Perhaps chief of these is his brief assertion (written when he was in his mid 20s!) that a prime source of alienation lay in the way in which modern knowledge is fragmented and organised. This is a dimension of alienation which neither he nor later commentators have developed in any detail. Pursuing this concern has led this study to adopt a realist philosophy of knowledge. As outlined earlier, this does not on its own provide a guarantee of accurate understanding. It leaves most of the hard work to be done but it at least begins to indicate how broad areas of understanding (physics, the natural sciences, the social sciences and the like) might relate to one another. Secondly, Marx's endorsement and embrace of modernity (including his recognition of the positive features of modern society, science and technology) are important correctives to much backward-looking green utopian thinking. Third, his insistence that in changing nature we change ourselves is surely right. Many of us, including many environmentalists, have become used to thinking of nature as 'something out there', a landscape that we consume or observe. Rather, our emphasis should turn to nature as something people work on and in the process 'humanise'. 'Nature' includes human nature, the capacities and potentials which constitute us as human beings. And in humanising nature through working on it with others we start to change ourselves in multiple, unpredictable and potentially emancipating ways. Finally, Marx's work warns us to remain aware of tendencies in modern society which may prefigure future social forms. As outlined in Chapter 8, cases in point are the new communications technologies and the emergence of large numbers of people now working outside formal employment. They too are working on nature to produce the things they need. The 'trick' as regards all these developments is that of capturing them and transforming them towards more emancipatory outcomes.

A brief Epilogue uses the arguments of this book to address an important on-going debate. Does humanism amount to speciesism and the systematic misuse of resources? Like other contemporary writers, this author remains optimistic about the potential for creating a form of humanism which recognises the needs of other species and the necessity of living within natural limits. But this potential is likely to remain unrealised if the social and technical divisions of labour continue to fragment and confuse the relations between different types of knowledge while marginalising the understanding that lay people have of themselves and their relations to the natural world. The central dilemma is that such divisions are a necessary and in many ways desirable feature of modernity.

1

SOCIETY, NATURE AND THE BALKANISATION OF ABSTRACT KNOWLEDGE

Over one hundred years ago Marx and Engels were pointing to the impacts of human civilisation on the natural world. There might be, they argued, one or two islands left in the Pacific which could still be counted as untouched by humanity. But essentially the whole of nature on earth had now become influenced by human activities. Nature had become 'humanised'.

Marx and Engels drew a number of conclusions from this. Perhaps best known, as mentioned earlier, is their celebration of humanity's conquering of nature. A strong theme in much of their work was that human emancipation lay precisely through such domination (Schmidt 1971, Grundmann 1991, Dickens 1992, Benton 1993, Pepper 1993). Nature, harnessed to the needs of human society, meant final freedom from the struggle by human beings to survive. It also meant that people were using their creative capacities towards achieving their own liberation. But dominating nature meant not only using it to human ends but increasingly understanding it. Such understanding meant that humans were developing their latent powers. They were transforming themselves in the process of transforming nature. Marx and Engels's vision was thus forward-looking and in some respects highly optimistic.

But they also argued that the precise ways in which nature was being conquered could also have profoundly damaging effects. Capitalism, while offering emancipation in key respects, simultaneously alienated people in others. People become separated from nature, particularly as a result of the institution of private property and of modern production processes. The latter meant that nature had become reduced to mere raw materials rather than something to be valued and lived with in its own right.

These contradictory themes will be pursued and developed later in this study. But two further aspects of Marx and Engels's work on society and nature are especially relevant at this point. The first is that 'victories' over nature are by no means trouble-free. They might at first seem wholly unproblematic and beneficial but in the longer run such appearances could be illusory. As Engels now famously put it:

Let us not flatter ourselves overmuch on account of our human victories

18

over nature. For each such victory takes its revenge on us. Each victory, it is true, in the first place brings about the results we expected, but in the second and third places it has quite different, unforeseen effects which only too often cancel the first.

(1959: 12)

Second, both these authors were alive to the implications of such humanisation of nature for knowledge itself. Marx, in his earliest manuscripts, recognised that separate compartments of knowledge – one set for human beings and another for nature – could no longer suffice in a world where society was becoming increasingly humanised. Such divisions were obfuscatory in a world where the two were being combined in increasingly complex ways.

The idea of one basis for life and another for science is from the very outset a lie . . . . Natural science will in time subsume the science of man just as the science of man will subsume natural science: there will be one science.

(1975: 328)

Apart from a few such lines, however, Marx was never to take up this theme again. But much later in the nineteenth century Engels attempted to demonstrate what such a 'one science' would look like. His unfinished work *The Dialectics of Nature* (Engels 1959) was an attempt to show how the physical, natural and human worlds interacted. His attempt can be seen as a triumph of dialectical thinking over the ways in which the non-human world actually works (Harvey 1993). There is something in this argument. It was certainly ambitious and of course reflected the overly-mechanistic scientific outlooks of his era. But at the same time it can be seen as a remarkably early prefiguring of many of the concerns now being expressed by some scientists (Woods and Grant 1995). Contemporary chaos theory and theories of complexity are centrally concerned with the interactions between the parts and the wholes of systems. Individual elements such as atoms or neurons are permanently unstable in their form; they are said to be continually shifting between chaotic and stable regimes. Chaos theory suggests that complex systems of all types have emergent features and regularities which are characteristic features of the dynamic interplay between the structures of the whole system and the elements which constitute them (Gleick 1987). Such a view very much parallels Engels's thinking in *The Dialectics of Nature*, this of course being originally influenced by Hegelian dialectics.

As suggested above, however, severe difficulties start when attempts are made to impose dialectical ways of *thinking* onto systems in which the actual, material relations between the parts and the whole are highly complex and composed of elements, unlike atoms, which are capable of conceptualising their circumstances and taking action. Chaos theory is now being extended well beyond the physical world to the study of biological and even social and economic systems. As Gleick puts it:

19

Now that science is looking, chaos seems to be everywhere. A rising column of cigarette smoke breaks into wild swirls. A flag snaps back and forth in the wind. A dripping faucet goes from a steady pattern to a random one. Chaos appears in the behavior of the weather, the behavior of an airplane in flight, the behavior of cars clustering on an expressway, the behavior of oil flowing in underground pipes.

(1987: 5)

But there are real problems in discovering chaos and the inherent principles of order 'everywhere'. For, as we move from theories of physics (from where the theory emerged) towards the world of real observable effects, we must inevitably encounter a vast range of mediating and complicating social, cultural and environmental factors which must affect the behaviour of the elements under observation. Cars driven by presumably thinking human beings are made analogous in some of this literature to atoms. Studying 'the behaviour of oil flowing in underground pipes' becomes detached from the effects of world oil prices. In short, there is danger of reifying 'holism' of the kind originally implied by contemporary thinking in physics. Indeed, there comes a point where pure science, along with the Creationism associated with 'Big Bang' thinking, starts to acquire a quasi-religious significance, one which has been wholly removed from how the world actually works.

This book argues for a recovery of Marx and Engels's original insights and thinking, but one which avoids slavish copying of their work or extending dialectical analysis in an unthinking fashion. It builds on their work in ways which have not really been attempted since. Several themes above (the combination of human society and nature, 'nature's revenges' and 'one science') are particularly worth pursuing. As we will discuss further in Chapter 5, nature is indeed becoming increasingly 'humanised'. And this increasingly refers to internal nature: the constitution of human beings themselves. Some of nature's potential counter-attacks now seem to be occurring as a result of such intervention.

On the other hand, and very paradoxically, it is now very clear that the intellectual bases we have for understanding them are becoming increasingly inadequate. Indeed, as the following section of this chapter will discuss in more detail, there are now *several* bases for understanding human life and several for understanding the physical and natural worlds. Such diversity is in many respects a great strength. It means that very considerable progress has made by individual disciplines in helping human beings to understand themselves and their relationships with their environment. At the same time, such fragmentation or balkanisation of knowledge through its containment in watertight compartments has proceeded apace. This same process also lies in the way of human emancipation.

This is partly a result of what MacNaghten and Urry (1995) call 'the Durkheimian desire to carve out a separate realm or sphere of the social which

20

could be investigated and explained autonomously'. But at the same time it is a process which, as we will see later, has a powerful social and political basis outside the objective of scientists and intellectuals themselves. Either way, the process means that there is rather little useful holistic understanding of what is taking place. Progress has certainly been made as a result of fragmented and highly specialised knowledges, but in key respects we remain unclear of our relations to nature because of an inadequate understanding of how these knowledges *connect with one another* in the process of producing the concrete outcomes in which we are interested. The result is a kind of alienation from nature which Marx's early work briefly mentioned and which Engels's later work tried to overcome.

This chapter pursues these themes, outlining what many see as contemporary 'revenges' of nature on society, the fragmented understanding of these processes, the social processes underlying this understanding and a conceptual basis for a new unfragmented view.

NATURE'S REVENGES OR A CRISIS IN UNDERSTANDING? ON THE FRAGMENTATION OF ABSTRACT KNOWLEDGE

As many in the environmental movement point out, postwar development has so far been largely dedicated to unbridled production and consumption, with technology largely devoted to these ends. This applies both to the capitalist West as well as the Soviet Union and its East European satellites. At 1987 prices the gross world product has expanded from $5 trillion in 1950 to about $18 trillion in the mid 1990s. There are of course several immediate *caveats* to be made about this. There was a global downturn in the early 1990s. There are also enormous disparities between societies. In China, for example, the economy has expanded very rapidly as a result of introducing a form of market-based allocation of resources. At the same time, parts of the former Soviet Union have declined very precipitously. Furthermore, if environmental costs had been included in the calculations of world production (those, for example, of medical costs arising from environmental pollution) then these levels of growth would have been much less or even negative. Finally, there is some indication that physical constraints to such growth are now emerging, in particular those of the forests, grasslands and fisheries (Brown *et al.* 1993).

In short, large-scale economic growth has been occurring under modernity, even if certain limits are now becoming apparent. However, perhaps even more important than physical limits are the apparent 'revenges' resulting from this economic growth. Many of these results of economic growth are well documented (see, for example, Elsworth 1990, Mannion 1991). One of the best known is the 'acid rain' resulting from the burning of enormous quantities of coal and oil. This in turn generates large amounts of polluting gases. Acid air pollution affects the environment in a number of ways and, through diverse pathways, 'kills human beings, animals, trees, vegetation and lakes over enormous areas' (Elsworth 1990: 1). Unlike all of nature's revenges it is truly international in scope. 'It is', in Elsworth's words, 'exported between countries in millions of tonnes'. One result is what Beck (1992a) calls the 'democracy' of environmental pollution. It can be highly indiscriminate towards different social classes, despite the attempts by the more affluent to escape the worst effects.

Forms of environmental degradation other than acid rain pose, however, a number of difficulties. In particular, they are subject to a great deal of uncertainty about the relationships between environmental change and human activity. This is largely the result of fragmented understandings. And these not only include divisions between the physical, natural and social sciences. They also entail, as we will see, divisions between different scientists within the same discipline.

It is possible to point to historically very long-term cycles in global warming. However, this outcome may be the result of a number of different causal processes and relationships. Is it part of a recurring cycle of warming and cooling which has little to do with the activities of human beings? Or is it the product of industrialisation and mass consumption? It seems that world temperatures are now higher than they have ever been since records started to be made. At the time of writing the hottest year ever recorded was 1990. And the six next hottest years ever measured worldwide occurred during the 1980s. These increases have been occurring slowly and erratically, indeed there have been some declines of late (see Figure 1.1). But the world does seem to have slowly warmed up by about 0.5 degree C during the last century. And, as Gribbin and Gribbin put it, 'even this tiny increase in world temperature is a big change compared with natural shifts in global weather patterns' (1992: 9).

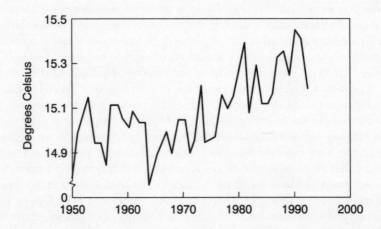

Figure 1.1 Global warming: one of nature's revenges? (from Brown *et al.* 1993)

But again, is this the product of a natural cycle or of human intervention? Once more it must be again admitted that understanding of the complex processes involved remains very far from complete. The general mechanisms are now quite well understood. But the hitherto quite cautious Intergovernmental Panel on Climatic Change (IPCC) has recently adjudged that the most recent evidence on global warming indicates 'a detectable human influence on global climate' (Lean 1995). Furthermore, they suggest that malaria, dengue fever and yellow fever are beginning to move out of their traditional areas as the climate heats up. They predict, however, that Western Europe could become colder as the changing climate affects the Gulf Stream. Meanwhile, large-scale floods are predicted for low-lying areas many of which are already poverty-stricken and unable to take satisfactory precautions. Bangladesh is one such region. Some of these changes can, it seems, now be observed. Seas are said to be now rising. And it is estimated that by the year 2000 they will be nearly 15 centimetres higher than when measurements began. The world's richest countries are committed to stabilising emissions of carbon dioxide by the year 2000 but IPCC argues that, because the greenhouse gases persist in the atmosphere for over 100 years, there can be no early escape from these revenges. There remains the question, however, of how good these alarming predictions really are. Why are they being made now? We will return to this shortly.

Just as significant are predicted extremes of all kinds in weather patterns. On the one hand there does seem to have been a rise in the number of droughts. Significantly, these are not limited to African countries where the possible revenges of nature have been exacerbated by civil war. The mid-west area of the USA ('the breadbasket of the world') has, for example, experienced an increasing number of crop failures (Gribbin 1990: 92). At the same time, it has been predicted for some time by climatologists that global warming will result in storms becoming more common and severe. Strong storms feed off warm water as it evaporates from the ocean and vapour rises into the air. From there it condenses back into liquid water and falls as rain. Gribbin and Gribbin describe the physical processes taking place.

> When the vapour turns back into liquid it gives out just as much heat to the air as it took to evaporate the water in the first place. This heat is the energy that drives the winds of the hurricane.
>
> (1992: 60)

But it is once more extremely difficult, given the divided form of current understanding, to assert hard and fast causes and effects. In particular, the physicists make little connection between their analysis and the ways in which the human social world actually operates. This is a core problem in developing an adequate understanding. Despite continuing uncertainties, however, many authors are persuaded that the greenhouse effect is now actually occurring (see, for example, Gribbin 1990, Gribbin and Gribbin 1992). During the past few years, hurricanes which have occurred appear to have been far stronger than any

23

observed before. To an increasing extent such extremes are seen as early signs of global warming. But, again, it is clear that knowledge remains inadequate. Lay understanding mirrors science itself in being almost wholly ignorant as to whether or not profound environmental change is actually occurring and whether this is the result of human intervention. In the end, individuals are left to their own devices. At a wholly anecdotal level a hurricane (though British weather authorities prefer to call it The Great Storm) destroyed this author's house in 1987. Perhaps this is the main reason why in the end he at least finds the evidence so persuasive!

The general physical and chemical mechanisms underlying all this seem to be getting better understood. Gases that human society is putting into the atmosphere are trapping heat that was previously escaping into space. The so-called 'greenhouse gases' trapping heat in the atmosphere are carbon dioxide, methane and the chlorofluorocarbons (CFCs) that also destroy the ozone layer. These gases are a product of those forms of production and consumption that modernity holds so dear. These include industry of all kinds (including agriculture), power stations and cars. The felling of forests is likely to further contribute to this process. Over the long term such destruction can be seen as massively contributing to global warming.

> When forests are leveled, the elements that composed the wood and tissue are partially converted into greenhouse gases. Then when forests are regrown, an equivalent amount of the elements are recalled into solid matter. The net loss of tropical forest cover worldwide during 1850–1980 contributed between 90 and 120 billion metric tons of carbon dioxide to the earth's atmosphere, not far below the 165 billion metric tons emanating from the burning of coal, oil, and gas. These two processes together have raised the concentration of carbon dioxide in the global atmosphere by more than 25 percent, setting the stage for global warming and a rise in the sea level.
>
> (Wilson 1992: 293)

But while the general processes and their possibly disastrous outcomes are understood in a broad sense, there is still very little understanding of concrete events 'on the ground'. A key factor underlying such failure to understand is that there are now very substantial social, economic and political interests offering their own self-interested scientific analyses of what is taking place. As late as the 1970s there seems to have been a broad consensus between scientists and government agencies on global warming, one which remained cautious about suggesting that it was the product of human society. Now the consensus is breaking down (Boehmer-Christiansen 1994b). Some scientists are suggesting that the end of the world is nigh, perhaps in an attempt to attract substantial research-grants. Similarly, some national and international government bureaucracies, many of which are also subject to budgetary constraints, will have an active interest in taking advantage of the uncertainty to promote their own interests. (Boehmer-Christiansen 1995a,b). Meanwhile, the scientists associated with the fossil fuel industry and the oil exporters also exploit the uncertainties to promote their particular products.

In these ways 'environmental crisis' remains in quotation-marks. It is a social construction. But does this matter? For example, some 'revenges' may well be happening despite the fact that they are being articulated by certain vested interests. The problem is again that of the fragmentation of interests and the difficulty of linking abstract science with knowledge of the particular social and environmental circumstances of geographical regions.

The mechanisms associated with another possible revenge, the thinning of the ozone layer, are also now becoming relatively well understood. But again, there is so far little understanding of how these mechanisms combine with local conditions and the well-being of different species. In this case the science principally involved is chemistry. Ozone, a variant of oxygen, can be poisonous to life. If it occurs near to the ground (as a result of, for example, industrial pollution) it can be hazardous to human health and to plants (Elsworth 1990). But at a safe distance it remains essential to the well-being of humans and other animals (Gribbin 1988). The ozone in the stratosphere protects the earth from the ultraviolet radiation and extreme heat produced by the sun. It is not, however, particularly stable. Chlorine in particular speeds up the breakdown of ozone molecules, this leading to the depletion of the ozone layer. Chlorine is one of the constituents of chlorofluorocarbons (CFCs), these being used as blowing agents in foam used to make hamburger cartons, other forms of packaging and insulation materials for houses. Their use has expanded massively since the 1940s (Elsworth 1990). It seems possible that there may be other humanly produced threats to the ozone layer. These include the large-scale use of nitrogen oxide for farmland fertilisation.

The resulting possible 'revenges' of the thinner ozone layer on humans also seem to be increasingly well documented. The incidence of malignant melanoma has been increasing throughout the world and it seems at least possible that increased exposure to ultraviolet radiation is associated with the suppression of the human immune system, the body's natural defence mechanisms. One effect of this is to increase the incidence of a range of infections by the herpes virus, hepatitis and skin infections caused by parasites (Gribbin 1988). As with many modern forms of disease, however, it is important to remember that the human life-span is meanwhile increasing. Nature's revenges are not in general killing people earlier. Paradoxically, we are leading longer lives. The problem is more that we are leading *unhealthier* longer lives.

In short, possible revenges may be taking place. Furthermore, they might be dangerous to animals and plants as well as to humans. Other kinds of potential revenge resulting from the humanisation of nature should be mentioned here. It seems at least possible, for example, that chemicals in the food chain may be linked to the considerable recent rise in testicular, breast and womb cancers and declining sperm counts in humans and other animals. Human-made chemicals are apparently mimicking the female hormone of oestrogen and it is this which may be leading to these reproductive abnormalities.

It also seems possible that a number of the very virulent viruses now ravaging the human population (AIDS and Marburg being two well-known examples) are a result of human civilisation penetrating further into the rain forests and humans coming into increasing contact with other species able to carry these diseases without themselves dying (Preston 1994). Similarly, a number of the old diseases such as malaria, cholera and tuberculosis are making a comeback (Garrett 1995). Antibiotic medicines initially seemed to have conquered infectious diseases. But bacteria and new viruses have now evolved which are resistant to these modern medicines. Indeed, it seems possible that human intervention may in certain key respects be making things even worse. The causal powers of microbes are such that they mutate in order to survive against their competitors. Antibiotics, which are made of natural chemicals, are intervening in this naturally occurring process, prompting the emergence of especially strong mutant variations. These enhanced mutations are able to withstand wider temperature variations, overcome more elements of a host's immune system and kill host cells in even more effective ways than their predecessors.

Such biological revenges on humanity could turn out to be more extensive than such better-publicised threats as global warming. Furthermore, human societies are now promoting especially favourable conditions for these counter-attacks. International travel and, in particular, the growth of large cities are described by Garrett as 'microbe heavens'. Unclean food, foul water and widespread sexual activity all provide extra opportunities for the powerful new microbes to spread. However, fragmented institutions (in particular separated private companies and regulatory bodies) are not able to cope with this increasingly global set of threats. The social and spatial division of labour is once more not up to the increasingly global scope of these virulent new revenges.

Some potential revenges do now, therefore, seem to be taking place. Economic development and population growth are revealing further limits to external and internal nature (Benton 1989). But again, there remains remarkably little understanding of the details of how processes in the natural world are combining with those in the modern social world. This book will be arguing that it is indeed the modern division of labour that does much to explain how it is that human societies are doing such damage to themselves and to nature. The fragmentation between knowledges has much to be responsible for. And this includes not only a failure to systematically monitor what is taking place but, even more importantly, a failure to *understand* whether or not major environmental revenges are even taking place. We will also be giving particular prominence to the *spatial* division of labour in modern society. This has meant that there is now little connection between the environments in which people live and the industrial and agricultural systems on which they depend. This division is another source of confused and potentially disastrous relations with nature. People can no longer use their own *local* lay knowledge and tacit understandings to monitor, understand and control the consequences of their own actions.

Uncertainty, as we have seen, fuels a wide range of explanations and ideologies. Some people still insist that there are no real environmental problems. And, given our failures to adequately understand what is taking place, they deserve to be taken seriously. As mentioned in the Introduction of this book, these views come almost entirely from institutions and organisations promoting optimism, free-market economics and notions that state intervention poses severe threats to individual liberty. They argue that all the environmental threats are wildly overestimated. As we have seen, they hold what has been called the 'melon' theory of green politics: it is green outside and red within. The environmental threats are said to be the product of left-wing thinkers who, still smarting for the defeat of communism, are now re-grouping and returning disguised as environmentalists. Furthermore, the critics of environmentalism argue that such thinking is another way of introducing heavy top-down governmental action to control people's hearts and minds, another supposed predilection amongst the Left. As we will discuss further in Chapter 7, some elements of the Left have indeed been quite legitimately searching for new rapprochements between the ecological move-ment and socialism (see, for example, Gorz 1994, Dobson 1995). And indeed there seems no particularly logical reason why the promoters of 'freedom of choice' should become so distressed by people choosing priorities different from their own.

The type of critique and conspiracy theory offered by the free-market anti-environmentalists should, in the light of the relative ignorance outlined above, be taken seriously. However, ignorance, or more accurately confusion, should surely not be seen as offering a *carte blanche* for business as usual. While the apocalyptic visions of irreversible environmental degradation may still turn out to be over-stated there is still plenty of evidence of widespread environ-mental destruction. Furthermore, these processes are now having major *social* and *political* impacts. This particularly applies to developing countries. The processes were particularly well documented in the Brundtland Report (World Commission on Environment and Development 1987). It argued persuasively that environmental degradation was one of the main sources of social and political unrest, particularly in Africa and the Far East. Thus environmental degradation actually is widespread but its extent and permanence are not the only points. The parallel central issues are social and political and these should be of as much interest to the 'business as usual' school as anyone else.

The anti-green polemicists should also take account of the fact that the scientific literature on the environment is actually written by people covering a wide range of political opinion. An example is E.O. Wilson. On the one hand, as a great documenter and promoter of biodiversity, he is one of the great heroes of the environmental movement (Wilson 1992). On the other hand he is the same E.O. Wilson who came under massive attack from the Left for his application of sociobiology (Wilson 1975) to the human species. This was a highly reductionist attempt to explain behaviour amongst humans and other species largely in terms of their attempts to preserve their genes and ensure their transmission to future generations.

Again, it is presumably not even in the free marketeers' interests to ignore the revenges and costs being perpetrated on people, crops and so on. It is difficult to avoid the conclusion that they are using the manifold uncertainties deriving from the unsatisfactory state of knowledge to promote their own particular social and political priorities. But this is certainly not to say that the Left has nothing to learn from the Right. They too have on occasions fallen into the trap of linking environmental crisis to an unthinking repetition of old ways of thinking. How might socialists, more specifically, green socialists, learn from the Right and from developments since the day that Marx, Engels and other key thinkers on the Left were writing? How might our knowledge be improved and how might this relate to future forms of green political strategy?

For a start, socialism could also start to become more forward-looking and optimistic; developing, that is, its own utopias. Similarly it could become far more responsive to science, seeing it as not just in the hands of oppressive forces but providing key insights and holding the possibilities of emancipation for humans and other species. But it is with the recognition of the importance of the division of labour where they have perhaps most to learn. Paradoxically elements of the Right, especially the so-called 'New Right', have been far more adept in recognising the power and robustness of the division of labour, especially the *social* division of labour.

Hayek is especially important in this regard (see Hayek 1988, Sayer 1995). He uses the word 'catallaxy' to refer to the millions of widely dispersed, varied, connected and exchanged knowledges between small institutions and households. This catallaxy has evolved spontaneously into very complex and variable forms. Furthermore, Hayek argues persuasively that such a system would be impossible to fully understand, still less control. It is therefore over catallaxy, very roughly equivalent to Marx's social division of labour, that the Left has perhaps most to learn (Sayer 1995). But there are problems in terms of adopting the whole of Hayek's 'package'. Clearly he wholeheartedly rejoices in such variability of cross-cutting, shared and spontaneous knowledges. But if the arguments of this book are correct, such diversity is also problematic. The disadvantage is surely that there is little knowledge in common about, for example, the relations between humanity and the natural world. Again, Hayek might celebrate this very diversity. And, applying his argument to the relations between people and nature, there are certainly many good reasons for recognising the potential and actual vast variety of knowledges. But underlying such diversity there are common physical and natural processes. We should therefore go beyond celebrating diversity as a wonderful thing in its own right. If the broad premises of critical realism are correct, the diversity and complexity spring from key underlying relations and processes working out very differently as they combine with the circumstances of different places and different historical eras. In short, diversity should not therefore be celebrated at the expense of understanding and exposing these more general processes and their combinations with contingent factors and processes.

SOCIETY–NATURE RELATIONS AND THE INTELLECTUAL DIVISION OF LABOUR

'Environmental crisis' emerges from the above as not only about environmental degradation. It is as much a crisis of understanding and resulting human alienation. But, assuming that real degradations are occurring, how are we to account for the revenges of nature on society? Assuming that at least some of them are occurring, it is initially tempting to adopt the argument first advanced by Marx. This says that capitalism is to blame. The argument is that capitalism is indeed impairing the very conditions necessary for its own survival. Marx, as is well known, was concerned with the inner contradictions of capitalism, contradictions which in the end would result in the downfall of capitalism itself. Perhaps the best-known of these is the contradiction between the productive forces and the social relations of production. Here, it will be remembered, the suggestion was that there are in-built crisis-tendencies within capitalism. Marx's central argument was that competition between firms would lead to the increasing substitution of workers by machines. In the long run this would lead to a declining rate of profit in the economy, since profit came eventually from the exploitation of labour power, people's capacity to work. These processes would first hit smaller firms, and production would therefore be primarily located in very large-scale industrial enterprises. These would generate a massive working-class with nothing to lose but their chains in overthrowing the system. As economic crisis set in they would expropriate the small numbers of people who owned the means of production. Capitalism, in short, was digging its own grave through generating its own internal contradictions.

Less well known, however, is Marx's spelling out of the contradictions between capitalist society on the one hand and internal and external nature on the other. Internal nature again refers to labour power and the capacity of people to work. These, Marx argued, are systematically undermined by capital: the physical and mental well-being of workers, combined with the physical conditions in which they were expected to work inevitably led to an undermining of the very capacity for labour which capital needed. As regards external nature, the argument here is that the external physical conditions needed by capital are systematically undermined by accumulation. Marx's view of the

29

impact of 'capitalistic agriculture' on the land was another instance of capitalism (almost literally in this case) digging its own grave. The following could, without too much difficulty, be extended to the contemporary ways in which the biosphere is being altered.

> All progress in capitalistic agriculture is a progress in the art, not only of robbing the labourer, but of robbing the soil; all progress in increasing the fertility of the soil for a given time, is a progress towards ruining the lasting sources of that fertility.
>
> (Quoted in Grundmann 1991: 78)

Adopting this perspective it could be said that crisis is continuously and actively *needed* by capitalism. Crisis, whether it is that deriving from the contradiction between the social relations and social forces of production or of the relation between capitalism and internal and external nature, leads to the dynamism of capitalism. Rapid restructuring takes place without profoundly changing the underlying relations (particularly the separation of wage-labour from capital) associated with the capitalist mode of production. Contemporary society is perhaps now on the verge of another restructuring: one in which capitalism is adapting to environmental limits, slowly adjusting towards managing the environmental costs of mass production and consumption by adapting production systems and consumption patterns towards some form of sustainability. This is clearly indicated by Mol (1995) in his analysis of different sectors of the Dutch chemical industry. This 'ecological modernisation' will inevitably be a very costly undertaking, and it is still unclear how and whether this can be achieved without at the same time undermining profitability. It is also not clear whether it will be implemented in societies where governmental regulatory regimes are relatively lax. (For the now growing discussion around this general issue see, for example, O'Connor 1988, Faber and O'Connor 1989, Leff 1992, Martinez Allier 1993, Ravaioli 1993, Recio 1992, O'Connor 1994.)

This leads back to the main argument of this book, and one touched on earlier in this chapter. Understanding the mechanisms by which capitalism combines with nature as the cause of environmental crisis is clearly necessary, even essential. But it is insufficient. It is laying too much at the door of capitalism. Too much explanatory weight is being given to capitalism, important as our mode of production obviously is.

There is another problem, an even more fundamental one, affecting our understanding. This is the division of labour necessarily associated with modernity of all kinds. An advanced division of labour is, and will remain, a central element of any kind of modern society, whether it is capitalist, socialist or some social form of which we are as yet unaware. This applies not only to the labour in places of paid work (the technical division of labour) but work in society more generally, the social division of labour. Short of some global catastrophe which entails starting all over again with very primitive divisions

30

of labour, it is impossible to imagine a future form of society which will not involve a very extensive division of labour.

A key result is our failure to understand how social processes as understood by the social sciences combine with ecological and natural systems as understood by the natural and physical sciences. We are back to the question of 'one science' briefly mentioned by Marx a century and a half ago and later attempted by Engels. The situation now, however, has marched well beyond the 'two sciences' (one for 'man', the other for 'nature') as originally outlined by Marx. We now have three main forms of knowledge. Even this, of course, underestimates the extent of the debates *within* these areas of scientific work.

It surely goes without saying that an adequate appreciation of humans' relation with nature entails not only an understanding of the mechanisms within the physical, natural and social worlds but, just as importantly, of *how these interact with one another*. How can these interactions be envisaged? Some sense of coherence can be recovered by adopting a 'critical realist' perspective (Bhaskar 1978, 1989, Collier 1989, 1994, Sayer 1992). This entails recognising that there are real causal mechanisms and powers within the physical, biological and social worlds. It also entails recognising a stratified way in which these mechanisms and powers are organised and relate to one another. Figure 1.2 represents this perspective, of course in highly diagrammatic form. It can be seen as a basis of the 'one science' to which Marx originally referred. It does not, however, say anything about how these causal mechanisms actually operate. In that important sense the initiative still lies with theorists working in the physical, natural and social sciences.

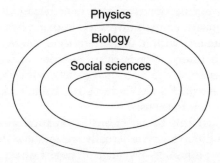

Figure 1.2 Relations between the realms consisting of entities governed by the various sciences (after Collier 1989)

All human activities, relations and mechanisms are set within general biological processes and mechanisms. These latter are the underlying mechanisms affecting the growth and development of organisms (see, for example, Darwin 1950, Goodwin 1994). These mechanisms are real, according to this

31

'realist' view of knowledge, in the sense that although the descriptions we make of them are in principle revisable they exist independently of the concepts we use to describe and explain them. Humans, then, are a type of animal subject to the laws and mechanisms outlined by natural science and, although they may sometimes wish to think otherwise, they remain subject to them. At the same time, humans are constituted by other real processes such as the laws of physics. Thus different kinds of mechanism operate at these different layers of nature. All this is not to argue, however, that humans do not indeed have powers or capacities which go beyond or transcend those of the human world. These include powers to use complex discourses. Meanwhile, all biological mechanisms, including of course those of non-human organisms, are in turn determined by the laws of physics.

To put this another way, all human entities are biological, but not vice versa. And all biological entities are physical but not vice versa (Bhaskar 1978, Collier 1989, 1994). Bhaskar, Collier and Sayer (1992) usefully refer to the 'emergence' of mechanisms at more complex levels from those at more simple levels. Thus biological mechanisms are rooted in chemical and physical processes but they cannot be explained by, or reduced to, such processes. They emerge from them, having their own causal powers and properties. Similarly, human society has its own properties and tendencies. These are rooted in and emergent from biological mechanisms and ecological systems, which in turn are rooted in more basic physical and chemical processes. And as most forms of social theory insist, social mechanisms in the human world cannot be reduced to those at these more basic levels. They are again best envisaged as emergent from them, again having their own potentials, their own 'life', so to speak. It should be clear from this that 'mechanism' is not referring to a particular type of 'thing' such as humans, animals or plants. Rather, physical and chemical mechanisms are contained within, and are in some degree influencing, the behaviour of all such things. Nor is this a question of scale. Physical and chemical mechanisms are not just about the globe while, say, psychological mechanisms operate at a small scale. Rather, all such mechanisms are operating at a number of scales simultaneously.

Again, of course, all this by no means automatically tells us what the mechanisms at these different strata actually are and how they relate to each other. Critical realist philosophy does not propose answers of this kind and certainly cannot be relied on as a magic solution. Again, it is best seen as an ontology; asking what *kinds* of things there have to be for knowledge of these things to be possible and for an understanding of how the social and natural worlds relate to each other (Bhaskar 1989, Collier 1989, 1994, Sayer 1992). Realism does not express a view on the theories operating at each strata. This means there is still much room for debate about the mechanisms operating within the different strata, especially those at the level of human society where a number of mechanisms combine and where the mechanisms or laws affecting human society are less well understood than those of, say, physics or biology.

Despite these complexities and difficulties, the relatively simple overview represented by Figure 1.2 is surely the kind of understanding to which Marx and Engels were leaning. As we have seen, however, Engels rushed to the conclusion that the mechanisms of nature themselves acted dialectically. The explanatory strategy outlined here is the dialectical *analysis* of nature and its relation to the human world. It is not imposing on nature a prior assumption that nature itself works like this. Rather it is an approach to understanding how nature works and how human society relates to nature.

Scientific endeavour, according to this view of knowledge, consists of 'digging deeper' (Collier 1994). Having established one generative mechanism, whether in the social, natural or physical sciences, the research process is one of progressively excavating in order to further illuminate the generative mechanisms determining or affecting what can be observed. The same principle should apply in studying the relations between the different strata of knowledge. But in practice, as we will see shortly, this is an infrequent occurrence.

Thus although each of the mechanisms of each outer layer in some sense determines those of the inner layers, a two-way process is also taking place. Humans can affect, and seem to be increasingly affecting, how biological mechanisms and ecosystems actually work in practice. We will encounter some of these later. Similarly they can transform, and in recent decades seem to be increasingly transforming, the precise ways in which physical mechanisms actually work out in practice. An example seems to be the thinning of the ozone layer. This general research-strategy does not only apply to humans, of course. An understanding of physical nature also depends on an understanding of how other animals use and adapt plants, stones and so on to their own ends. Nevertheless, the laws of physics are not dependent on, or generated by, the laws of biology. Again, we are involved in a two-way process, but an *unequal* two-way process. In later chapters of this book we will be looking at how biological mechanisms within humans and other animals are being used and adapted by human intervention. But the underlying biological mechanisms have not been fundamentally changed. They are still there but their powers are being adapted in different ways, sometimes for good, sometimes for ill.

Debates about knowledge within each of these strata or layers are partly, of course, about the precise ways and extents to which the laws of physics determine biology and the precise ways in which biological laws affect human behaviour . . . and so on. These debates are over what we mean when we say that, for example, the laws of physics and chemistry explain those of biology. They are clearly very important but the more important and indeed central point here is that all too often the division of intellectual labour systematically denies such a coherent and connected understanding. This is because each stratum tends to be considered in isolation. The idea of layers of nature and layers of mechanisms as outlined above has gone missing. Similarly, the notion of 'emergence', with one type of understanding being dependent on or underwritten by (but not reducible to) another, has gone astray. And the two-way dialectical interplay between these different levels has become largely ignored.

Rather, it is assumed that there is an ultimate foundation of knowledge and, furthermore, one which happens to be within the realm of knowledge under consideration. Meanwhile the mechanisms having causal effects across all or some of these spheres remain unexamined. In short, each realm has been developed as a distinct and self-contained science. Furthermore, it is a science of certain kinds of things: atoms and particles in the case of physics, chemicals in the case of living organisms, and humans in the case of the human sciences. Again, all this is at the expense of illuminating the powers and mechanisms determining and being affected by processes across *all* of the strata diagrammatically represented in Figure 1.2. Thus, although clear and important advances have made within each of the realms, the way they have been constructed constitutes a serious block to understanding the whole. Such a block is the core to the alienation (or lack of understanding) of people in modern societies. The advanced capacities they have for understanding their relations to the natural world are denied.

PHYSICS, THERMODYNAMICS AND SOCIETY

To make some of these points more specific we can turn to the theories associated with each of the three realms in Figure 1.2. Let us start with physics. The extraction of raw materials, their separation and assembly during the production process, the transportation of commodities, their consumption and their eventual waste all involve many processes, including of course distinct kinds of social relations, technologies and work on nature. They are firstly constrained by the laws of thermodynamics, which regulate the mechanisms by which energy is transformed from one state to another.

The First and Second Laws are most relevant to our purposes. The First Law states that energy can be neither created nor destroyed. It can indeed only be changed from one form to another. As Lee puts it:

> When a tree grows or when a shed is put up, the energy used is imported from elsewhere. When the tree dies or the shed decays, the energy as such does not vanish; it is merely transformed so that the tree eventually becomes soil, dust and so on.

(1989: 72)

The Second Law is concerned with how energy takes various forms and becomes unavailable for useful work. The energy of a piece of coal, for example, may be the same before and after it has been burnt. But once it is burnt, the ashes or waste created cannot be burnt again. Entropy has been increased. Before it is burnt the energy in the coal is very concentrated. Afterwards, it has been transformed into a form in which energy has low concentration. Another way in which the changing form of energy is expressed is in terms of its order.

34

Energy moves from an ordered (non-random) to a disordered (randomised or dissipated) state. Thus energy which is highly concentrated and available for work is also at its most ordered. And energy which is least available for useful work is also at its most disordered. To quote Lee again:

> Commonsensically, we can grasp this point through the general recognition that things left to themselves sooner or later become disordered. And to restore order requires an expenditure of energy in the tidying, cleaning, repairing and rearranging process.
>
> (1989: 73)

In summary, transformations of energy can be characterised as shown in Table 1.1.

Table 1.1 Transformations of energy

High concentration	→	Low concentration
Available; free	→	Unavailable; bound
Ordered (non-random)	→	Disordered, randomised, dissipated
Low, negative entropy	→	High, positive entropy (entropy increase), heat death, waste, pollution.

(after Lee 1989)

Physics provides an understanding of the mechanisms involved in the creation of entropy or 'waste'. It merges into the sciences of biology and ecology which we will consider in more detail shortly. As is well known, the waste produced by non-human transformation of energy is largely taken back into the ecosystem. The carbon dioxide produced by an animal's breathing is reabsorbed by the ecosystem's plants. The 'waste' produced by the animal is worked on by a variety of organisms. These break down the waste into small components which in turn become part of the soil. And this in turn enables plants to grow, which the animal eats. Nature's 'revenges' are in part a result of new kinds of productive systems which introduce new substances which cannot be broken down. They are also produced on such a large scale that reabsorption by ecosystems can no longer take place.

Physics, and the laws of thermodynamics in particular, can be considered as hard and reliable knowledge. Einstein wrote, 'it is the only physical theory of universal content of which I am convinced, that within the framework of applicability of its basic concepts will never be overthrown' (quoted by Lee 1989: 19). For the foreseeable future it will remain an essential component of any understanding of how human society relates to nature. Very major difficulties start, however, if we think that physics on its own provides guidelines to future forms of society.

Lee (1989), for example, appears to believe that it is possible to construct a new civilisation and set of values based on thermodynamics. She argues that present-day society celebrates and supports 'the expression of selfish inclinations to the extent of even denying that human beings are capable of altruistic ones' (p. 197). Altruistic inclinations are, she suggests, systematically repressed. Individuals are pressured into acquiring wealth, possessing goods and exercising control over others. Competition is supported at the expense of cooperation. All these 'ecologically insensitive' values are, Lee argues, 'not consonant with the laws of thermodynamics and the principles of ecology'.

Lee is favourably disposed towards some form of socialism. But she argues that Marx's triumphalist view of nature is incompatible with the thermodynamic principles and ecological systems. Instead, she looks to utopian socialists, and in particular Fourier, who advocated scaled-down levels of production and consumption. Clearly, many of her arguments against Marx are well taken. (For a discussion see Hayward 1990.) But the utopian socialists do not offer even a preliminary way of understanding the relations between physics, biology and human society. Furthermore, it is only through such an understanding that environmental degradation and human emancipation can start to be made. If we take a stratified view of the complex relations between society and nature as proposed above, it is clear that we need to be very careful about starting to 'read off' a particular kind of society (however desirable) from the laws of thermodynamics and the principles of ecology. Indeed, since there is a large number of mechanisms mediating between the laws of physics and the workings of a modern capitalist economy, it is impossible to extrapolate from the laws of physics any particular form of society. It is by no means self-evident, for example, that competition and property ownership as practised in human society actually are hostile to the principles of thermodynamics. Physical principles may determine society in the sense that they are principles within which any society must operate. And the ways in which these principles operate can also be influenced by society. This is now becoming all too evident. But no particular kind of future society, socialist or capitalist or any other, can be simply derived from these principles.

The same can be said of an increasing number of other authors who are trying to derive social forms from the principles of modern physics. Quantum physics insists that atomic phenomena are determined by their connections with the whole. Thus what appear to be isolated elements such as atoms can only be understood in terms of their relations with one another. This leads Capra, for example, to argue that 'modern physics can be characterised by words like organic, holistic and ecological' (1983: 66). He is suggesting, through making a deft but highly misleading analogy between quantum physics and a possible new society, that his utopian way of life is justified on the basis of the new physics alone.

Similarly, Zohar and Marshall (1993) argue for a 'quantum society', a society which is 'firmly rooted in nature' (p. 1). They are saying that because humans must live in accordance with the laws and principles of physics they should learn from physics and be sensitive to the kind of 'holism' which is apparent in the workings of the physical world. Thus because an electron or a photon is now seen by physics to be in constant dialogue with its environment, so similarly a modern society must be one in which individuals and their relation to nature must also be envisaged as in a constant dialogue. In the end, a metaphor based on quantum physics is again being used to envisage and idealise a future society. Zohar and Marshall are transferring an obviously insightful theory of the physical world to their preferred utopia. This is highly deceptive since it once more remains wholly innocent of social, political and even biological mechanisms. A shortcut to a better form of society is seen simply as a product of being aware of, and somehow putting into effect, 'the new physics'. Marx's 'one science', and its later extension through modern realist philosophy, recognises that any 'whole' is likely to be much more complex than an expression of physical and ecological principles and their direct mapping onto future human societies. Thus these simplistic accounts will not suffice.

SOCIETY MODELLED ON THE LIFE SCIENCES?

The life sciences are in danger of being seduced by very similar temptations. Considerable understandings of relationships between organisms and their environment are now being made. But wholly unjustified analogies are being forged between such sciences and an appreciation of how human society might or should operate. Ecology is of course the study of the relation of living organisms to their environment. It is often viewed in terms of a self-balancing system: an ecosystem, being the complex web linking animals and plants and enabling flows of energy to take place. The word 'population' is used to describe individuals of any species that live together within any designated area. The word 'community' is used to include all the populations living in a particular area and it is the community and the non-living environment which are seen as functioning together as an ecosystem. But, as we will shortly see, the problems again start when these concepts are mapped straight onto human societies, past and future. There is again little sense of 'emergence', with biological mechanisms not only being linked back to physical laws but also human societies' having their own considerable autonomy despite the fact that they are founded on biological principles and relations.

It is important to note that some of these problems even apply to those involved in the natural sciences who are adopting the kind of ontology being recommended and developed in this study. Biologists, some of whom not only take their cue from theoretical physics but are now adopting a broadly realist position, increasingly see the mechanisms underlying development of organisms and the emergence of species as a result both of their interaction with their environment and of the powers and propensities of organisms themselves (see, for example, Lewontin 1982, Levins and Lewontin 1985, Dickens 1992, Goodwin 1994, Kollek 1995). Organisms' potentials are thus seen as unfolding in relation to their environment. At the same time these potentials have been formed in relation to their environment. A dialectical relation between organism and environment is therefore an emergent key theme in contemporary biology.

These perspectives form part of extensive and sometimes even bitter debates within the natural sciences, particularly between those promoting the above systemic, dialectical and realist overview and those insisting on genes as providing a basis for understanding an organism's form and behaviour. It is instructive to note, however, that even the 'dialectical' or 'realist' biologists adopt a view of the relations between organism and environment which can still considerably over-play the biological at the expense of the social (see, for example, Goodwin 1994). This again serves to underline the basic point here about fragmented or balkanised knowledge serving to provide misleadingly simple explanations. Similarly, it again helps to emphasise that realism is in itself not a royal road to understanding. Again, the hard work as regards examining the interactions between causal powers, emergent tendencies and the precise relationships between naturally acquired powers, on the one hand, and the social and political world on the other remain to be done.

But this process of using the principles of ecology to inform our understanding of human society has a quite long history. Contemporary forms of environmental philosophy and activism have often appealed to the principles of ecology and biology, especially those adopting the systemic and inter-relational view. Furthermore, these are promoted as offering ways forward for new forms of society. This particularly applies to the so-called 'deep greens'. Their key theme is 'living as if nature mattered'. Devall and Sessions (1985) base their 'natural philosophy' on:

> a proper understanding of the purposes and workings of nature and do not try to impose an ideology upon it. We seek to transform society based on this understanding.
>
> (p. 37)

In short, the deep greens are trying to draw from the inter-relatedness inherent to and articulated by modern biological and ecological science and extend it to the ways in which humans should live with one another and the rest of nature. The human and the non-human realms are seen as ontologically inseparable. As Fox (1985) insists:

> We can make no firm ontological divide in the field of existence. There is no bifurcation in reality between the human and the non-human realms .... To the extent that we perceive boundaries, we fall short of deep ecological consciousness. (Quoted by Devall and Sessions 1985: 66)

A similar point is made by Arne Naess, the founding father of deep ecology. He too is assuming that principles for human society can be drawn for ecological science and, by extension, from the laws of physics.

The essence of deep ecology is to ask deeper questions. The adjective 'deep' stresses that we ask why and how, where others do not. For instance ecology as a science does not ask what kind of society would be the best for maintaining a particular ecosystem – that is considered a question for value theory, for politics, for ethics. As long as ecologists keep narrowly to their science, they do not ask such questions.

(Quoted by Devall and Sessions 1985: 74)

Why is this wrong? First, it again remains innocent of social mechanisms: the social relations, production processes, markets and politics which constitute real human societies. These are taken to have been somehow subsumed during the transition to the new society. The transition between the natural and the social has once more been made too rapidly. Human society certainly could relate better to ecological and physical systems. But theories of these systems have nothing to say about precisely how human society (or societies) should be formed. What precisely would a society which is harmonious with nature actually look like? Would it be run by the state? And if so, are state bureaucrats to define what is harmonious with nature? Would it be a product of the market? If so, does this leave the social relations of production untouched? The unsatisfactory words 'man' and 'mankind' used by the deep greens only serve to confuse the (social) situation even further.

Second, the particular kinds of understanding of ecology offered by the green movement are often very selective about what actually is natural. Species have regularly died out and ecosystems are continually subject to flux. So how would we know when a 'balanced' relationship with nature had actually been achieved? Furthermore, a peculiarly bucolic ideal is assumed to exist within nature when the reality can be seen as far nastier, at least for some species. Martell (1992: 30) sums up many of these points when he outlines the 'problematic' idea from the deep greens that norms for social and political organisation can be drawn directly from nature itself.

First the principles they attribute to nature – equality, diversity, symbiosis, etc. – are debatable because nature often goes against these principles (as any David Attenborough documentary will demonstrate). In other words, they have an over benign one-sided view of nature. This leads to the second problem which is that nature is contradictory and does not imply any single set of principles.

THE SOCIOLOGY OF THE ENVIRONMENT: NATURE'S REAL POWERS EXCLUDED

Finally we come to the inner ring of Figure 1.2, understandings of human society. If the sciences of physics, ecology and biology have remained blissfully ignorant of the human social world, the reverse holds just as much for much contemporary social theory. As Dunlap and Catton (1994) have pointed out, sociology has (following a lean period in the 1980s) increasingly addressed itself to environmental issues. But there is little sign that even this discipline has seriously opened up its boundaries to include insights from such clearly related disciplines as biology.

There are now, however, signs of real progress. An example is Murphy's recent application of Weberian thinking to the relations between society and nature (Murphy 1994). He argues that modernity is characterised by a process of rationalisation. And this includes the attempted rationalisation of nature. The consistent ideal of modern society has been to impose, with the aid of technology and science, an order over nature. This has been the modern way, Murphy argues, of dispelling nature's mysterious and magical elements. And rationality enables predictability and calculability to take place. By now attaching economic values to the environment, for example, it becomes possible to calculate the consequences and costs of human intervention. The assumption has consistently been that nature is 'plastic', it is infinitely malleable and subject to understanding and control. However, Murphy's key point is that it is not plastic. Rather, it is elastic in the sense that the environment can 'stretch' before it finally breaks. Much the same applies to human beings. They too are not infinitely malleable. And finally, nature has its 'revenges', as the 'elastic' of which it is made recoils on those who are testing its limits.

Murphy's study is a remarkable one, not least for its deliberate attempt to fuse social relations and processes with knowledge of the powers of nature. It has some close parallels with the analysis offered in this study. The processes of 'rationalisation' in modern societies are closely linked to the creation of complex divisions of labour and the fragmenting of labour processes. Murphy's Weberian analysis remains wanting, however, in the sense that to fulfil its own promise it will need a realist ontology to make these links between society and nature. Such an ontology would mean that the 'elasticity' of humans and the environment would not need to rely on metaphors with plastic and elastic and could eventually be specified in terms of specific mechanisms and powers. In this way sociology would indeed start to combine with other forms of science.

Marxism has remained relatively sensitive to these connections, though it has latterly been largely supplanted by other forms of sociology. Even Marxism, however, has had severe relapses. For example, Engels, despite his own considerable sympathy to an analysis of society in relation to nature, was in practice quite hostile to attempts actually to create an ecological social theory. He argued, for example, against Serhii Podolinsky, the Ukrainian ecological socialist, who was trying to measure the inputs and outputs of industrial production in terms of energy (Martinez Allier 1987). Engels understood the principles full well but rejected Podolinsky's ideas on two grounds. He felt that the assessment of energy budgets for industry would be very difficult. But he also felt that the whole question of physical energy was of minor importance compared with the energy productivity of human labour itself.

It is easy, with the benefit of hindsight, to see why Engels should have downplayed in 1882 the importance of the demands of industry on the environment. Perhaps less admissible is a dogmatic assertion of the over-riding importance of labour. At all events, less excusable are environmental sociologists, over 100 years later, still trying to contain their analysis within sociology itself. Giddens (1994) and Beck (1992a,b,c, *et al.* 1994, 1995) are two of the most influential contemporary sociologists working on environmental questions and, although they have certainly produced very valuable work, they also illustrate some of the difficulties. Giddens has recently asserted that nature has 'ended'. He argues that in modern society nature is no longer a phenomenon external to human social life. (He seems here to be making a very similar point to that made by Marx about 100 years ago.) At the same time Giddens, along with Beck, argues that contemporary society is characterised by a range of intense anxieties. These partly stem from the supposed 'end of nature'. But they also stem from the end of tradition and of science.

Modernity is seen as characterised by high degrees of 'reflexivity', individuals reflecting on themselves and on their positions. Part of this reflexivity, according to Beck and Giddens, involves sustained challenges to science and tradition. Modern, or 'post-traditional' life consists of continuous challenges to all forms of knowledge. The old universals and guarantees have gone, each form of knowledge needing to justify itself in relation to competing claims and knowledges. All these challenges to certainty, Giddens in particular argues, lead to new forms of angst and uncertainty amongst the general population. A key result is 'life politics' in which individuals are continually trying to reassert who and what they are in relation to changes to nature. These changes may be on a global scale or they may be, as in genetic engineering, modifications to the internal nature of living beings.

Finally, Beck argues that we live in a 'risk society'. This refers to the increased incalculability of consequences and damage under modernity, the fact that threats increasingly affect everyone and yet cannot be nailed down to any particular individual or organisation. As Giddens argues, the old certainties are seen as breaking down, these including science itself. Furthermore, while it was previously possible to insure oneself against (relatively predictable) risk, this is impossible in a society where new technologies (including nuclear power and the chemical industries) are threatening society in extensive and unpredictable ways. Again like Giddens, the lack of insurance is not only economic.

> In all the brilliance of their perfection, nuclear power plants have suspended the principle of insurance not only in the economic, but also in the medical, psychological, cultural and religious sense. *The residual risk*

41

SOCIETY, NATURE AND ABSTRACT KNOWLEDGE

society has become an uninsured society, with protection paradoxically diminishing as the danger grows.

(1992b: 101, Beck's emphasis)

Beck's work provides of course a number of very useful insights. This particularly applies to his discussion of the ways in which modernity is associated with reflection by people on their own circumstances, on the nature of knowledge and on any notion that the application of science necessarily leads to social and environmental progress, however defined. But in the end, they remain confined to the purely sociological field. Although he is not very explicit about this, Beck seems to be assuming that all knowledge is no more than a social construction. He is not recognising any real causal mechanisms 'out there' independent of human discourse and social construction. Indeed, the supposed uncertainty over science to which he refers seems to confirm this stance. Beck seems quite confused. On the one hand he is, like Giddens, saying that all forms of knowledge are under constant interrogation and challenge. On the other hand, his notion of a 'risk society' must assume that there actually *are* real mechanisms out there causing real and likely environmental disaster. Both Beck and Giddens (and Beck in particular) tacitly rely on a realist ontology in order to make their points while simultaneously denying that such a form of knowledge can exist. Caroline New makes just this point with reference to Beck.

For us to make or assess an apocalyptic claim about environmental threat requires us to believe that reality exists and has certain characteristics and structures independent of human discourse.

(1995a)

One way and another these influential sociologists are writing about human society's relation with nature without recognising the possibility of an independent 'nature' of the kind constructed by other disciplines such as physics or the natural sciences. Furthermore, they are making assumptions about physical, biological and ecological processes which remain wholly inexplicit. Either way, they have managed to contain an understanding of the relations between human society and nature within sociology itself. This may be good news for a sociology which continues to promote its own discipline but it does rather little to address the urgent need for a better understanding of how society relates to nature. This applies too to the notion of 'life politics'. Paradoxically, an understanding of such politics actually manages to exclude life itself in the form of biology. However mediated, human beings' practices are a product of, or are 'emergent from', biological processes which they of course share with other species (Benton 1988). In sum, contemporary social theory has not learnt the lesson expressed very lucidly by Murphy (1994: ix).

Nature does matter, even for sociology. The sociological thesis of the social construction of reality is viable only if tempered by an ecosystemic sociology that takes into consideration of nature. The relationship between social action and the dynamic processes of nature will have to be incorporated into sociological theory. A restricted focus on only social action just will not do.

Giddens and Beck recognise, and are actively involved in, the undermining of the scientific enterprise and its metanarratives. They seem less keen, however, to apply the same critical criteria to their own academic discipline (Irwin 1995).

Even more surprisingly, these writers (like many other social scientists) manage to avoid outlining the *social* mechanisms by which human beings combine with the natural world. What are the processes underpinning the socialisation of nature and the creation of 'the risk society'? Beck and Giddens remain largely mute on this point. Marx, for all his faults, specified the process by which capitalist society combines with nature to produce commodities for sale. It is best summarised by the circuit of capital (Figure 1.3).

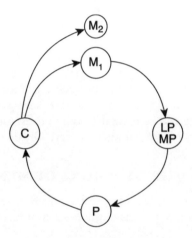

Figure 1.3 The circuit of capital (M_1 = money invested, LP = labour power, MP = means of production (including raw materials from nature), P = labour process, C = exchange of commodities, M_2 = profit)

Money (M_1) purchases technology, or the means of production, and labour power. These combine with raw materials taken from nature and other commodities in a labour process to produce commodities for sale on the market. These commodities are then sold and consumed. The resulting money is either recycled back into the process (purchasing new labour power, raw materials etc.) or is taken as profit by the investor. This relatively simple process is surely a key element lying behind the 'humanisation', 'socialisation' or 'end' of nature under capitalism. Furthermore, the incorporation of nature into the circuit of capital is even more profound than indicated by Figure 1.3. It concerns not just the input of raw materials into a pre-given process. Rather, the powers of nature are themselves being used as production processes. And this incorporation is steadily increasing. Genetic engineering, for example, now allows animals to be used to mass-produce such commodities as 'human' blood and 'human' milk.

Marx, and indeed later Marxists, under-emphasised other forms of labour process in modern society, especially, of course, those in households. But, if we broaden out Marx's emphasis to include all forms of labour to produce the things we need, we are surely going a long way towards pinpointing the key mechanism underlying the creation of the 'risk society', at least as it is created under capitalism. Humans may or may not be now creating more risk than in the past (sociologists do have a distressing tendency to periodically announce wholly new forms of society) but in societies based on capital-accumulation a central underlying mechanism for the past three hundred years or so is that outlined in Figure 1.3. How this combines with other non-capitalist forms of labour and with other physical and ecological mechanisms is the extremely difficult question which contemporary sociology has largely managed to ignore.

This again brings us back to the main argument of this book. How does the technical and social division of labour relate to nature and possible environmental crisis? This is of course a massive question. There are many dimensions to it and they will be at least partly covered in later parts of this book. Most important here is the rise of mental labour and divisions between different types of intellectual work. What are these and why do they occur?

EXPLAINING THE DIVISIONS OF MENTAL LABOUR

Why are we left with the discrete and abstract forms of knowledge (represented by Figure 1.2) as the main forms of guidance to understanding the relations between society and the environment? Environmental issues are, above all, interdisciplinary, and an explanation of such fragmentation has to be made.

First, it has to be said that such divisions are a product of the ways in which nature and human society are themselves organised. This stratification which distinguishes between physical, biological and human social mechanisms is in part a reflection of the ways in which the world actually works. There are intrinsic divisions here which are not just a product of the ways in which academic institutions are organised. Nevertheless, and bearing in mind that stratification insists that each stratum (laws of the physical world, the natural world and the social world) is emergent from its predecessor, this does not excuse the construction of watertight divisions between areas of the human and natural worlds.

A full explanation would also involve an extensive analysis of the rise of science and, in particular, the rise of particular *kinds* of science. Three closely

44

related processes have been at work. First we have the relatively familiar process whereby groups of people promote and attach themselves to certain areas of knowledge. As Weber in particular argued, a 'social closure' process takes place, whereby certain areas of expertise are created and barriers are placed around this knowledge in order to protect the rewards and prestige of those involved (Parkin 1979). Such autonomy and separatist policy is often justified by the group's claim that the protection and regulation of their distinct form of knowledge is necessary for the general good, for society at large (Cozzens and Woodhouse 1995). A struggle is therefore taking place, some people attempting to manoeuvre themselves into positions of power through the creation and protection of knowledge, if necessary at the expense of others. Divisions of knowledge can therefore be seen as the straightforward attempt by organised workers to 'protect their patch', organising themselves around a particular area of expertise and, at the expense of other people less able to organise themselves, reaping rewards in terms of autonomy and monetary gains. As Rueschemeyer (1986: 104) puts it:

> Experts who possess knowledge which helps in solving urgent problems of others can exert a price, and that price may well be much more than a good fee; it nearly always includes honour and esteem and often influence and power, especially if the experts use their common expertise and social honour as a foundation for collective organisation.

The second and complementary process is the incorporation of science into industry. While people, and professional elites in our case, are attempting to improve their life chances through processes of knowledge-creation and social closure, they are also necessarily involved in the way that society and economy are constructed.

Writing in the mid-nineteenth century Marx observed that, with modern industry,

> the varied, apparently unconnected, and petrified forms of the industrial processes now resolved themselves into so many conscious and systematic applications of natural science to the attainment of given useful effects.
>
> (Quoted in Braverman 1974: 155)

In a remarkably prescient way Marx was outlining here the ways in which science has become incorporated into capitalism. By the late nineteenth century, capitalist industry was indeed actively using such sciences as physics and chemistry to change the characteristic features of its products. The (mis)use of labour is the most important pre-requisite for a capitalist enterprise but the second most important input is science itself, 'turned', as Braverman puts it, 'into an adjunct of capital'. This process did not really start until the late nineteenth century, which makes Marx's comments all the more stunning. Rapid advances in modern science were made. At the same time, mental knowledge started to acquire a premium, with science being developed on a massive and professionalised scale. As a result, the labour process started to be extended well beyond the simple application of labour to technology and the materials of nature (Sayer and Walker 1992). In Germany, and then particularly in the USA, large-scale research programmes were established in universities staffed in the main by securely sinecured professors. And it was at just this time that capitalist industry itself started to benefit from this scientific–technical revolution (Freeman 1982). As Braverman (1974: 167) puts it, this late form of capitalism should be understood in its totality as a mode of production into which science and exhaustive engineering investigations have been integrated as part of ordinary functioning. The key innovation is not to be found in chemistry, electronics, automatic machinery, aeronautics, atomic physics, or any of the products of these science–technologies, but rather in the transformation of science itself into capital.

Such economic investment in science by capital further legitimates the divisions which elites have established. But perhaps the most important point to make here is that they strongly influence the *form* of the sciences they have created. Any labour process converting nature into products, capitalist or otherwise, must have some understanding of the causal powers of nature. If it did not, the results of its interventions would presumably be a series of unmitigated disasters for all concerned. Nevertheless, it seems obvious that the prominence of some forms of science must be in part attributable to social and economic needs. One process is very much apparent today with, for example, a particular form of biology (that which still sees organisms as little more than assemblages of DNA) now being very heavily invested in and exploited by capital. We will discuss this process later in this book, but the main point is that a science which analyses by taking things apart and re-composing these parts in different ways is attractive to capital and is likely to be invested in. After all, many of these parts can all be owned. All this is in marked contrast to a biology which emphasises wholeness, causal powers and qualities rather than quantities. Such a science does not attempt to reduce behaviour and forms to such parts as genes and genetic structures. Admirable as it is, it is of far less interest to capital. Thus abstract ideas are not so much the problem, it is the form of abstraction where the problems start.

But again, this emphasis on sub-division into discrete parts may not simply be attributable to the needs of capital. It can also be seen as the product of a broader and relatively independent process, the creation of a division of labour. Presumably there would be a tendency within any kind of complex production process to divide the process up into discrete, manageable and ultimately controllable parts. Breaking down organisms into genetic or other components must at least assist this process.

It may well be asked how the social sciences, the inner ring of Figure 1.2, fits into all this. A very similar set of professionalising processes has occurred. Starting about the same time as the natural and physical sciences, but not gathering full momentum until about the turn of the century, social theory also started to set itself up as an independent science, one which paralleled the non-human sciences. Importantly, these were based on interpretations of what the natural and physical sciences were like. The equation between natural and social evolution was a tempting one to make. Not only was it made by social scientists such as Comte and Spencer but it actually helped to inform Darwin's theory of evolution itself (Dickens 1992). Meanwhile, other sociologists were constructing a science based on what they perceived to be the theories of physics (Platt 1993). Paradoxically, however, such imitations of the natural and physical sciences have not led the social sciences to significantly question their philosophical assumptions. If anything the reverse. As Collier puts it:

> They have seemed unable to sever their umbilical cords, substituting an unconsciousness of their philosophical assumptions for an independence of their philosophical origins.
>
> (1994: 207)

In the above ways, then, a number of distinct sciences were formed and, in the comparatively recent past, a separate science of society was created. The latter was one which, for reasons of social closure, remained almost wholly distinct from the sciences of biology and physics but which, paradoxically, drew from them. The human species became seen as the product of human society alone. Humans were necessarily envisaged by this new science as no longer part of nature in the sense that they were not seen as a natural species. Their behaviour and their relations were a product of human society alone. No appeal could be made to the natural sciences as part of this new science asserting an autonomy from the other sciences (MacNaghten and Urry 1995).

The new science of the new, self-contained, sociology also adopted a stereotypical view of how science itself proceeded. The supposedly scientific notions of objectivity, rationality and openness to falsification were read into science and built into the new sociology. These presumably too lent authority to the new elites. Finally, even these sociologists received social backing (mediated by the state) as they became seen, particularly in the USA, as capable of addressing an emergent series of 'social problems' arising from industrialism. This was assisted by the sociological professionals also presenting themselves capable of addressing and solving these problems as apparently apolitical experts (Manicas 1987).

Scientific elitism and its increasing incorporation by capital are therefore key elements in trying to explain how the fragmentation of abstract or intellectual knowledge has taken place and how, in particular, the separation between human society and nature became envisaged. But there is one more key element. And this is perhaps even more fundamental than any of those discussed so far. This is the separation of abstract understandings from other forms of knowledge. These include lay knowledge, understandings that are not well informed by abstract ideas. But it also includes tacit knowledge; forms of skill and judgement which people develop on the basis of their everyday life and work but which cannot be easily described or encoded in the form of words, written documents or other impersonal means (Polanyi 1958, 1967, Collins 1985, Wainwright 1994, Hobbelink 1991).

All these professional groups and the incorporation of their knowledge by industry are predicated on this one process. It is the marginalisation of tacit and lay knowledge acquired during work and which is largely unrecognised. We will encounter a number of examples of this later in this study. They include, for example, the knowledge that indigenous farmers have of their land, the knowledge which women have of their own bodies, knowledge of preparing and cooking food and the knowledge that children have of their environments. In all these instances we are discussing the skills of subordinated groups that have been downgraded in significance and which have remained largely unrecognised.

Marx was alluding to just one particular version of this when he referred to the fragmentation between mental and manual labour in the workplace. But it is misleading to refer to manual labour as if it were not also a mental form of work. Rather, it is another form of activity which remains largely unrecognised. And such recognition is a result of the active concentration of knowledge by dominant classes. Referring to the division of labour at the workplace ('the technical division of labour') Braverman (1974: 425) emphasises the very active way in which abstract knowledge is withheld from the worker.

> The more science is incorporated into the labor process, the less the worker understands of the process; the more sophisticated an intellectual product the machine becomes, the less control and comprehension of the machine the worker has. In other words, the more the worker needs to know in order to remain a human being at work, the less does he or she know.

But the same process of alienation extends to all areas of social life. To, that is, the social division of labour as well as the division of labour at the workplace. Contemporary attitudes to knowledge, dominated as they are by the sciences of various kinds, systematically deny or decry the importance of lay, tacit and non-professional forms of knowledge. Such understandings and skills (which, as much of the environmental movement of course points out, are often derived from direct experience in localities) become downgraded as insignificant or even useless. This latter, then, is the final part of the jigsaw in trying to explain the fragmented nature of contemporary environmental knowledge. We will discuss this in much more detail in the next chapter, but as a key process it is worth emphasising here.

This, in combination with other processes such as the active appropriation and protection of knowledge by professionalising groups, has been a key mechanism in the elevation of abstract knowledge to a dominant position. It is a process which has gone relatively unexplored, but it is one which inevitably applies to all modern societies, capitalist and socialist alike. What Sohn-Rethel

(1975, 1978) calls 'alienated knowledge' particularly thrives in a society based on the buying and selling of commodities. Knowledge becomes considered not for its internal qualities and not in its social and environmental context (Sayer 1992). Rather, it becomes 'a pure object world', one apparently divested of social and environmental relations and considered predominantly as a quantity or quality to be exchanged in the marketplace. Furthermore, and most importantly for this argument, these are generalised quantities and qualities. They can in principle be bought by anyone, at any time and in any place. It is therefore hardly surprising that generalised and abstract knowledge acquires such a considerable significance in a market economy. To put the matter rather bluntly, it is easier to sell abstract knowledge than concrete knowledge on a mass-market. A book, television programme or compact disc describing how ecological systems work in general, for example, is likely to find more buyers than such a product about the knowledge of these issues held by a limited number of people. Sales will be particularly disappointing if these people have been made socially or politically marginal. Nevertheless, none of this is to say that abstract knowledge necessarily has to be socially oppressive. Furthermore, the ontology suggested by critical realism (that of a stratified nature composed of a number of inter-related mechanisms) is both quite abstract and yet one which is not difficult to understand by lay, non-specialist, people.

CONCLUSION: CAPITALISM, NATURE AND MODERNITY

The distinguished biologist E.O.Wilson is one amongst many who has argued that environmental crisis entails the creation of new kinds of connected knowledge.

> The solution will require cooperation among professions long separated by academic and practical tradition. Biology, anthropology, economics, agriculture, government and laws will have to find a common voice.
>
> (1992: 298)

This chapter has been trying to explain, albeit in a preliminary way, how this situation has come to pass and how to find what Wilson calls 'a common voice'. The particular kind of unity outlined here, however, may be far too 'political' for Wilson himself.

There is, however, one final element to this discussion which could convert E.O. Wilson to this line of thinking. The argument so far has been couched in terms of the orchestrated division of labour and the role of capitalism in effecting such a division. Even this, however, remains a partial picture. For, as argued earlier, the division of labour has been and will surely be a central characteristic of *any* kind of advanced society. In a modern society no one person can spread her or himself across the increasing number of specialised tasks that need conducting in modern society. Appealing (as of course some environmen-

49

talist do) to older, pre-industrial, societies with their less-developed divisions of labour, is no more than a pipe-dream. As regards the technical division of labour, a complex production process will again entail some kind of coordination, with 'mental' labour in some way supervising this process. Marx, to his credit, recognised this need. This despite the fact that he saw, especially in his early work, the division of labour as the basis of private property and therefore needing abolition (Rattansi 1982).

Again, the division of labour is indeed closely related to property ownership in capitalist society. Factory owners are highly likely to own the means of production as a means of ensuring that they maintain over-all control over the producers and the commodities coming off the production line (Sayer 1995). Similarly, Marx and Engels argued persuasively that the ownership of women was central to early forms of the division of labour, wives and children alike being what Marx and Engels called in *The German Ideology*, 'the slaves of the husband' (Marx and Engels 1969: 294).

But there are two points to make about this. First, as Coontz and Henderson (1986) point out with reference to recent historical research, the subordination of women's productive and reproductive powers has not taken place in isolation from other social processes and other elements of the social division of labour, especially those of class. But second, the division of labour (and especially the technical division of labour) cannot be laid at the doorstep of capitalism alone. The importance of recognising the necessary division of labour in any kind of modern society has been emphasised by those analysing the previously 'communist' societies (Sayer and Walker 1992, Sayer 1995). The latter of course made extensive use of managers and technical experts using specialist scientific knowledge. In many respects they would have been at home in a capitalist factory.

Recent work on industrial pollution in the previously communist East European countries shows, for example, that the division of labour established by these societies was by no means in the right form when it came to dealing with environmental problems. Such problems are of course worse in some parts of East Europe than in many parts of the West. And research on these state socialist societies also suggests that the division of labour may itself be a major problem in trying to establish a sufficient understanding and an adequate policy. One commentator on Poland's water and environmental system says, for example, that 'it cannot be described as anything else but chaotic' (Zvosec 1984: 105). No fewer than seven federal bureaucracies were (and perhaps still are) simultaneously responsible for its management. Similarly, as Tamas (1992) has shown, factories in East Europe have often been characterised by a disastrous split in the way that they are managed. On the one hand some managers are charged with controlling their factories in such a way as to guarantee maximum production. On the other hand, other managers were charged with controlling industrial pollution. In the end it was the former group who consistently won out. Production, and at prices which competed

50

with those in the West, eventually gained the ascendancy and, for example, pollution filters were not checked or even removed. Again, the division of labour (combined with professional protection of skills and expertise) directly inhibited the protection of the environment and the health of workers, citizens and other species. As we will briefly discuss in the next chapter, similar divisions of labour can persist within capitalist enterprises.

Unsuccessful forms of environmental control in the old state communist regimes can of course be attributed to the bureaucratic inefficiencies of those particular regimes. But the argument here is that they are more than this. They are an indication of the difficulties inherent in any advanced modern society. A transition from capitalism to some other type of modern society will by no means overcome the problems deriving from complex divisions of labour. Such divisions are a necessary feature of a modern industrial society. A coherent overview and successful management of the relations between society and nature will therefore always be up against such fragmented knowledges, bureaucracies and competing power relations.

But this only leads us to another issue for the understanding of such relations. Contesting mental or managerial workers are, in the end, centralising and defending particular types of more general or abstract knowledge against the tacit knowledge and capacities developed by their subordinates in the process of their everyday work. But the type of abstract knowledge with which managers deal is in turn a product of these same forms of protectionism. This again implies that alternative forms of abstract knowledge could prevail in forms of work which were more democratically organised. This chapter, drawing on critical realism, has suggested what these alternatives might be about. But the difficult business of defining what exactly the links are between the different powers and mechanisms at each stratum of the social and natural world (the actual way in which, for example, human social relations are emergent from biology) largely remains to be achieved.

Meanwhile, what about those lay people whose knowledge has been limited to understandings based more on the experience of everyday life? And what about the continuing wars they are having with the intellectual workers? We will now address these tendentious questions.

2

UNDERSTANDING ALIENATION
From the abstract to the concrete

What would a thorough understanding of society–nature relations look like? How can we understand contemporary alienation from nature? This chapter tries to answer these questions, concentrating particularly on the relations between abstract and concrete knowledge. These links, which are based on a reading of critical realism, are important if we are going to understand not only people's alienated relations with nature but also the prospects for more emancipated forms of understanding. They are also important, this chapter will suggest, if we are to adequately understand the alienation of other species. In all, these links need to be made in order to understand the full scope of environmental politics. Realist epistemology, which focuses on the range of causal mechanisms and processes which generate concrete events, strongly suggests that such politics are by no means only about the environment. They are as much about social relations. And when we turn to the actual practice of green politics we find that this is indeed the case. It is as much about the social relations of class, gender and other sources of oppression, particularly the division of labour in modern society. I will shortly give two examples of this, one concerned with the relations between humans and animals, the other with the resistance of indigenous peoples to modernity. The division of labour, along with other processes such as the penetration of market relations, will again emerge from this as a common alienating process for both humans and other animals.

CRITICISING AND DEVELOPING EXISTING WORK

So far there is some superficial resemblance between the analysis outlined in the last chapter and that being currently offered by certain influential German sociologists. Luhmann (1989), in particular, has referred to problems of what he calls 'ecological communication'. Basing his work on Parsons and systems theory he argues that contemporary society has become divided into relatively independent 'autopoietic subsystems'. He suggests that modern societies are no longer controlled by centralised and hierarchical control-systems. This is good news insofar as the individual is released from suffocating top-down influences. This occurs, according to Luhmann, as society becomes constituted by an array of relatively independent and 'self-referential' systems such as the economy, the law, science, the political system and so forth. It is bad news, however, in the sense that the very complex and even highly dangerous circumstances into which modern societies are now moving no longer have overarching systems of control or even languages with which the subsystems communicate. Social and political steering mechanisms do not produce the desired effects. When national, and increasingly international, crises start to emerge (those associated with the environment being one such), all this spells social and environmental trouble.

Beck (1992a,b,c, 1995) offers a related analysis, though with less emphasis on systems theory. On the one hand there are 'superdangers' emerging from modernity, especially those resulting from the humanisation and manipulation of nature. On the other hand, the subsystems (which have in large part evolved to deal with increasingly complex forms of society) are operating against a rational system of control over, and management of, these systems. According to Beck, however, the 'autopoietic subsystems' outlined by Luhmann have become increasingly merged. The very dangers emerging from modernity mean that 'the economy' becomes increasingly part of the erstwhile 'political' sphere. Similarly 'science' becomes increasingly 'political', the legal system becomes increasing political *and* scientific ... and so on.

Luhmann and Beck's work clearly offers a number of useful insights, especially regarding the problems of control in complex modern societies as a result of the increasing combination of society and nature. There are also some similarities between their work and the present analysis in which the advanced division of labour is posited as a central reason for humans in modern societies' being unable to understand and thereby control the possibly serious problems which they themselves are creating. Luhmann's 'autopoietic subsystems' can be seen as another way of referring to the division of labour. Furthermore, Beck makes the very helpful point that much of contemporary environmental analysis should be seen in terms of capital–capital relations rather than relations between capital and labour. This is because in addition to companies causing environmental degradation there is an increasing number of enterprises which have a very active interest in dealing with the same problem.

> One gets an inkling of the global market forces being unleashed here from the impact of the nuclear shock on the growth of the Geiger counter industry; or from the exponential growth in industrial pharmaceuticals, fostered by a worldwide hope of a cure for Aids.
>
> (Beck 1995: 138)

Sometimes, to add further confusion, the division of labour within one company may entail some divisions attempting to make profits from environmental pollution while others are profiting from finding ways of cleaning up. The problematic divisions of labour within East European factories are mirrored in supposedly more advanced Western companies.

But there are a number of differences between the approach of this study and that of Luhmann and Beck. Technical and social divisions of labour are a matter of struggle and negotiation, as indeed Beck's version of the argument implies more firmly. Knowledge and power relations lie behind these so-called 'subsystems'. They are, on the one hand, therefore, unstable and problematic. The division of labour is not, in Sayer and Walker's words, 'an inert set of specialized slots into which people fit like pegs' (1992: 1). On the other hand, they are not wholly negotiable. This particularly applies to the technical division of labour where the social relations and processes necessary for industrial production (in particular, the separation of labour and its management by capital) must be held broadly in place for a capitalist society to reproduce itself. Further, as discussed earlier, an extensive division of labour must be a feature of any modern future society.

In short, the subsystems referred to by Luhmann and Beck are the result of hard-fought relationships between classes, genders, races and other groups such as adults and children. Furthermore, the language of systems analysis is doing rather little to help us understand these conflicts. The subsystems are being reified as if they were concrete 'things' when they are in reality the product of complex social and power relations and, in some respects at least, subject to transformation. They therefore need analysis and understanding rather than treatment as self-evident objects.

Furthermore, if we are to really understand the 'superdangers' arising from the humanisation of nature we need to know much more about the causal powers operating at each stratum of nature and how human intervention is affecting those powers. If we do not do this we are in real danger of adopting apocalyptic visions on the basis of really very little understanding. An example is in Beck's most recent work where he asserts that genetic engineering is 'undoubtedly putting the "essence" of man, his anthropology' into the sphere of public policy-making (1995). As I will outline in Chapter 5, however, genes should not be considered the 'essence' of human beings. This is to revert to old reductionist forms of biology. The chemical components identified at one stratum of nature are being confused with the causal powers at the biological level. The essence of humans and all other organisms is constituted by the causal powers generating their form and development. These powers are inherited through their genes but this is not the same thing as saying genes are their 'essence' or that genetic engineering is profoundly changing this 'essence'.

The argument and the differences between the two approaches should become even clearer when we come to look at the relations between different types of knowledge, especially between abstract and concrete types of information. Science, economics, knowledge of the concrete, lay understandings and so on are all operating at different levels of generality or abstraction. They offer explanations of different types and with varying levels of reliability. These differences need 'unpacking' and, if we are to gain some real purchase on what is taking place, they need explicit recognition. This process of prioritising and combining different types of information is insufficiently recognised by much social theory dealing with the environment. But such a recognition is a feature of the critical realism which guides this study.

Abstraction, on the one hand, is useful for identifying structures, the underlying patterns of nature and society which give rise to the generative causal powers of nature or society. There is of course a large number of such powers and they combine with one another to contribute to the course of events which we can observe in the world. Such combination is sometimes said to be 'overdetermining' the more concrete levels at which deeper, structural, processes are experienced. For example, as we will see later, the alienation of animals from external and their own internal nature is a product both of capitalism and of the speciesist practices of human beings. Similarly, what might be interpreted as a purely environmental struggle is just as much a product of the rise of modernity and the market.

On the other hand, the concrete objects and events we can observe and analyse should be seen as another category of knowledge. They are the product of combined generative structures. But they are also the result of contingent processes and events. How underlying structures combine, how they affect concrete events and whether indeed they affect these events at all, will depend on a range of contingent factors. These include, in particular, the particularities of place and time. To give an example, while it might be generally true to say that animals' subordination is a result of a number of deep-lying structural processes such as capitalism and the speciesism generally associated with modernity, there may be contingent facts (say, extensive legislation in one country) which protect animals. Thus contingent factors can often be very important in terms of explaining concrete outcomes or conjunctures. As Sayer puts it:

> According to conditions, the same mechanism may sometimes produce different events, and conversely the same type of event may have different causes.
>
> (1992: 116)

Concrete analysis, therefore, is research into how causal structures and mechanisms combine with contingent processes and relations to produce real, material, conjunctures or events. As Marx put it:

> The concrete is concrete because it is the concentration of many determinations, hence unity of the diverse.
>
> (1973: 101)

But how does knowledge of the concrete relate to the meanings, experiences and beliefs that people, especially lay people, hold? It is at the concrete level that these generative structures and mechanisms are actually experienced and lived through. At the same time, as we will discuss in more detail in Chapters 3 and 6, meanings, language and so forth are constitutive of, or bound up with, these deeper-lying structures. On the one hand it would be a mistake to conflate theoretically informed understanding at the concrete level, as proposed by critical realism, with experiential knowledge and discourse. The latter necessitates some understanding of abstract knowledge as well as brute experience of what is taking place and it is a subject we will pursue later. At the same time, expression of lay experience and beliefs must in some respect reflect the material circumstances in which they are working. The question of meanings, experience and language is a distinct matter which must be considered separately from real material processes. But there are definite and necessary links between the two and, unsurprisingly, people's own accounts do reflect the multiple causations to which they are subject. It seems that another stratum, that concerning psychological mechanisms within the individual subject, would be the best way of linking our understanding of the concrete events with the ways in which someone actually interprets and communicates these events. (For further discussion see Collier 1994, Chapter 7.) Again, we will briefly discuss this later.

TOWARDS A GENERAL THEORY OF ALIENATION

The above discussion suggests that we need an understanding of alienation which recognises the complex processes underlying concrete outcomes or 'conjunctures'. At the same time, we need an overview which is epistemologically and ontologically well founded. This means an understanding of alienation which is broader than that usually attributed to Marx.

This is not the place to rehearse the development of the concept of alienation in detail. (For full discussions see, for example, Schacht (1971), Schaff (1980), Geyer and Schweitzer (1981), Schmitt (1983).) Suffice to say that with Marx's understanding it once had a tight (indeed, as I will shortly argue, sometimes over-tight) definition. It is now used very loosely to distinguish the contemporary human condition, but the word has passed into common parlance in a way which often leaves it largely bereft of meaning. Schacht (1971: lix) writes of the concept of alienation in the present day as follows:

> Reference is constantly made to it in connection with the growth of superficiality and impersonality in interpersonal relations, the compartmentalization of our lives, the stunting of personal development, the widespread existence of inhuman or neurotic personality traits, the absence of a sense of the meaningfulness of life, and the 'death of God'. There is almost no aspect of contemporary life which has not been discussed in terms of 'alienation'.

Whether or not it is the salient feature of this age, it would certainly seem to be its watchword. In spite of the term's great popularity, however, few people have a very clear idea of precisely what it means to say of someone that he or she is 'alienated'.

Given this amorphousness, Marx is a good place to start even if, in the end, his analysis now needs building on. As we shall see, his understanding of the relations between humans and nature is potentially richer than many contemporary 'Marxist' approaches to society–nature relations might suggest. And relations with nature are at the core of his theory.

Human beings, Marx argued, have certain essential characteristics. They have a 'natural being' which they share with many other species. This includes, for example, eating, drinking and sexual reproduction. They also have a 'species being'. Unlike other animals they are self-conscious and creative. They are also social. They need other members of their own species to develop adequately *as* human beings. Work is also central to their species-being. They need work of some kind to fulfil their innate creative capacities. Finally, Marx argued that they need a close association with external nature. Nature, he wrote, 'is man's inorganic body'; the central idea being that nature is continuous with and an integral part of persons, albeit not part of their organic being. They again need it to develop *as* human beings (Marx 1975). But it is important here to remember that humans are not bound by these biological and social needs. One of their chief characteristics, according to Marx, is that they are always discovering new powers and capacities within themselves. In this sense at least Marx is firmly in line with Sartre's later assertion that the essence of humans is that they have no essence. They can always transcend their biological–inherited needs and propensities in the sense of developing new capacities.

Marx argued, however, that modern capitalism has also left a very considerable price to pay. The price is, he argued, that humans have consistently had aspects of themselves alienated. Marx is best known for his analysis of the ways in which the commodities which humans make are systematically alienated from them. People may need work, and creative work at that. But under capitalism the products of people's labour are removed from them. They become owned and used by someone else. The efforts that humans have put into the things they make or sell are thereby taken away or alienated. Furthermore, industrialisation and the tendency to de-skill labour means that their creative capacities are ignored or misused. Similarly, humans may need one another to develop adequately as human beings, but the division of labour and the degree of competition engendered between people, especially at the workplace, systematically deny connections between people.

In much of Marx's writing, therefore, the industrial production process was the key to understanding alienation. This also applies to nature. In his earliest writings Marx argued that private property is the main culprit in alienating people from nature. But in his later writings he pointed to industrial production and the use of the raw materials of nature to make the things we need. Despite all the great material benefits accruing to humans, nature becomes merely a set of inputs into a production process. It is not regarded as a worthwhile thing in itself. Human beings, a species uniquely sensitive to aesthetic qualities, have even managed to insensitise themselves from the beauty of nature. As Marx puts it:

> The dealer in minerals sees only the commercial value, and not the beauty and peculiar nature of the minerals.

> (1975: 353)

There are, however, a number of dimensions to alienation in Marx. The most general one, and hence the one with greatest application, is the sense of loss or absence of something which is essential to humans' well-being. Paradoxically, it forms a very small part of Marx's work and has had virtually no development since. Bhaskar (1994) describes this more general meaning, though he skirts around the difficult question of what it actually *is* that is essential to human beings. Alienation, he argues, means 'separated, split, torn or estranged from oneself' (p. 114). It means being estranged from something that is essential or intrinsic to one's nature.

This more general sense, one which has gone largely unrecognised in Marx's theory of alienation but the one which is being adopted here, is the process by which people's understanding of themselves and their relationships to the world are removed. Once more, the result is a profound failure to *understand* our own circumstances.

As we have seen, the resulting paradox is that on the one hand humans are the one species which has managed to create the world largely in its own image. And yet in doing so they have simultaneously managed to turn one of their primary capacities, the advanced capacity to understand nature and the changes they are making to it, against themselves. The form in which such knowledge is available and is manipulated ensures that their appreciations remain in limbo.

FROM THE ABSTRACT TO THE CONCRETE

An understanding of people's alienation in modern society, and indeed that of other species, therefore needs to be multi-dimensional. Without becoming all-inclusive and hence again vacuous it needs to see how a number of structures and processes combine to produce the events to which people and other animals are subjected. A way of summarising the arguments of this chapter and linking them to the discussion in the last chapter of separated abstract knowledges is to refer back to the realist ontology as outlined earlier.

Figure 2.1, which is taken from Sayer (1992), sums up, in his words, 'the hierarchy of types of concepts which might lie behind a conceptualisation of a concrete event or conjuncture' (p.140). Its main intention is to show how more general processes combine with one another and with contingent conditions to produce these 'concrete events and conjunctures'. Sayer has chosen Marxist theory to illustrate this way of understanding concrete, observable, events.

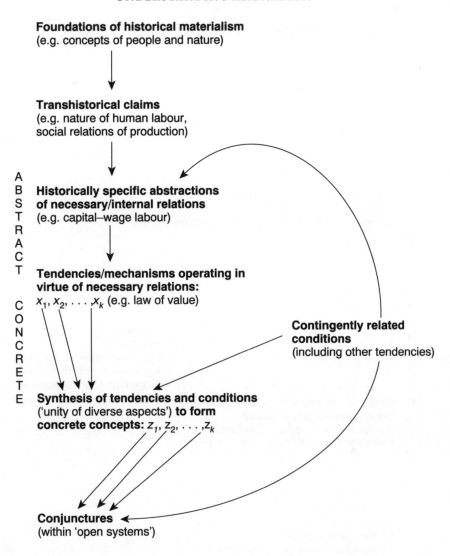

Foundations of historical materialism
(e.g. concepts of people and nature)

Transhistorical claims
(e.g. nature of human labour,
social relations of production)

A
B
S
T
R
A
C
T

**Historically specific abstractions
of necessary/internal relations**
(e.g. capital–wage labour)

**Tendencies/mechanisms operating in
virtue of necessary relations:**

C
O
N
C
R
E
T
E

$x_1, x_2, \ldots, x_k$ (e.g. law of value)

**Contingently related
conditions**
(including other tendencies)

Synthesis of tendencies and conditions
('unity of diverse aspects') **to form
concrete concepts:** $z_1, z_2, \ldots, z_k$

Conjunctures
(within 'open systems')

Figure 2.1 The relations between abstract and concrete (from Sayer 1992)

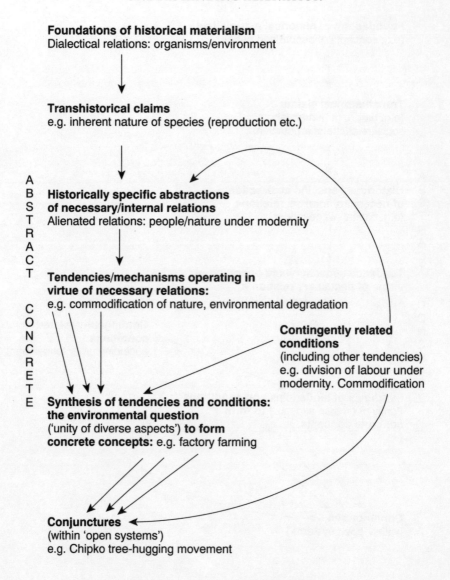

Figure 2.2 The relations between abstract and concrete:
factory farming and the Chipko movement

There is no particular reason for linking this approach to Marxism, although as Sayer points out, Marxism is particularly well developed in terms of formalising how the abstract and the concrete are related to one another.

As Figure 2.1 shows, at the most abstract levels are the principles of historical materialism. These include concepts of the relations between society and nature. Still at a relatively abstract level are 'transhistorical claims'. These would include the materialist argument that for human culture to exist people must be able to feed themselves, have shelter and reproduce. 'Tendencies' or 'mechanisms' refers to those processes which are a product of underlying structures. The example used by Sayer is the tendency, under capitalism, for money to flow towards the most profitable sources of investment.

All these processes, which are understood at fairly high levels of abstraction and theoretical knowledge, are conceptualised as combining to produce the concrete concepts and conjunctures at the 'lowest' level. Meanwhile, contingently related phenomena are again introduced on the right hand side of the diagram. This refers to other kinds of knowledge and information which affect how causal powers, liabilities and tendencies work out in practice. The research task typically entails moving between these different levels, trying to gain a better understanding of underlying 'necessary/internal relations' while linking them to contingent conditions and concrete conjunctures and events.

Applying this framework to our own particular concerns with the relations between society and nature (see Figure 2.2), research again takes the form of movement between the more abstract and the concrete. The former includes, for example, a general understanding of organisms (humans as well as animals) as developing dialectically in relation to their environment. This latter includes, of course, other organisms. Generally at this more abstract level we are concerned with understandings about underlying relations, generative mechanisms and processes. It is at this abstract level, for example, that we would recognise the need of all species to reproduce sexually and have shelter if they are going to survive. Our understandings at this level can of course always be subject to challenge but they can be considered relatively reliable. But meanwhile we must appreciate the contingently related conditions and tendencies which affect, and combine with, these more general processes. In our society, for example, we are particularly concerned with the great extension of the social and technical division of labour and the steady commodification of all areas of human and, as we will see, animal life. Finally, at a more concrete level, we are able, as a result of combining knowledge of structures and contingent information, to start introducing concepts which refer to the synthesis of these many conditions and tendencies. Figure 2.2 sums these up as 'the environmental question'. This concept is of course constituted by a diverse array of 'concrete concepts'. One mentioned in Figure 2.2 is 'factory farming', a process we will discuss in detail shortly. Finally, we are able to offer theoretically well-informed explanation of 'conjunctures'. One example, which will also be discussed shortly, is the specific episode of the Chipko 'tree-hugging' movement. Note that for all aspects of the contemporary environmental question there are a number of underlying processes and relations in common. These include, of course, assertions about the relations of organisms to their environment and the alienated relations of people from nature under modernity. But, more concretely, they also include the increasing division of labour and the increased penetration of the market into relations between people and nature.

Example one: humans and other animals

If, for example, we are trying to understand a concrete event involving the mistreatment of animals, this would again entail taking on board a hierarchy of general concepts lying behind such an event or 'conjuncture'. On the one hand it would once more entail an understanding of the general dialectical relations between organisms (human and animal) and nature of the kind originally outlined by Marx in relation to humans. It would also assert, still at a quite general level, that there are certain mechanisms involved which transcend time and space. Animals, for example, can be seen as having a species or natural being, internal structures and powers which will persist and affect their growth and development during their lifetimes.

At the same time, and now becoming more concrete and contingent, modern capitalist societies bring not only people but many animals into the circuit of money capital, treating them as inputs to a process of commodity production. These more specific forms of intervention begin to affect the actual ways in which an animal's structures and powers actually develop in practice. The particular way in which capitalism treats animals, for example, often uses (sometimes in a highly distorting way) an animal's species and natural being as it is exploited as a commodity. It affects the precise ways, for example, in which animals reproduce. Genetic engineering is a case in point.

In these ways, therefore, the animal's powers can be seen as simultaneously subjected to a diverse array of social processes and relationships. 'Contingently related conditions' (such as, for example, the extent to which animals are given rights in different societies) may well affect how these particular relationships and tendencies operate in practice. All these relationships and tendencies combine if we trying to understand a particular event such as, for example, a particular episode of the mistreatment of animals.

Our thinking on the relations of humans and animals to nature can be usefully combined with a Marxism which continues to focus on forms of exploitation specific to capitalism. Indeed, a number of contemporary writers are recommending such a combination. Influential examples are Benton (1993) and Birke (1994). Another is Noske (1989) who very explicitly argues that the types of alienation outlined by Marx can be extended to understand the use made by contemporary society of animals. She is striking exactly the right note if we are attempting a materialist, and critical realist, approach to the relations between contemporary society and animals. Her analysis can, however, be somewhat extended.

In line with the general thesis outlined earlier, the distinctions between 'communist' and 'capitalist' societies are marginal for the purposes of understanding the plight of animals (and, by extension, industrial workers) under modernity (Noske 1989). Both use a supposedly 'objective' and separated science and technology harnessed to Taylorist work practices. The powers of animals, much like those of industrial workers, have been increasingly subjected to mechanisation, rationalisation and automation. These processes are indicated in Figure 2.2 as 'tendencies/mechanisms operating in virtue of necessary relations'. Modern societies are combining with (many would say exploiting) the capacities of animals to grow and provide resources such as meat and milk. Animals have long been, of course, part of the technical division of labour, their work being alienated by their masters in what Marx called 'a master–servant relation' (1973: 500). But their lives are themselves subjected to an increasing division of labour in human society. Stockmen and women, for example, were once mainly responsible for monitoring the whole life of an animal, its health, behaviour and its relations to other animals. Such management by humans has now, however, given way to a number of specialist sciences. The routine administration of antibiotics, hormones, disinfectants has resulted in higher productivity and, in many instances, improved levels of health and nutrition for the livestock concerned (Bower 1987). But at the same time, animals are losing someone who has, to use Bower's word, 'empathy' with the animal's needs as a living being. The animals also lose a number of their own natural capacities: their ability, for example, to seek and choose their own food. The parallels with the way in which modernity affects human beings are striking.

Furthermore, as is the case with human beings, animals have now been 'specialised', divisions of labour being created even between animals of the same species. For example, some cattle are for beef and some for milk. And some chickens are for humans to eat while others are raised for the production of eggs. The 'species-being' and 'natural-being' of animals are being treated as disaggregated wholes, only parts of which are dealt with by human beings, primarily for human beings. The results can be horrendous. Pigs, which out of shear boredom start biting each other's tails, have their tails docked. Chickens, normally socialising in flocks of up to a hundred members, cannot establish a 'pecking order' among the thousands of their kind on the floor of a modern broiler or turkey house. They end up by pecking each other to death. Typically, the technologists have responded to the high rate of casualties among chickens by inventing the Automatic Debeaking Machine which slices off the tip of the birds' beaks with a hot blade (Noske 1989: 16).

Factory farming therefore leads to a number of forms of alienation amongst animals, paralleling those outlined by Marx for humans. They are even being alienated from their own products. They are, for example, made to have the maximum number of offspring and are then removed from their young as soon as possible. They are also 'de-skilled' in the sense that they are made to perform one or two basic tasks. The causes and consequences are again outlined by Noske (1989). Calves, for example, are only supposed to fatten, either in confinement crates or on metal-slat floors. The fact that crate calves lose the ability to stand at all or that metal-slat floors cause permanent lameness is of no concern to the management as long as it does not interfere with the fattening process – the calf's assigned task (p.19).

Animals are also alienated from their fellow animals. Humans are social beings and they develop as humans in relation to others of their species. For animals too, communication, contact, social play and social learning are all-important. And yet the modern industrial production of animals either systematically removes them from members of their own society or greatly distorts these societies by crowding them together. Contemporary farming practices even alienate animals from other human beings, computerised mechanisation dispensing with stockmen, for example. All this leads to the objectification of animals: their treatment as things, without relations to other living beings.

Similarly, capitalism even systematically alienates non-human animals from nature. They are 'sheltered' from the natural environment, but only in ways which are primarily oriented towards profit-making mass-production. Cattle internal systems, for example, have evolved to cope with grasses, stalks and other roughage but they are actually fed with high-energy grain. This causes a variety of health problems. Similarly, calves suffer from anaemia as a result of being fed on high-protein milk and no iron. Not only are farm animals separated from nature but they even suffer when they are exposed to nature. Pigs, for example,

> are prone to a kind of shock reaction, known in the pig industry as Porcine Stress Syndrome. The pigs can literally drop dead when they are moved to a new pen or transported to the market. Broiler birds may suffer the so-called flip-over syndrome, whereby the bird jumps into the air, sometimes emits a loud squawk and then falls over dead.
>
> (Noske 1989: 20)

So the powers of animals in contemporary society are also being extensively estranged from external nature and from their own, internal, nature. And it is not too far-fetched to see them alienated by modern factory methods, live transportation and animal experimentation in other, possibly even more profound, senses. They are not only alienated in these very physical senses but also in the sense of an understanding of their predicament's being removed. Of course, humans cannot appreciate what form such understanding takes. They can only guess, in the end, by making parallels with human beings. But once we have progressed beyond the stage of seeing animals as simply machines and, some animals at least, sharing with humans the quality of some kind of consciousness and awareness, there must be a sense in which their own skills and learned tacit knowledges are also being subjugated and marginalised by human beings and in the interests of human beings alone.

The central methodological point here is that the mistreatment cannot be seen as simply a result of 'speciesism' as much of the literature on animal rights suggests. (For an example see Regan and Singer (eds) 1976.) It is once more a complex combination of capitalism, modernity and speciesism. (For a path-breaking discussion see Benton 1993.) The division of labour, between people and between animals of the same species, emerges as a key process. One factor which facilitates such combination is the fact that in all modern forms of society people are systematically removed from contact with, and under-standing of, non-human species. No-one wishes to romanticise the association with animals before the advent of modernity. But the contemporary ways in which we are physically removed from the natural world are important preconditions for excesses such as factory farming. It takes events such as the driving of live animals through public streets for most people to realise what is taking place.

But there is one final twist as regards the alienation of animals. All these forms of estrangement can also be seen as themselves leading to *human* alienation. As such, they are a basis for human politics and mobilisation. Assuming that human beings need an adequate understanding of nature to develop their capacities as humans, then these forms of subjugation may not only be wrecking animals' lives but those of humans. Similarly, a concern for animals' well-being is not necessarily in contradiction with anthropocentrism. As much of the contemporary animal rights movement suggests, ending the alienation of animals can also ultimately serve human spiritual ends. As O'Neill suggests in support of what he calls 'an environmental ethic',

> Care for the natural world is constitutive of a flourishing human life. The best human life is one that includes an awareness of a practical concern with the goods of entities in the non-human world.
>
> (1993: 24)

Paradoxically, then, human beings are denying their own innate powers and capacities through restricting and subverting those of other animals.

Example two: indigenous peoples' resistance to modernity

Another example of how a movement between abstract and concrete knowl-edge assists our understanding of people's alienation from nature starts with ecofeminist work on the relations between women and nature. Ecofeminists such as Shiva (1988) argue that women are frequently 'the guardians of biodiversity'. It is often they who know most about the details of local farming practices, soil qualities, seasonal weather variations and so on. They are frequently the mainstay of local agricultural and forestry systems. And it is both their lay and their tacit knowledges which are often marginalised by the more general or abstract knowledges associated with 'the green revolution' and the creation of monocultures. The difficulties start, however, when Shiva and others finish up totally rejecting abstract knowledge because of the way it is used by capitalism and male-dominated institutions.

The central part of the difficulty is not so much abstract knowledge itself but the form of such knowledge and ways that scientists, including indeed social scientists, propose its use. Too often they jump from abstract analysis of causal processes in closed experimental systems to recommending applications in complex open systems where all kinds of contingent factors could trigger unintended and malign consequences (Collier 1994). It is one thing, say, to do successful general research on pesticides but quite another to apply these understandings to particular kinds of food in particular environmental and social contexts. Emancipation, as indeed Marx suggested long ago, lies not in resisting general understandings of how the world works but in harnessing abstract knowledge and using it towards alternative, more emancipatory, ends.

The underlying complex *combination* of processes affecting environmental degradation (and, with it, the marginalisation of both lay and tacit knowledges) again, therefore, needs constantly to be remembered. And, indeed, actual forms of resistance often recognise such complexity. What is occurring in such struggles? The environmental movement often over-romanticises what is taking place. Resistance is often not necessarily to protect nature and local practices. More materially, it is also undertaken by marginalised peoples to protect themselves from *social* domination. The collapse of old forms of social order and again the rise of the market and the division of labour should be central to our understanding.

Let us take, as an example, the famous case of the Chipko 'tree-hugging' movement. Here we find that it is indeed only partly an environmental movement. As Guha, in his study of the Chipko struggle points out:

> The most celebrated environmental movement in the Third World is viewed by its participants as being above all a *peasant* movement in defence of traditional rights in the forest, and only secondarily, if at all, an 'environmental' or 'feminist' movement.
>
> (1991: xii, Guha's emphasis)

This struggle in the central Himalayas has received much attention from environmentally conscious Westerners looking for signs of hope. It has also been widely celebrated as resistance of local women to the 'scientific' management of the forests by the state authorities in the interests of commercial exploitation. The protesters proposed what was actually a long-standing form of 'management', one which entailed the periodic burning of the forest floor with the object of creating fresh crops of grass and for animals amongst the forests. This was clearly incompatible with 'scientific management', and the authorities in effect closed off the forest to animals as well as to humans.

Detailed work on the Chipko movement shows, therefore, that the protest was only in part about being separated from their own knowledge and environment by 'scientific' management. It was just as much, if not more, a resistance by peasants to colonialism and the world market in timber. The hierarchy of types of concepts as laid out in Figures 2.1 and 2.2 suggests that there is likely again a complex set of combinations, although it says nothing about the relative importance of such combinations in generating concrete events. Research on the Chipko movement shows the actual combinations involved in the famous 'tree-hugging' of the people involved.

Guha makes clear, for example, that the struggle was as much about resistance to the growing division of labour under modernity as a struggle over environment alone. The women involved were not engaged as *just* women. Rather, they saw themselves as guardians of rights and privileges to the forest (for agriculture and the raising of animals) which were being denied by the state-sponsored commercialisation of the forest. Such guardianship had little to do with any supposed affinity between women and nature as proposed by some ecofeminists. (For a discussion see Plumwood 1993, Chapter 1, Jackson 1993a.) It had much more to do with the fact that the men were 'selling out' to the new market economy and in many instances even leaving the area and sending back money which they had earned elsewhere. A 'community spirit' persisted, one which was the product of an old peasant way of life in which the forest kings allowed the peasants rights of access to the forest. But, as Guha points out, increasing commercialisation, individualism and education in the Garwhal district

> definitely contributed to the erosion of the community cooperative spirit.... Although the community spirit is still present, as shown by Chipko, there is, simultaneously, a growing differentiation within the village due to the impact of commercialisation. There is, too, a sense of disruption of the traditional social fabric that the opening of Garwhal has brought, as well as anger at the comparative underdevelopment of the hills.
>
> (1991: 165)

The resistance was therefore a defence of a moral economy against a cash economy. It was only partly about nature and only partly about women. It was about a complex combination of relations and processes, perhaps the most important being the new position in the global division of labour which was being forced on them. Interestingly from our viewpoint, the abstract 'science' adopted by the colonial and later the indigenous authorities was in due course adapted to local lay knowledge, with a limited amount of burning allowed. This seems to be a case in which not only local, lay, knowledge but tacit and unarticulated skills did, in part at least, challenge and adapt the abstract scientific ideas being imposed from above.

A problem with some feminist analysis, including many versions of ecofeminism, is that it relies too much on gender on its own to offer explanations. Gender, more specifically the powers and capacities of reproduction, again combines with class, property relations and other structures of power in complex ways to produce not only difference but great variety in experience. Jackson makes the same point when she argues that ecofeminist approaches

> fail to recognize the diversity of lived environmental relations which different women experience, or the power structures in societies which mediate environmental relations and the ebb and flow of competing environmental ideologies.

> (1993b: 663)

Critical realism, as we have seen, distinguishes between different levels of abstraction and between underlying mechanisms and contingent circumstances. It allows the 'unpacking' of the experiences of women, and indeed men, to take place. It therefore makes no claim, as do many ecofeminists, about 'women's experience' in general. It would, however, want to open up what we actually might mean if we refer to the causal powers of women. These would particularly include women's reproductive capacities. These real powers are 'emergent' from the biological being of women. But of course the forms such capacities take (and whether they are emancipatory or otherwise for women) vary widely according to their combination with other relations such as class and property and the contingent circumstances in which the woman in question is living.

TYPES OF KNOWLEDGE, DISCIPLINES AND POLITICS

Three summarising points will conclude this chapter. One concerns the relationship between abstract and concrete analysis and different disciplines. The second concerns the difference between lay knowledge and theoretically informed concrete knowledge. The third concerns the political implications of this analysis.

It is clear from the above that scientists can simultaneously work at different levels of abstraction. A chemist, for example, can study both the concrete details of complex chemical compounds *and* periodic tables describing in much more abstract terms the constitution of chemical elements. Similarly a social scientist can study the details of a political movement while exploring some of the underlying tendencies (such as the tendency under capitalism for the rate of profit to fall) underlying such movements.

But does social science necessarily operate at more concrete levels? It is also clear from the above that abstract knowledge is not only associated with biology and other forms of science. It is of course possible to have abstractions of selected aspects of *human society*, an example being the circuit of capital. Nevertheless, it is still true to say that the sciences such as physics and biology

68

have the most to offer in terms of the most general understandings of the structural relations and mechanisms affecting or 'underwriting' all aspects of life. This can be seen as a comment on the supposedly advanced state of the sciences vis-à-vis the human social sciences (Collier 1994). It may be that it is only a matter of time before students of the human sciences establish structures and causal mechanisms affecting human society which are analogous to those uncovered by scientists of the physical and non-human world. However, abstract understandings of human social mechanisms and associated tendencies are of course always subject to transhistorical claims about the non-human world, even if these 'transhistorical claims' may themselves be subject to change during the long evolution of nature itself. Generalisations about human society are most likely to be about particular kinds of society such as feudalism or capitalism. And in the case of human society we are talking about 'open systems'. It is not possible to develop theories about the social world in a test tube. As soon as the theory is tried out in the real social world it is swallowed up in the many other mechanisms associated with that same world. This means that theories of the social world are limited to the relatively concrete. Perhaps the nearest we can get to a claim about a transhistorical mechanism in the social world is the increasing social and technical division of labour. This is a product of modernity and not directly attributable to one type of society such as capitalism.

It is therefore at the upper strata and in the realms of physics, chemistry and the natural sciences that the strongest claims about underlying and relatively permanent structures can be made. There are, however, several important points to remember about information at this more abstract level. First, these entities or organisms are envisaged as having *latent* or *potential* forms of behaviour and development. How they actually emerge and, most important here, the precise ways in which they actually become manifest will depend on contingent circumstances. An organism such as a plant or person, for example, has the power to grow and develop. But precisely how it does so, and indeed whether it does so at all, depends on less abstract, contingent, information.

How concrete events are experienced by people, or written or communicated about, is a separate, though linked, question. It is one to which we will return in Chapter 4. The point here, however, is that there is an important distinction to be made between everyday knowledge and skills (which are usually only developed as far as the demands of everyday life require) and theorised concrete knowledge of the kind implied in this chapter and by Figures 2.1 and 2.2. Everyday knowledge is what everyone engages in making and communicating all the time, and it will of course be developed differently according to the historical and environmental conditions in which people are located. It is this type of skill and knowledge which should be referred to when we are talking of the ways in which many people's understanding of the relations between themselves and nature becomes alienated in modern society. It might offer an understanding of nature's powers and might indeed be the basis for using such powers in, for example, the growing of food. As we have also argued, such lay knowledge is also entwined within the manipulation and use of real causal powers. But it is not usually, and does not usually need to be, full-blown theorised concrete analysis of the kind alluded to in Figures 2.1 and 2.2.

Finally, this chapter has been arguing, with the aid of a realist analysis of concrete events, for the notion of alienation being widened. This would entail a systematic understanding of how a *number* of causal processes combine to remove a person's or an animal's relation with nature, with its own capacities and with the products of its work. The other side to the same coin is that emancipatory struggle needs to recognise such complexity. But how is this to be achieved? Sayer and Walker sound the right note when they argue in relation to feminist politics that

> the only way out this impasse is to confront the intransitive and irreducible nature of each major structure of oppression in its own right, while realizing that gender, division of labour, and class are constructed simultaneously and reciprocally.
>
> (1992: 40)

We now consider the fraught question of the relation between 'the intransitive and irreducible nature of each major structure of oppression' and the ways in which people understand these same structures. This is a difficult area but it is one in which much fashionable social theory is leading us astray.

3

REALISM, CONSTRUCTIONISM AND THE PROBLEM OF 'NATURE'

Recent years have seen a growing debate over what is the most appropriate form of conceptual framework for understanding human society's relations with nature. One argument, stemming from the postmodern insistence that there can be no absolute truths or discourses, asserts that the environment (and our relations with it) is a purely social construction. It is simply a product of language, discourse and power-plays. Our description of the environment, according to this view, has no reference to real and material processes 'out there'. The environment or nature is only what society (and some groups more than others) care to make of it. Furthermore this type of construction gets used to inform our understanding of *human* societies. A second argument is that there are indeed real causal mechanisms, processes and relationships 'out there'. They exist independent of our own understandings, language and theoretical constructs even though the observable forms they take are dependent on contingent social and natural conditions.

The purpose of this chapter is to extend and critically assess these arguments. It will first suggest that the dichotomy 'constructionism versus realism' is in some respects misleading. All concepts have evolved from human societies. Therefore all knowledge must in some sense be a social construction. No knowledge has fallen out of the sky with a label attached pronouncing 'absolute truth'. Similarly this chapter will also argue, with reference to recent work from critical archaeology and feminism, that the two apparently opposing forms of understanding can actually live side by side with each other quite happily. The arguments of both realism and social constructionism are now quite sophisticated and well known.

But the two positions have become rigidified, not to say fossilised. There is, in Soper's words 'a kind of communicational impasse between the two perspectives' (1995: 7). This is largely, it must be said, because of divisions of intellectual labour between, on the one hand, scientists such as biologists and physicists and, on the other hand, certain social scientists. Unwittingly or otherwise, the latter in particular have been responsible for attempting empire-building. The implicit claim from what we will later be calling 'strong' social constructionism is that since all knowledge is socially constructed, it is primarily the social scientists to whom we should turn for understanding.

This chapter will argue that such claims are inadequate. But more assertively, it argues that the fact that knowledge is socially constituted does not entail that knowledge is *only* socially constituted. In other words, there exist powers and mechanisms in society which are not simply a product of language and discourse. More assertively still, it will argue that strong emphasis given to discourse by social constructionism may, in the end, not be worth the amount of intellectual effort currently being put into it. All it seems to be saying is that the ways people understand and communicate over the natural world are socially constructed. This is largely uncontroversial, although it is of course valuable to know how different interests 'construct' the environment in pursuing their interests (Hannigan 1995). Our priorities should now turn, however, to the more urgent task of developing better understandings of the causal mechanisms underlying how the social and natural worlds actually work and combine with one another.

CONSTRUCTIONISM VERSUS REALISM: SOME RECENT DEBATES

Insofar as academia is capable of having a stand-up row, it is over this issue that sociology has become most heated. *Vide*, for example, the argument between Tester (1991) and Benton (1993). Tester, from the social constructionist camp, argues that 'nature' is what humans care to make of it. Nature, in the end, is what human beings construct to make sense of themselves. Consequently, the form of its construction will vary according to the state and form of the human predicament.

> A fish is only a fish if it is socially classified as one, and that classification is only concerned with fish to the extent that scaly things living in the sea help society define itself. After all, the very word 'fish' is a product of the imposition of socially produced categories on nature.... Animals are indeed a blank paper which can be inscribed with any message, and symbolic meaning that the social wishes.
>
> (Tester 1991: 46)

But, from the realist camp, Benton argues that this is a wholly absurd position. He is tempted to parody Marx's comments about the person who:

> believing gravity to be a product of human consciousness, felt himself to be sublimely proof against drowning. Perhaps, if we were to impose the socially produced category of fish upon the viper its bite would lose its venom? Of course, views like Tester's, daft as they are, are currently very

fashionable among intellectuals. But I do not propose to provide a sustained philosophical analysis of these views here . . . .

(Benton 1993: 65–6)

None of these arguments would count for very much if they had no material effects on the lives of humans, other animals and inorganic nature. These seemingly rather abstruse debates could be ignored if we are also prepared to ignore the effects that human beings are having on the environment. Yet this is not the case. This insistence that 'nature' is a purely social construct surely runs the real risk of repeating and reinforcing the very kinds of anthropocentrism that are one of the key targets of modern environmental thinking (Dunlap and Catton 1994). A fish is certainly understood in different ways by different societies. In certain instances, for example, it may assume forms of religious significance which would be unrecognisable in other societies. On the other hand, a fish surely also has a real physical being, one which can be (and in many instances is being) damaged. It simply ceases to be a fish if it is surrounded by a toxic environment that kills it. A fish which has lost its life or its capacity to swim is by no stretch of the imagination *just* a social construction. In short, there are real differences between how people *construe* fishes, but this is a wholly different matter from how a fish is physically constructed. This is the nub of the argument here.

SOCIAL CONSTRUCTIONISM AND REALISM: A FALSE DICHOTOMY?

It is, however, important to assert here that both types of theory are indeed social constructions. Our understandings of the world must be products of persons and power relations in the social world. To this extent at least the dichotomy 'social constructionism versus realism' is misleading. There are in practice a number of versions of social constructionism. Dittmar (1992) refers, for example, to 'strong' and 'weak' constructionism. The 'strong' version is represented by, for example, Tester. It denies the importance of nature as an object external to human experience. The 'weak' version recognises that all knowledge is socially constructed, but it would argue that some abstractions can be extremely robust forms of social constructionism, in the sense of standing the test of time. 'Weak' social constructionism can be seen as analogous to what Cole (1992) calls 'core knowledge'. Again, it recognises that all knowledge is both socially constructed and contestable. On the other hand, all knowledge of the social and natural worlds need not be considered endlessly contestable. Some concepts and theories can be considered verified through repeated experience and intersubjective agreement.

It is this latter which can be equated with realism. A realist knows as well as anyone else that her or his work is located within a particular society, that its practitioners have particular values and motives and that science, like all other

73

forms of production, is conducted by individuals working in a collective fashion. In these ways it is indeed 'socially constructed'. On the other hand, they would argue that science is about much more than this. As we have seen, it is about establishing deep-lying causal structures and mechanisms. What these theories of these mechanisms actually consist of is yet another matter. A realist has no particular predilections as regards which is the best theoretical account. As one set of mechanisms is established, science is about 'digging deeper', establishing further structures and causal powers behind the layer of mechanisms already established. This is the nub of what is sometimes called 'transcendental' realism (Collier 1994).

But a realist goes further than this. While recognising such forms of 'social construction' he or she would not see these as problematic. 'This poses', to use Greenwood's words, 'no threat to the linguistic and epistemic objectivity of theoretical descriptions' (1994: 30). The mechanisms and structures established can still be real, causal and extra-discursive, even though they have been established in social contexts. Thus social constructionism as developed by realists is indeed establishing relationships, causal powers, and mechanisms which can be relied on in explaining changes in the human and natural worlds. But it is important to note here that realists do not rely solely on constructions of such phenomena to explain concrete events. As we have seen, they typically look to the *combination* of such mechanisms with other information derived from the particularities and contingencies within which such mechanisms are operating. Thus a fish may, for example, have certain in-built propensities to develop in a certain way. But the actual way in which it grows and indeed whether it grows at all will depend on a range of other factors, including the pollution of the seas, whether it is caught and so on.

Strong social constructionism, by contrast, denies that there are features of the world which exist independent of discourse and social construction of the kind mentioned above. The central point here is that strong social constructionism makes at least two fatal elisions. This means that it is wrong to treat the two forms of constructionism together as straightforwardly compatible. First, strong constructionism runs together the fact that something is physically made with the fact that it is construed, interpreted or understood. Similarly, it elides the distinction between, on the one hand, the things made by people and, on the other hand, what we make *of* these people's constructions. Researchers, academics and intellectuals in particular actually make very little. They are, however, in the business of interpreting. We are prone, however, to make (strong) constructions *of* other people's constructions. Whether the rest of the population shares these constructions is yet another matter. We should remain very doubtful about this, and we will return to this matter later.

The basic problem with social constructionism of the 'strong' variety is that it falls for the *non sequitur* that because knowledge is necessarily socially constructed it cannot be objective in the sense of providing a practically

74

adequate account of extra-discursive phenomena. Greenwood (1994) is a social psychologist promoting the adoption of realism to his discipline. He makes this point when he argues that:

> To claim that emotions are socially constituted – to claim that they are intrinsically social – is also to claim that they are social constructions, in the following respect: that they are constructed or created out of the joint commitment to certain arrangements, conventions and agreements by those who are parties to them. This is not, however, what is standardly claimed by social constructionist theorists: they claim that emotions are social constructions in the sense that they are constituted by, or are nothing more than, socially constructed *theories of emotion*.
>
> (p. 149, Greenwood's emphasis)

As we have seen earlier, knowledge and information are, according to a realist framework, stratified. At the more abstract levels are theories and conceptions concerning underlying generative structures and powers of objects. These are the necessary ways of acting of an organism or object in virtue of its nature. At a less abstract level is knowledge or information which is contingent to particular historical and social conditions. In this sense it is less 'important' than the more abstract information concerning structural laws. It is certainly, however, not less important in helping to understand observed phenomena. Indeed, contingencies may be more socially significant in some instances. Finally, then, there are those concrete phenomena which can be actually observed. They are 'conjunctures': the product of underlying relations and powers of objects *and* contingent structures and processes.

In the case of the life sciences, for example, a realist account refers to the innate powers and propensities underlying the growth and development of an organism. It is these powers and propensities, constituted in both humans, other animals and inorganic nature and evolved through interaction with their environments which constitute nature in a 'weak' social constructionist sense. But precisely how these powers and propensities develop (and indeed whether they develop at all) is dependent on contingent conditions, including the other organisms to which they are exposed. And in the case of human social systems, the realisation of such capacities is affected not only by contingencies but by people's ability to reflect on all these processes and to intervene in order to change them.

An example of weak constructionism is Darwin's theory of evolution. Darwin's ideas, as has often been pointed out, were socially constructed in the sense that they emerged from the very specific social milieu of industrial capitalism. And it is often forgotten that mid-nineteenth-century biological theory often borrowed from the ideas of prominent *social* scientists such as Espinas and Spencer (Dickens 1992). And, as Marx wrote in a letter to Engels, Darwinism was in some very important respects a social construction.

It is remarkable how Darwin recognises in beasts and plants his English society with its divisions of labour, competition, opening up of new markets, 'inventions' and the Malthusian 'struggle for existence'. It is Hobbes's 'bellum omnium contra omnes', and one is reminded of Hegel's Phenomenology, where civil society is described as a 'spiritual animal kingdom', while in Darwin the animal kingdom figures as civil society.

(Quoted in Schmidt 1971: 46)

On the other hand, it was (and remains) an extremely *good* social construction. While the theory of evolution has certainly been modified, the basic underlying mechanisms outlined by Darwin in the mid-nineteenth century have indeed remained relatively robust explicators for a long period of time ever since. As I will outline later, however, new 'weak' constructions are now beginning to modify Darwin's original ideas. These too are the product of particular groups of people, values and so forth.

So is the distinction between realism and social constructionism a spurious one? It is if we implausibly insist that realist concepts are not socially constituted. It is not if we take seriously the notion that, despite this, there are indeed reliable 'core' forms of knowledge about relations and processes on which we can depend and which our social constructions can illuminate. This is not, however, to reject the strong form of social constructionism as socially unimportant. For the many ways in which individuals and society are constructed in the form of language and communication are centrally important in legitimating and, as it were, scaffolding the ways in which causal powers are put to use. I will now develop this theme with particular reference to the category of 'nature'.

ON THE DIALECTICS BETWEEN REALISM AND STRONG SOCIAL CONSTRUCTIONISM

Human societies use, employ and modify the capacities and potentials of living beings (human and non-human) in a number of ways. (For an extended discussion see Benton 1993.) These include the capacity for movement and activity which can be, in some instances quite literally, harnessed to the purposes of man. This applies also of course to the capacity of human beings to labour. Other capacities such as growth and development can be used to human ends. Instances include the internally generated potential for growth and development of animals, these of course being central to the farming industry. Human societies also of course use parts of animals to create shelter and warmth for the human species. Similarly, the reproductive capacities of animals are subject to careful management in the pursuit of profit by modern farming.

As we will discuss in much more detail in Chapter 5, *in vitro* fertilisation and genetic engineering are amongst the most recently developed ways in which the inherited powers and developmental tendencies of organisms are modified in the interests (or at least in the intended interests) of human beings. As again we will see later, the modification of organisms' biologically inherited powers is now being extended to human beings. This applies particularly of course to recent developments in the new reproductive technologies and future developments in bioengineering. In all these instances, then, the genetically inherited propensities identified by a realist analysis are being exploited (often by powerful social groups and institutions) towards ends forced on animals. Furthermore, as we have seen some feminists arguing, the manipulation of women's reproductive capacities removes control and understanding of their own bodies.

These various means by which the powers and capacities of organisms and groups are exploited or used in society necessarily imply forms of social dominion by one group of humans over other groups, human or otherwise. And perhaps the most important way in which such power is exercised is indeed through a 'strong' form of social construction. It is here where the postmodernist and social constructionist tendencies of the 1980s have achieved the most extensive insights and should not be dismissed. The social constructionists of the 1980s, and indeed those of earlier decades, have shown how much of Western thinking opposes nature to culture and, in doing so, marginalises those groups such as women, black people and non-human species as 'nature'. Again, social constructionism in the form of discourse has real and material effects (Soper 1995). And as Plumwood (1993: 4) has recently put it:

> The category of nature is a field of multiple exclusion and control, not only of non-humans, but of various groups of humans and aspects of human life which are cast as nature.

The core of the dominating element tends to be middle-class white males and it is important to remember this when considering the claims of strong social constructionists. And, as has often been pointed out, 'the rest' is typically classified in discourse as an 'other', an unruly or disorderly 'nature', one which can therefore be legitimately subjected to control and modification. The dominant element is usually classified as 'culture' (Sydie 1987, Plumwood 1993) in contradistinction to the 'nature' which is managed and made subject to surveillance.

As Dunlap and Catton (1994) have pointed out, a strong form of social constructionism has indeed been a dominant feature of society–nature analyses during the last decade or so. Again, some, but not all of this has come from feminist scholarship. Perhaps the best-known work on the relations between society and nature is that of Haraway (1989, 1991). In her studies of the (strong) social construction of primates she persuasively shows how what we consider to be 'nature' is indeed very much a product of dominant values and relationships in modern society. At the same time, however, she appears to defend in a qualified way a sense of an objective knowledge about the biology of humans and other animals.

Another important text is Carolyn Merchant's *The Death of Nature* (Merchant 1980). It is with her book that discourses over nature can again be seen *in relation to* human intervention deeply affecting the real powers and capacities of human and non-human nature alike. Her argument is that around the sixteenth and seventeenth centuries in Europe a substantial change took place in people's consciousness of the natural world and their relationship with it. Before this time, the relationships between people and the cosmos were conceived as 'an organic unity'. All parts of the cosmos were seen as connected, related and mutually interdependent. The cosmos itself was seen as a live organism or unit, with human societies (including its oppressive hierarchies) as part of this same organism. Modernity picked up on and developed a wholly different set of concepts, world-views which reflected the increasing mechanisation of the social world. From this time on, and unevenly, the universe became equated with mechanism. It became envisaged as a machine, one constituted by discrete parts. Furthermore a world-view of this kind lent itself to the notion that the universe itself could be controlled and exploited. Perhaps it is wrong to say that these were wholly new concepts. Rather, what happened with the advent of modernity was a subtle re-working of old ideas which go back at least as far as the early Judaeo-Christian tradition. Essentially, 'man' became re-positioned as central to the rest of the universe.

In these ways, then, the holism of the mediaeval era became supplanted by a new or at least renovated discourse or 'social construction'. Again, whether and how these social constructions became a regular feature of popular or 'lay' discourse seems a separate matter. Merchant, like many social scientists, has relied for her account on the accounts of influential people such as priests and writers. It is their social constructions to which she refers and much less to the lay population at large. Meanwhile, of course, a realist view of science would insist that, for all these changes in discourse, nature was still stratified as an ordered series of generative mechanisms. It took nineteenth and twentieth century science to start establishing the laws describing these mechanisms.

The important point for Merchant (and for other ecofeminists such as Plumwood (1993)) is that these new constructions of the universe had major implications not only for how women became conceptualised but for how they, or more precisely their powers of production and reproduction, have been *used*. The fact that they gave birth to children (and became increasingly involved in raising them) combined with the fact that they became increasingly excluded from the production process, meant that they themselves became equated in discourse and action with 'nature'. Their sexuality and reproductive capacities became a threat. If culture was to prevail then nature, in the form of women, needed surveillance and management. The result was what Plumwood calls the 'backgrounding' of women. Their capacities for reproduction were not only relegated compared with production, but since they were constructed as part of nature this was, or so it seemed, a part of the natural order of things. Like the rest of nature they should be subjected to male 'reason'.

78

The scene was thereby set for women's real causal powers and capacities to become increasingly dominated and used by men. Plumwood, and of course many others, argue that such backgrounding of both women and nature remains dominant today. It not only accounts for the marginalisation of women's own capacities but for a particularly exploitative attitude towards the non-human world. But like all ideologies and 'strong' forms of social constructionism, such apparent 'naturalisation' remained to be challenged and, in part at least, overthrown.

The language of a primordial 'nature' has been extended not just to gender but to race and class. This becomes particularly clear if we examine the literature on colonial domination. (See, for example, Bond and Gilliam 1994.) The nineteenth and early twentieth centuries of course saw the widespread exploitation by European countries of labour and resources in such continents as Asia, Africa and Latin America. Key features included the concentration of production and capital into large monopolies, the rise of a globally mobile 'finance capital', and the territorial division of all the globe's territories amongst the great capitalist powers. So social and political relations were again in play, with the capacities and powers of indigenous peoples and resources being exploited by capital, with the active assistance of the dominant European nation-states.

The reciprocal of this process was that those societies which were being exploited became named by dominant social orders as the closest to 'nature' and the furthest from 'culture'. As Bond and Gilliam (1994: 9) put it in relation to Africa:

> The most recent source of slave labour and raw materials became the lowest rung on the cultural ladder constructed by European scholars and rulers.

Again, note in passing that such constructions were primarily made by dominant social classes and academics. Such elites did a great deal to make indigenous peoples' understandings and tacit knowledges culturally invisible. The result was that they had no apparent history or culture of their own.

Thus in complex, varying and contested ways the subordinated cultures became constructed by their societies as 'nature'. Two typical forms were locals as either 'noble savages' which needed to be preserved and in some degree emulated or as barbarians which needed to be civilised as a matter of urgency (Ramos 1994). Like many such constructions they were not only contradictory but unstable (Soper 1995). But the important point to note is that both the above constructions represented indigenous peoples and their tacit, difficult to articulate, skills as 'inferior' or non-cultured. Again such constructions could be challenged but such colonising language and discourse became in part adopted by the subjugated themselves. Such constructions are subtle and flexible and open to a number of different interpretations (Bond and Gilliam 1994).

Again, the obvious point is that 'the real world' is characterised by complex interactions between class, gender and race. The social construction of 'nature' becomes particularly transparent when, for example, we look at the history of pornographic violence conducted by men towards the reproductive and emotional powers of black women. Collins's account of the use of *black* women as sex objects by men summarises much of this study's argument so far.

> Exploiting black women as breeders objectified them as less than human because only animals can be bred against their will. In contemporary pornography women are objectified through being portrayed as pieces of meat, as sexual animals awaiting conquest.

> (1990: 167)

Other kinds of social relation besides those of gender, race and class could be subjected to the same kind of analysis. Children, for example, have been (and to some extent still are) constructed by dominant social orders as 'nature'. All this has again been a prelude to their exploitation and abuse. On some occasions in the early middle ages, Church and State attempted to stop infanticide and the abandonment of children when it became argued that children after all had souls. And having souls, of course, meant that they were human as distinct from 'nature' (Lyman 1991).

I have so far only considered the ways in which strong forms of social construction assist in various forms of social domination. It is important to make the point here, however, that to be persuasive and to be at least partly endorsed they must have some degree of practical adequacy in the way they 'carve up' the world and assign properties to it. To assign children or indigenous peoples to 'nature', for example, (and to thereby imply that they have not been fully subjected to 'culture') has a massively over-simplified grain of truth about it. In other words, gibberish is not practically useful. There must be some kind of correspondence between these constructions and the actual and material properties to which they refer if they are to generate any kind of endorsement or practical action.

Similarly, constructions of the strong variety sometimes provide, albeit quite rarely, windows or insights into real causal processes themselves. An example of this was offered earlier in relation to Darwin. Here we found a set of ideas and analogies which were very much influenced by the workings of Victorian capitalist society providing important and robust insights into the workings of the non-human world. A similar process is taking place now with the emergence of contemporary developments in the life sciences as represented by, for example, the work of Goodwin (1994), Wesson (1991), Lewontin (1982) and Dickens (1992, Chapter 4). These developments are sometimes referred to as 'the new biology' but they do not supplant Darwinism. Rather, they add to it.

Darwin's theory envisaged species blindly and randomly varying and evolving in order to fit their external environment. Natural selection was seen as occurring in this way. The new emphasis recognises other sources of order and change (Wesson 1991, Kauffman 1994, Goodwin 1994). Organisms are seen as having their own internal powers. These include powers of self-organisation, self-maintenance and self-government. Furthermore, the relation between organisms is seen more dialectically. Organisms change their environment, they do not simply adapt to it. Furthermore, they interact with one another socially.

In short, we are no longer dealing with Hobbes's 'bellum omnium contra omnes'. Species are no longer envisaged as helplessly mutating pawns. The key word is agency, whether of individuals or cooperating partners. Now, it is important to emphasise here that this new perspective does seem to be offering real insights into the causal powers and tendencies of organisms, providing radically new insights into how organisms develop and grow. (For examples see Goodwin 1994, especially Chapter 5.) But the key point here is that this is again a social construction in the sense of being the product of a particular set of people promoting particular values in a particular historical context. This time, however, it is a construction which recognises and postulates powers and capacities which are not *only* a product of the society in which they were formed. They have led to new insights into the causal powers of organisms and their relations with their environments.

The authors and thinkers behind this new form of biology are as much resisting ways of envisaging *human* forms of society as they are resisting particular forms of biological science. In particular they are resisting socio-biology or neo-Darwinism. As is well known, this relies on genes to explain many forms of behaviour such as aggression, territoriality and dominance, and even altruism. According to sociobiologists all such forms of behaviour can be ascribed to the genes' attempts to reproduce themselves in future generations (Wilson 1975).

The critique of sociobiology, and more specifically, its reductionist attempt to ascribe forms of behaviour to genes is now well established (see, for example, Rose *et al.* 1984). Furthermore, as indeed Rose *et al.* point out, sociobiology or 'neo-Darwinism' can be seen, as Marx spotted for Darwin over one hundred years ago, as an apology for capitalism. The aggressive individual, the demand for property and so on can all be seen as biologically innate. Capitalism is the 'natural' form of society. But it is important to point out that 'the new biology' as represented by Goodwin, Lewontin, *et al.* also has its own social programme, as well as its own biological project. In insisting on the agency of the organism, on the notion that individuals develop in relation to one another and the assertion that organisms change their environment and do not passively adapt to their environment, the representatives of the new biology are promoting a new kind of human society. This is one which opposes the kind of society in which Darwin lived and in which the neo-Darwinists and ourselves still live.

'The new biology' is not therefore socially innocent. It is indeed another construction, one laced with values about how society is or ought to be constructed. There is of course no harm in this. It simply needs recognising. Nevertheless, it is again more than *just* a social construction. It refers to real causal powers and mechanisms. These exist independently of discourse and lie behind the growth and development of organisms. When, however, the representatives of the new biology start to project their thinking into how modern societies are to be transformed they can rapidly become idealistic and detached from how the real social world actually operates (see, for example, Goodwin 1994). This is because they give inadequate emphasis to the actual material ways in which human social relations both constrain and enable the development of organisms to take place. To say, for example, that humans do and should relate to one another is one thing. But there is rather little that can be done about this until we have an adequate understanding of the real material relations and processes blocking or encouraging such interactions. A realist framework of the kind sketched out earlier provides the broader context in which to locate these recent developments in the life sciences.

One upshot of this argument is to dismiss the many dichotomies which have bedevilled the social sciences generally and our thinking about nature and society more specifically. Such dichotomies as nature/culture, animal/human, body/mind and so forth are all deeply ingrained in Western thought. And they have done much to legitimate the processes by which humans have dominated animals, men have dominated women, and white people have dominated 'others' in the form of non-white races. (See Plumwood 1993 for further discussion.) Furthermore, they do indeed allude, in an extremely rough and ready way, to real material powers and processes. Instead, as discussed earlier, knowledge is best envisaged as a series of layers, ranging from the most abstract to the most concrete.

CONCLUSION: STRONG SOCIAL CONSTRUCTIONISM – WHY ALL THE FUSS?

MacNaghten and Urry have recently given special emphasis to the social construction of nature. They do so in the following way.

> There is no pure 'nature' as such, only natures. And such natures are historically, geographically and culturally constituted. Hence there are no natural limits as such, but each depends on particular historical and geographical determinations, as well as on the very processes by which 'nature' is culturally constructed and sustained, particularly by reference to the 'other'.
>
> (1995: 207–8)

If the arguments of this chapter and of this study generally are right, however, there are some significant problems with this argument. They again concern the distinction between the real causal powers of nature and the ways in which academics and other theoretically well-informed people understand or interpret nature. The word 'constituted' again seems to be rolling together the business of materially transforming nature's powers with its interpretation. Similarly, what do the scare quotes around the word 'nature' actually allude to? Are there really no natural limits as such? Are we not again back to the assertion that gravity is simply a product of human consciousness and this means we need take no account of it in our actions? Again, all natures are indeed social constructions. But some constructions are in a sense 'more equal' than others. Although they are always revisable, they are 'weak' social constructions referring to 'core knowledge' of the powers, capacities and tendencies of organisms and their development in dialectical relation to their environment. And nature here is not in quotation-marks. It refers to the real powers of human beings as well as non-human organisms. These are not just yet another 'nature'.

Writing from a realist perspective, this chapter has been discussing the relations between 'weak' and 'strong' constructions of nature. For strong social constructionists at least, the dichotomy between their perspective and realism is surely irreconcilable. Realists' appeal to structures, powers and causal processes which are independent of discourse will surely remain an unacceptable proposition to the strongest of social constructionists. But, as the above discussion has also been outlining, a realist can indeed handle *both* perspectives and view them as dialectically interdependent. Exploiting an organism's inherited powers both depends on and often legitimates the (strong) social construction of that organism as part of 'nature'. At the same time, 'strong' social constructions can act as a window onto more abstract understandings of the natural and social worlds. They can be envisaged as a check on those more general sciences which, while providing useful insights into the structures and processes of the world, still threaten to obliterate the differences and particularities of time and space. 'Strong' social constructions can offer still further insights into the processes and mechanisms affecting the experiences of people 'on the ground'. They can on occasion threaten the understandings of the causal mechanisms of nature and society, showing that such understandings are, after all, social constructions.

But, for a realist, much of the intensive contemporary celebration of discourse by strong social constructionists remains in the end a great deal of ado about rather little. We must again make a crucial distinction. This is between material processes and relations on the one hand and our understandings of, and communications about, these processes on the other. It is self-evident that the latter are indeed social constructions. Realists would certainly not have a problem with such a proposition. They are as interested in people's understandings and discourses as anyone else. They are especially interested in their material effects. But they are also even more interested, as will be indicated in Chapter 6, in the complex *relationships* between, on the one hand, the causal powers of nature and the material processes involved in these powers and, on the other hand, the particular ways in which people communicate to one another about these powers and processes. These are issues we will pursue later. Meanwhile, however, it is a moot point whether it is worthwhile building and maintaining a large-scale academic industry around the obvious fact that understandings and their communication are social constructions.

Perhaps more interesting, as the next chapter suggests in relation to contemporary people's understandings of science, are the differences in understandings between scientists and academics on the one hand and the lay understandings of the remainder of the population. This important distinction seems to have gone largely missing in the debate between realists and social constructionists. Furthermore, as we will see, the kinds of construction made by lay people suggests future research from a critical realist might concentrate on the innate psychological powers of human beings to make sense of, and communicate about, the many and diverse processes to which they are subject.

4

WHO WOULD KNOW?

Science, lay knowledge and alienation

What does lay understanding of scientific knowledge of the environment actually consist of? Do lay people broadly accept what abstract science has to say or are they rejecting it? It is symptomatic of the general argument outlined in this study that lay understandings of the relationship between society and nature are under-recorded. A specially commissioned Directive by Sussex University's Mass-Observation Archive illustrates the kinds of alienation to which the last two chapters have been referring. This chapter will argue that lay people are not so much dominated by abstract thinking as left with an inadequate understanding of their predicament and their relations to nature. They also do not necessarily share the theoretically informed social constructions which intellectuals and others attribute to them.

However, we can be more assertive than this. People do seem to be constructing and communicating about relations with nature which draw on and reflect their *social* experience. On the one hand people are necessarily involved in experiencing and monitoring diverse combinations of real causal powers and tendencies. These, as we have seen, are best understood through the analysis of concrete conjunctures. On the other hand, people are making sense of these experiences, giving meaning to them and communicating about them by drawing on icons and forms of experience with which they are more familiar. Perhaps we are encountering here another tendency which stems from the innate powers of human beings, that of constructing the world in ways which make some sort of sense to the person involved.

LAY KNOWLEDGE: A HOSTILITY TO SCIENCE?

We have already suggested in the last chapter that there may be a significant gap between the social constructions which intellectuals make and the interpretations and understandings of lay people. In the absence of adequate information, it is tempting to ascribe to lay people views similar to those held by academics. Much the same can be said of lay people's understanding of their relations with nature. Here again, their appreciations of abstract science are not the same as those often attributed to them by intellectuals.

A good starting-point and a preliminary hypothesis is Beck's work. His analysis of 'the risk society' (Beck 1992a, b, c) also has some close parallels with Giddens's understanding of the threats present in contemporary society (Giddens 1990, 1991). There are differences between these analyses but they have a number of themes in common. (See also Beck *et al.* 1994.) They are currently very influential views, but the correspondents to Mass-Observation Archive show that they are quite misleading.

Beck and Giddens suggest that an important new feature of contemporary society is the systematic and very widespread undermining of scientific knowledge. This is a key theme in their work and one on which this chapter particularly concentrates. People, Beck and Giddens argue, remain highly dependent on abstract knowledge for an understanding of their predicaments. But modernity, they suggest, is characterised by increased 'reflexivity', whereby people no longer take such abstract knowledge for granted. They increasingly subject it to criticism and refuse to take it as given.

This scepticism is said to have a number of causes. For Giddens it derives partly from the complexities of globalisation. Globalisation, he argues, tends to reduce the significance of everyday knowledge and to concentrate such understanding and expertise within 'abstract systems' which largely manage everyday life. At the same time, people are increasingly realising that expertise must have its limitations. No such system can, in the end, predict or dispense with risk. The result is a sense of deep personal insecurity and a distrust of the knowledge which has been detached from people's everyday experience.

For Beck too, scientific knowledge is coming under increasing critical scrutiny. Again, this is seen as a result of general public scepticism towards most forms of authority. But Beck, like Luhmann whom we discussed in Chapter 2, particularly stresses that science is under very intensive scrutiny as a result of the ways in which it has become thoroughly politicised and identified with vested interests. It is now, in his words, a 'branch office' of economics and politics. Its claims to detachedness have become thoroughly exposed. Far from being seen as a saviour of people's relations with nature it is now, according to Beck, a way in which essentially political and social questions have become scientised and hence concealed from the non-scientific or lay public. As Beck puts it:

> Science has *become the protector of a global contamination of people and nature.* In that respect, it is no exaggeration to say that in the way they deal with risks in many areas, the sciences *have squandered until further notice their historic reputation for rationality.* 'Until further notice', i.e. until they perceive the institutional and theoretical sources of their efforts and deficits in dealing with risks, and until they have learned self-critically and practically to accept the consequences from this.
>
> (1992a: 80, Beck's emphases)

Science, both Beck and Giddens argue, is becoming increasingly under-mined as people reflect on it and refuse to take its assertions for granted. The purpose of this chapter is to test and develop these ideas. But, in the light of global environmental risks, do people increasingly distrust science? Do they find their lay knowledge being increasingly supplanted by abstract scientific theories? How do non-experts interpret their society's relations with nature?

THE MASS-OBSERVATION ARCHIVE SURVEY

To address some of these questions a Directive was conducted by the Mass-Observation Archive. During recent years *Mass-Observation in the 1990s* has asked a large number of its correspondents to reply on specific topics. These are often on a topical and contemporary issue, and this particular Directive, entitled *Nature and the Environment*, took place at the time of the United Nations Conference on Environment and Development in Rio de Janeiro during June 1992.

The Directive had three main aims. The first was to seek people's feelings about the environment and economic development. The second was to establish how people found out about these issues, and the third was to ask people what could be done about development and environment. Only part of this directive, however, was directly addressed to the issues and themes discussed in the first section of this chapter. A substantial part of the survey was devoted to the role of the media in transmitting information about nature and economic development. As such it was not directly relevant to the theories and ideas discussed earlier. This chapter will therefore concentrate particularly on those sections and questions which apply to the issues in hand.

1 The Earth Summit assumed that there were substantial environmental and development problems in the world. Do you agree?
2 What in your opinion are the three most important environmental prob-lems facing the world today? What are the three most important deve-lopment problems?
3 Do you think future generations will face the same issues or will there be others that are more important to them?
4 Do you feel any of these problems pose a threat to you personally or to our way of life in the UK?
5 Or are they only relevant to remote areas of the world?
6 How useful is modern science? We are still very dependent on scientists to tell us about the environment, our relationship with it and changes to our behaviour if we are going to protect the planet. Does modern science have an adequate understanding of our relationships to the environment? How seriously should we take the explanations, predictions and proposals offered by modern scientists?

697 people were mailed. By the end of September 1992 the replies were reducing to a trickle and the analysis took place. 408 had replied, a response rate of 58.5 per cent, 294 of whom were women and 114 men. *All* the replies are dealt with in the quantitative sections of this chapter.

The Mass-Observation Archive correspondents have some very distinctive characteristics and these need to be borne in mind when considering the replies. They contain, as we will see, a large proportion of women and middle-aged and older people. Further, it is of course quite possible that those who replied are those who are most likely to have been agitated by the issues involved. As will become clear below, most of those who responded felt that there are indeed some major environmental and development problems. Possibly those who did not agree did not choose to respond.

It will be noted below that two main kinds of information have been derived from the Directive. One is quantitative in nature: for example, the simple numbers of people who said there were or were not substantial environmental and development problems. The second type of data is more qualitative. As I hope to indicate shortly, this latter is particularly useful for showing the often contradictory and fragmented responses to the questions. The quantitative results outlined below were often in fact quite difficult to deduce from the Directive. As will become clear, the Mass-Observation Archive correspondents often simultaneously endorse *competing* forms of abstract knowledge. They also recognise both abstract *and* lay or popular forms of understanding. All this means that responses which are reduced to purely quantitative knowledge do not adequately reflect the complexity and richness of the original replies. Furthermore, the way in which the questionnaire was constructed invites people to talk in the kinds of abstracted way they might find familiar in the media. This means that the prime emphasis here is on people's understanding of abstract science rather than on their own, personal and local experience. Nevertheless, some indication can be inferred as to the links they make between abstract and lay knowledge. This, as suggested in the last chapter, seems to entail language and communication mediating between, on the one hand, the real causal mechanisms involved in the creation of concrete events and, on the other hand, mechanisms innate to human beings which construct experience into coherent and understandable forms.

THE MASS-OBSERVATION ARCHIVE ENVIRONMENT AND NATURE DIRECTIVE: RESULTS AND DISCUSSION

Clearly, the overwhelming impression gained from the data in Table 4.1 is that people do agree that there are substantial environment and development problems. Women, it seems, are more likely to agree that such problems exist. This can be seen as in line with some of the arguments from ecofeminism discussed earlier. It can also be interpreted, however, as indicating that women

Table 4.1 Question 1: The Earth Summit assumed that there are substantial environmental problems in the world. Do you agree?

			% of respondents
Total Sample	Yes	368	98.1
	No	3	0.8
	Don't know	4	1.1
	No answer	33	-
Men	Yes	100	95.2
	No	2	1.9
	Don't know	3	2.8
	No answer	9	-
Women	Yes	268	99.2
	No	1	0.4
	Don't know	1	0.4
	No answer	24	-

are more deferential to scientific authority, while men are more prone to be contrary. Men do not necessarily have any good reason to be so antagonistic to science, but they perhaps feel (as Harrison *et al.* (1994) suggest) that they should assert their male right to have an opinion. For women and men alike, however, the greater proportion of those answering this question took it to be a self-evident fact which need hardly have been asked. A typical response was:

> Do I agree that there are substantial environmental and development problems in the world? Look outside your front door. Seems so obvious as to not need stating.
>
> (Part-time female teacher, age 55)

The above quote, however, raises the important question of whether a recognition of such problems is a product of people's personal experience of risk. Or is an understanding of environmental risk largely independent of personal perceptions of these problems? We can begin to answer these questions with the aid of Question 2: *What in your opinion are the three most important environmental problems facing the world today? What are the three most important development problems?* The ten most frequent responses to the part of the question concerned with environmental problems are listed below. They are divided by gender. The ranking system uses the following procedure. For each respondent there are three replies. This times the number of respondents gives the total number of replies. The total number of responses to each type of problem is then calculated. The ranking given in Tables 4.2 and 4.3 is this latter total as a percentage of the total number of replies.

Again, this purely quantitative analysis does not adequately reflect the complexity of the replies. Often, for example, the correspondents stressed the *connections* between these problems. The figures do, however, suggest that it would be difficult to argue that perceived environmental risk is a product of direct experience. Nor is it necessarily a result of understandings based on such

Table 4.2 (Question 2) Most important environmental problems, men

Pollution of air and sea	20.2%
Rain forests / deforestation	13.6%
Population numbers/growth	11.6%
Global warming	9.3%
Ozone layer depletion	7.4%
Nuclear waste / nuclear accident	5.4%
Private transport	5.0%
Resource depletion	5.0%
Loss of species	3.9%
Desertification	2.3%
(Other)	(16.3%)

Table 4.3 (Question 2) Most important environmental problems, women

Pollution of air and sea	23.4%
Rain forests / deforestation	15.7%
Ozone layer depletion	10.3%
Population numbers/growth	8.8%
Global warming	8.2%
Resource depletion	8.2%
Loss of species	5.1%
Toxic chemicals in food chain	3.4%
Drought	2.4%
Nuclear waste / nuclear accident	1.8%
(Other)	(12.7%)

experience. Pollution from transport, for example, has a relatively low ranking in people's assessment of environmental hazards. By contrast considerable emphasis is given to rain forest destruction and ozone layer depletion. This suggests that people do not need to be encountering risks in order to rate them *as* risks. Again, the perception of a 'risk environment' often has little to do with direct physical contact. They rely on other sources. These include iconic symbols of environmental destruction such as the supposedly pristine, exotic 'other' of the rain forest. But they also frequently depend on abstract scientific knowledge and its elaboration in various forms of media.

Some gender differences are again worth pointing out here. The relatively high (though in numerical terms still quite small) emphasis given to private transport by men presumably reflects their more extensive use of cars. The special mention of food and toxic chemicals in the food chain are likewise presumably a reflection of many women's continuing high levels of responsibility in civil society, especially those for food-production and child-care. One interesting difference is the particular emphasis given by women to ozone layer depletion. This again could well be a reflection of their still central role in the raising of children and a broader concern for future generations. The following response suggests, however, that it may also be a result of many women's more extensive involvement in family networks.

Ozone layer. 'We are all at risk from skin cancer. I don't sunbathe anyway. I smother the children in suncream. My neighbour, my husband's aunt and his father have all had malignant melanomas removed (all are in their sixties) and my aunt's cat had one on its pink nose.'

(Housewife / ex bank cashier, age 32)

Again, however, it would be difficult to argue that these different reactions to environmental risk are based solely on direct understanding of the risks involved. She, like presumably almost everyone else, knows very little about environmental risk on the basis of any first-hand experience. The cancers which the above respondent refers to, for example, may or may not be due to the thinning of the ozone layer. As we will see later, the sense of risk and danger to which she refers largely derives not from the danger itself but from the lack of sufficient knowledge. The cause of her feeling insecure is her own ignorance.

The ten most frequent responses to the second part of Question 2, that concerned with development problems, are listed in Tables 4.4 and 4.5. The ranking system is the same as that described for environment problems.

Table 4.4 (Question 2) Most important development problems, men

Population	17.5%
Famine/nutrition	8.3%
Poverty/wealth distribution: North–South	7.5%
Pollution	7.0%
Resource depletion	6.6%
Armaments / regional wars	5.4%
Industry/capitalism	4.5%
Third world debt	4.2%
Third world governments/politics	3.8%
Western lifestyles	3.8%
(Other)	(31.4%)

Table 4.5 (Question 2) Most important development problems, women

Population	20.7%
Famine/nutrition	12.1%
Poverty/wealth distribution: North–South	10.4%
Pollution	5.0%
Third world debt	4.6%
Resource depletion	4.2%
Education	4.2%
Industry/capitalism	4.0%
Armaments / regional wars	3.6%
Deforestation	1.7%
(Other)	(29.5%)

Clearly, the distinction between problems of environment and those of economic development (one alluding to the natural world and the other to the social world) was a difficult one for many correspondents. Many items (for example population, pollution and resource-depletion) occur in responses to both questions. One respondent went so far as to spell out the difficulties involved in separating environment and social development as proposed by the Mass-Observation Archive Directive. She drew a diagram (Figure 4.1) showing the key connections as she saw them. This Mass-Observation Archive correspondent backed up her diagram with the following statement:

> I cannot answer this question. Everything is inter-related, so climatic change is both an environmental and a developmental problem; nor do I think anyone can say which problems are going to be the decisive ones.

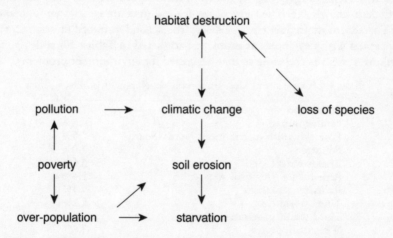

Figure 4.1 The connection between environmental and development problems
(by infant school teacher, age 63)

The rankings in Tables 4.4 and 4.5 again show that the sense of environmental risk resulting from development can hardly be seen as stemming only from direct experience and knowledge of such risks. They are often seen as produced somewhere else and frequently by people other than the respondents. Over-population, famine and North–South social divisions are hardly regular events in most Mass-Observation Archive correspondents' everyday lives. Listing these items as major problems is again largely a tribute to the various forms of media explaining global development and environment problems. At the same time, people are holding *multiple* appreciations: some global and general, some based on direct experience. In practice these are inter-weaving within people's awareness in highly complex ways.

The results for Question 3 are shown in Table 4.6. They are again divided by gender. The responses seem to indicate widespread agreement that modernity is characterised by universal environmental risks extending to future as well as present generations. It seems quite possible, however, that there may be more involved.

Table 4.6 (Question 3) Do future generations face the same problems?

				% of respondents
Men	Yes	63		86.3
	No	6		8.2
	Don't know	4		5.5
	No answer	41		-
Women	Yes	157		83.5
	No	11		5.9
	Don't know	20		10.6
	No answer	106		-

The number of people who did not answer Question 3 is quite surprising and intriguing. There is a range of possible reasons for this. Perhaps they see the risks as so obvious as to not need response. (One of the difficulties of this particular type of survey is that, unlike a questionnaire, it cannot press or remind people to answer every question.) Alternatively, and despite the fact that only a relatively small proportion explicitly stated that they did not know, the lack of response could be due to the fact that people simply felt quite unable to answer this question. A third possibility is that the threat is so global and extensive that people have mentally insulated themselves from the risk. Bearing in mind the extensive responses to other questions, however, this latter seems most unlikely.

It seems at least possible that the high numbers of people not replying is a result of the combination of the answer's being perceived as so evident as to not need a response while at the same time raising such large conceptual issues that people simply felt unable to respond. Again, Mass-Observation Archive Directives do not enable dialogues between researchers and correspondents to take place, and another type of questionnaire involving face-to-face inter-action would be needed to pursue these matters further.

The responses to Question 4 – *Do you feel any of these problems pose a threat to you personally or to our way of life in the UK?* – and Question 5 – *Or are they only relevant to remote areas of the world?* – are shown in Tables 4.7 and 4.8, again divided by gender.

The responses show that a majority felt that environmental threats affected them and the UK. But a perhaps surprising 44.6 per cent of men and 32.4 per cent of women did not feel personally affected or that the risk does not affect the UK. Unfortunately the form of the question made it difficult to distinguish between personal threat and threat to British society as a whole, but a tally was kept of the number of people who did explicitly mention that they themselves had directly experienced pollution or major environmental change. Only 4 men and 26 women explicitly mentioned direct and personal experience of this kind. This again suggests that people are largely dependent on global knowledge, especially of course that produced by the media, as a means of assessing the risks and threats to which they are subjected. It is by no means simply the physical or direct risk itself which is the problem.

Table 4.7 Responses to Questions 4 and 5 by men

Threat to me personally/UK		Threat to remote areas only	
Yes	40 (54.0%)	Yes	6 (9.1%)
No	33 (44.6%)	No	60 (90.9%)
Don't know	1 (1.4%)	Don't know	0
No answer	40	No answer	

Table 4.8 Responses to Questions 4 and 5 by women

Threat to me personally/UK		Threat to remote areas only	
Yes	98 (67.5%)	Yes	15 (12.2%)
No	47 (32.4%)	No	105 (85.4%)
Don't know	0	Don't know	3 (2.4%)
No answer	149	No answer	171

The fact that quite a large percentage of the population did not appear to feel to be at great personal risk could be partly accounted for by the fact that a large proportion of the Mass-Observation Archive's correspondents are either middle-aged or elderly. A frequent response amongst old, and sometimes not so old, people was that they did not personally feel at risk because they realised their lives were limited in length anyway. Here, for example is a 68-year-old charity organiser:

I don't think these problems pose a threat to me as, by the law of averages, I don't suppose I'll be around all that much longer.

For many older people the risk to self became transferred to the risks for future generations, especially grandchildren.

The particular sample suggests, therefore, that further research needs carrying out on this issue. Do younger people feel under greater levels of risk? Similarly, the high numbers of people not responding to the question on risk is quite puzzling. As with the question of hazards to future generations, further work needs to establish whether this silence again indicates that people either find the answer too obvious to need stating or that they have insufficient knowledge to respond or are deliberately ignoring an issue which is too large for consideration.

The answers to Questions 4 and 5 seem to indicate a considerable lack of certainty. A predominant impression is that people are very unsure about whether contemporary environmental problems are affecting them personally or Britain more generally. As we have seen, few of them seem to claim any direct experience of these risks.

On the other hand, they are very aware of a looming sense of threat and crisis. There is perhaps a larger metanarrative involved in understanding environmental change (Szerszynski 1993). Furthermore this may be important in developing the realist framework being adopted in this study. According to this view of imminent decline and disaster, previous eras are seen as harmonious, with the individual in an authentic relation with society as well as nature. Now all this is seen as changing towards one real and potential hazard. This can of course be simply ascribed to the fact that many of the correspondents are middle-aged or elderly. But something else important seems to be at work.

The type of narrative or construction is perhaps best summed up by a 53-year-old female 'carer for an extended family'. It illustrates the general argument here that environmental risk in advanced civilisations is often less a case of personal experience and more one which can best be described as a sense of impending doom based largely on inadequate understanding.

It is easy to feel that these problems are not a threat to me personally, insulated from the aspects of the world which I do not choose to face as most of us are. I, and thousands of other middle aged and middle to working class women are seemingly secure in our paid for cosy homes with water on tap, heating in winter assured and seemingly limitless amounts of food in a little cornucopia down the road named 'Gateway' or possibly 'Tesco' or 'Safeway'. We are absolutely removed from all unpleasantness, all hunger, dirt, cold, and exhaustion which must be the regular lot of countless millions that we read about in the handily delivered newspaper or see from the comfort of our sofas on the TV news. However, this insulation, this comfort, does not produce, for me, at any rate, a lasting confidence. Rather, as I go about my rather circumscribed life, I am aware of a dim foreboding within myself, an awareness of a creeping and insidious threat, somewhere else, somewhere out there, 'abroad', in a Third World but which seems to be moving inexorably closer.

There remains the central question, however, of how this sense of imminent disaster has come to lodge itself in many people's perceptions. Is it literally a sense of large-scale environmental crisis? Or is it a product of a more general sense of threat; one based on individuals' perception of their *social* positions in a globalising society and economy and projected onto their perceived relations with the non-human world? Is it a case of the landscape serving to remind people of who and what they are in society. As Szerszynski (1993: 186) puts it: 'It locates us in place, time and community'. Other Mass-Observation Archive studies on the environment seem to indicate the latter (see Dickens 1992, Chapter 7).

With the final question of the Mass-Observation Archive Directive we address the most central part of the ideas offered by Beck and Giddens. *How useful is modern science? We are still very dependent on scientists to tell us about the environment, or relationship with it and changes to our behaviour if we are going to protect the planet. Does modern science have an adequate understanding of our relationships to the environment? How seriously should we take the explanations, predictions and proposals offered by modern scientists?* Table 4.9 shows the results for the population as a whole.

Table 4.9 (Question 6) How useful is modern science? Population as a whole

Science offers a good explanation	35.6%
Science offers a good explanation, but:	
it is often used by governments/industry	12.8%
there are conflicting views *within* science	16.4%
scientists' views keep changing	5.6%
science is sensationalised by the media	1.2%
science creates new problems while solving others	5.7%
it doesn't tell us what to do	2.4%
it cannot explain everything	12.4%
it needs better interpretation to the layperson	2.8%
it is underfunded	1.6%
We should reject or be very suspicious of science	2.4%
Don't know	1.6%

It should be clear from Table 4.9 that people's attitudes towards science are far more complex than those suggested by Beck and Giddens. About one third of the respondents had no critical comment whatsoever to make as regards scientific knowledge. A common theme here was that the knowledge offered by science was far superior to that of lay people and needed accepting on those grounds alone. As a retired female factory worker put it:

> If modern science doesn't know about the environment and the thinning of the ozone layer etc., how on earth are the general public to know – and what can be done about it?

Or as one other respondent, a 49-year-old female clerk, wrote:

> Has *anybody* an adequate understanding of anything? Why pick on scientists? But yes, we should take their proposals very seriously because they at least spend time thinking about our relationships far more than the rest of us.

But even more importantly, nearly two thirds of the respondents to the Directive had a range of partial, ambiguous and sometimes contradictory views of scientific knowledge. The importance of the Mass-Observation Archive type of directive becomes clear at this point. It elicits very well the multiple and fragmented forms of understanding which most people seem to hold. Many people have a generally high regard for scientific knowledge. On the other hand, as Table 4.9 shows, they felt that science was compromised in a number of ways. Some felt, as indeed Beck and Giddens argue, that it is often used by industrialists and politicians for ends to which the scientists themselves would not subscribe. But, again, this by no means leads to a widespread rejection of science itself. As one male administrator and accountant put it:

> The modern scientist on the whole is a servant of big business once more and he must educate those in control and with ambitions of the consequences of their actions long before he can seek the right to influence the thoughts of the populace. I think we should accept the explanations of science, suspect the predictions and weigh carefully the proposals, for this can lead us and the planet into 'no-go' situations.

One of the largest and most characteristic responses is that science contains a number of conflicting opinions. Once more, there is no suggestion at all that science itself should be rejected. Rather, the impression is one of irritation over science's incoherence. The remarks of the Mass-Observation Archive can be seen as reflecting the fragmentations we noted in Chapter 1, with the knowledge of separate sciences (including that of social science) remaining within entirely insulated fields. This means that, in the end, no coherent advice is to hand.

> Science has given us so many wonderful advances without which our lives would be briefer, less comfortable and quite different, but when it comes to scientists and the environment, they don't seem to be able to agree on how best they can help us. I don't think it has done scientists' reputations any good that they have been indulging in something like open warfare over environmental problems. On the one hand are the gloom and doom merchants who tell us that global warming will destroy us in time and on the other hand are those who deny that it will have much effect at all. Likewise is the argument over the depletion of ozone. What are ordinary mortals to believe or do if we don't know what the truth is?
>
> (female teacher, age 41)

A related view is that scientific understanding keeps changing. One 45-year-old female Mass-Observation correspondent sums up the state of her knowledge with the rhetorical question, 'who would know?':

> One month the hole in the ozone layer seems to be gripping everyone's attention and then the subject drops out of the news and it is forgotten. It is difficult to know why there is not a regular update. Is

the situation irremedial (sic)? Would a worldwide effort mend the hole? Who would know?

But once more this does not seem necessarily to undermine widespread popular trust in the scientific enterprise. There is no suggestion of anything profoundly wrong with science itself. There are two remaining large categories in this multiple and sometimes ambiguous understanding of science. One is simply that science makes too many claims. It is again not the case that science is itself incorrect. Rather, the general population should have much less faith in scientists' apparent omniscience.

> I don't think modern science knows all there is to know about environmental problems. They are really only guessing at things half the time.
>
> (female receptionist, age 43)

> Very difficult to know how seriously we should take the explanations, predictions and proposals offered by modern scientists. On the one hand they're scientists and specialists and they should 'know'. On the other hand, science has largely taken the place of religion and everything 'scientific' is given an almost absurd level of respect and credence. Am I suggesting, then, that we go back to examining toads' entrails and looking for the philosopher's stone? No, but perhaps that science should be more answerable and less an unquestioned end in itself.
>
> (female personnel officer, age 46)

Second, there is the frequently expressed view that science is double-edged. It has brought, and is still bringing, many great advances. On the other hand, it has also brought about a number of disasters. But it would once more be difficult to argue that this leads to a widescale attempt to discredit or dismiss scientific effort as a whole. The following quotation is very typical of this ambiguous and contradictory position.

> To me scientists are very largely the cause of the mess in which we find ourselves: their chemicals pollute as do their nuclear power stations; their spacecraft clutter the stratosphere; their 'smart' weapons cause carnage in war and all the time they think they are improving on nature they are in fact contributing towards its destruction.... But one also has to admit, fearfully, that it is perhaps only scientists who can reverse the dangerous predicament into which they have led us.
>
> (female advice bureau worker, age 65)

It is therefore very difficult to find people within the survey who totally reject scientific knowledge. One, very rare, response is that the environmental knowledge advanced by outside authorities such as the government, environmental groups and scientists is a product of subversive forces who are trying to impose their political wills on an unsuspecting public. More typical is the assertion that scientists' ideas are just as subjective as those of lay people. As such, they are just as prone to criticism. Here is one example of this rare type of reaction.

> I think that most scientists have their own axe to grind and will make the facts fit their explanations the same way the unemployment figures are massaged.
>
> (female teacher, age 54)

More assertively:

> How useful is modern science? For whom? I don't think a discipline which enabled the atom bomb to be produced thereby killing hope for future generations has anything to tell me at all, apart from how to fuck it all up. I assume that scientists are just as likely to get it wrong as other people are.
>
> (female medical practice manager, age 51)

How do these figures break down by social group? Table 4.10 (showing the breakdown by gender) is intended to begin answering this question, though at this stage the relatively small scale of the sample starts to raise some potential difficulties.

Table 4.10 (Question 6) How useful is modern science? Breakdown by gender

	women		men	
	$n =$	%	$n =$	%
Science offers good explanations	62	36.4	27	33.8
Good explanations, but:				
often used by govLRts...	22	12.9	10	12.5
has conflicting views	30	17.6	11	13.8
keeps changing	14	8.2	0	0.0
is sensationalised	2	1.2	1	1.2
creates new problems	8	4.7	5	6.2
doesn't tell us what to do	3	1.7	3	3.7
can't explain everything	20	11.8	11	13.8
needs better interpretation	4	2.3	3	3.7
is underfunded	1	0.6	3	3.7
Science should be rejected	0	0.0	6	7.5
Don't know	4	2.4	0	0.0

It is difficult to draw too many general conclusions from Table 4.10, especially since the numbers in the intermediate categories are small. A relatively low percentage of women wish to reject science altogether, although the different percentages involved are by no means considerable. Similarly, for reasons we have discussed earlier, men seem to treat science with higher levels of suspicion.

It would of course be valuable to know how views of science relate to such divisions as age and class. Unfortunately, as we have seen, the correspondents to the Mass-Observation Archive are in the older age brackets. Furthermore, this sample of the population contains relatively few working class people. All this makes it difficult to draw firm conclusions on these matters. However, a broad impression left by the correspondents' replies is that professionals, managers and older people are likely to give more credence to the abstract knowledge than those in clerical and more routinised jobs. Furthermore, those in full-time domestic work seem very likely to be hostile to scientific understanding. But such conclusions must be tentative. Further work is needed on these important questions.

How can all the above results on people's attitudes to modern science be summarised? The evidence, despite the relatively small scale of the survey, once more suggests that the arguments advanced by Beck and Giddens are far too generalised. It is far from clear that a wholesale rejection of science is taking place. Attitudes towards scientific knowledge of the environment are far more ambiguous, contradictory and partial than Beck and Giddens's theories would suggest. It is tempting to suggest that the thorough-going critique of science in which many critical sociologists regularly engage is being inaccurately projected onto the population as a whole. Many of the Mass-Observation Archive correspondents are looking to science as an authoritative guide to the extent of environmental crisis. At the same time, they know that science is indeed subject to social and political pressures. It is socially constructed, being often a product of agendas other than simply providing the objective facts. Such social construction includes, for example, results which attract more research funds or the 'discovery' of risk-levels with which private industry can actually cope (Boehmer-Christiansen 1994b, Levidow 1994a). The Mass-Observation Archive correspondents know much of this. At the same time they are not prepared to simply reject scientific authority. They again combine it in often complex ways with their own practical knowledge. But can we make any sense of this complexity?

CONCLUSION: ANOTHER CAUSAL MECHANISM?

It is tempting to suggest that the Mass Observers have a wholly chaotic conception of human beings' relation to their environment. But the apparent chaos can be seen as a result of combining of what Szerszynski (1996) calls 'modern' and 'neo-modern' views of science. The first contains an idea of science as in perfect correspondence between knowledge and reality. The second advances an idea of science as an evolving and fallible enterprise. The Mass-Observation Archive correspondents' very cautious attitude towards science (sometimes it is offering understanding, sometimes obscurity) again seems to betray great uncertainty. 'Alienation', in the sense we are using the word in this study, is characterised not by direct oppression but by just such uncertainty, or failure to understand.

The kinds of analysis offered by Beck and Giddens seem wrong, or at the very least far too generalised across the whole population. The outcome is far more complex and messy than Beck and Giddens's arguments suggest. But that is how it is. Furthermore, such 'messiness' is the product of conflicting attitudes to abstract knowledge combining with practical understandings and interpretations of how human society is interacting with the powers of nature.

Nevertheless, we can perhaps be somewhat clearer than this in understanding what is taking place. The understandings articulated by the Mass-Observation Archive correspondents are obviously social constructions. Unsurprisingly, however, they are far more complex and less informed by abstract theory than the constructions usually made and articulated by the academic community. The understandings lay people actually adopt often involve a projection of the relatively familiar, and indeed messy, social world onto the world of nature. So perhaps we are encountering here another causal mechanism, this time built deep into the human psyche. This could be one whereby people are unconsciously constructing the largely unknown ways in which human societies are intervening in nature in familiar terms. Such a mechanism would mean that people are constructing a world in which they still feel relatively secure. Collier (1994: 224) argues that critical realism as applied to psychoanalysis would

> propound an epigenetic theory of development, that is, one which recognizes the interaction of a real environment with a really existing world of fantasy, including misperceptions of the environment. Here, as in the case of socio-linguistics, critical realism's notion of stratification and multiple determination serves as a corrective to one-sided explanations.

Perhaps with the correspondents to the Mass-Observation Archive we are witnessing the results of such 'multiple determination': the causal mechanisms of society and nature are combining with the mechanisms innate to human beings which help people to make sense of their circumstances. Concepts, language and communication are the means by which such sense is made. Metaphors and analogies borrowed from familiar social experience are being projected onto processes and relationships which remain beyond comprehension. 'Environmental misperceptions' are the result.

5

INDUSTRIALISING NATURE'S POWERS

This chapter brings together some of the key themes outlined earlier in this book (especially critical realism, the powers of nature, the division of labour and the subordination of lay and tacit knowledges) around some more substantive concerns. It gives special attention to the role of industrial work in the conversion of nature's powers. Clearly an emphasis on industrial production is not the only way in which societies convert nature into the things they want. We will later come to other forms of production such as those conducted in the informal economy. But this kind of labour process is certainly one of the most important ways of understanding how the powers of nature are used. It provides us with a core understanding of how human beings, through their own activities, regulate and control the properties of nature towards their own ends.

The productive basis of human beings is the basis of their society and history, and it seems peculiar that so little environmental analysis has started at this most fundamental of levels. Yet, considering that such a perspective exposes many of the ways in which contemporary society is organised, it is perhaps not so surprising after all. This chapter will therefore pursue the theme of labouring on nature. It will take two sometimes linked topical areas as case-studies: the new reproductive technologies and genetic engineering. It will conclude by investigating some common themes. These are the relations between lay knowledge and the division of labour and whether or not these new technologies should be seen as emancipatory.

WORKING ON NATURE: A DIALECTICAL PERSPECTIVE

All forms of work are necessarily work on nature. Individuals not only work on nature to create the things they need but they have ideas about what nature is, about their impacts on nature and what their society is trying to achieve by manipulating it to their ends. Often these ideas are a combination of 'official science' on the one hand and of local, lay and tacit knowledges on the other. For most people in modern society the relation between their work and nature is

102

mediated and indirect. Between their work and their impact on nature are a great range of processes, technologies and infrastructures. This particularly applies, of course, to the so-called 'service' industries in which people are, for example, transporting or selling the goods made in factories. They are also actively involved in the transformation of nature, although their relations to nature are if anything more remote and alienated from nature than those of the industrial workers transforming raw materials. Finally, we must remember that the technologies people use to manipulate and to try and control nature have been created through other labour processes on nature. And technologies mediate the relations between persons and the non-human world.

The relations between people and nature in modern society are highly mediated by the division of labour. This again means that people's knowledge of the non-human world becomes less a matter of depending on the knowledge gained in everyday life and more a product of learning from people such as scientists, whose main role is in the creation of abstract knowledge. Despite all these mediations, however, the outcome of working on nature will be the humanisation of nature, its manipulation and the projection of human under-standings and intentions onto it.

Changes in how nature's powers are used can also lead to changes in how human beings understand nature. As we have seen earlier, it can modify their understandings of the natural world. In the era of the enlightenment, for example, nature became harmonised by the more powerful social classes with the dominant social and ideological relations of the time. As Yoxen (1986: 30) puts it:

> In the eighteenth century, an age of classification in botany and zoology, the emphasis was on harmony and systemic order. Nature was a catalogue of organic forms, each fashioned by an ingenious creator, each with a place on a Chain of Being that stretched from inanimate matter to God. The scientist's tasks, confronted with this majestic scheme, was to classify its elements, to contemplate the subtlety of the connections that held it together and to reveal the harmonious functioning of particular parts.

By the late nineteenth century, the dominant metaphor or social construc-tion had changed again. And this reflected the dominant ways in which society was now working on nature. Nature came to be considered as 'red in tooth and claw', the central mechanism being the competitive struggle for existence. As we will explore shortly, this metaphor is itself now being modified. It is being changed to a contradictory one in which nature is envisaged by scientists and others as, on the one hand, a manageable system and, on the other hand, a collection of replaceable and manipulable parts.

But in adopting such alternative views of nature, people have not over-ridden the underlying properties of nature. Again, nature has its own powers and tendencies independent of people's accounts. As Benton (1993: 66) has put it:

No matter how 'deep' we go into the structure of the materials and beings with which we work, it remains the case that the transformations both *presuppose* the causal constancy of structure and causal powers at a *deeper* structural level and are limited by the nature of that deeper-level structure.

(Author's emphases)

To be sure, however, these powers continue to be explored and better understood. In interpreting nature in different ways, and in using the powers of nature according to these interpretations, people create new insights into these powers and how they can be deployed towards human ends. Furthermore, since human beings are themselves part of nature, they learn something more of themselves as a natural being through studying nature. Can human beings withstand the 'revenges' that they now seem to be inducing? Or are they (which seems unlikely) infinitely flexible? Conversely, what can be learnt about hitherto unknown human capacities? Does working on nature tell us anything new about, for example, the human body or potentials of the human species which have not yet been realised? Through working on nature more can come to be known about, for example, human beings' remarkable potential for not only creating but actively using new ideas about nature. Human beings therefore not only reach natural limits but make something new of themselves as a result of humanising nature. They realise new powers with which they were born but which they did not know they had. This latter consideration is often forgotten in contemporary environmental debates, many of which concentrate wholly and negatively on the harmful effects of working on nature.

In short, labouring on nature should be seen as a cyclical process. A labour process starts off with certain ends in mind and certain material and conceptual means of achieving these ends. But the ends become in due course the means. Working on nature leads to new conceptual and material bases. And these become the springboards for new ways of working on nature, manipulating it, and changing the ways humans live. Working on particular variations of plant or animal through biotechnology, for example, creates a new variant of the species. This variant becomes the basis for a new round of agricultural production and research.

Second, and as implied above, human beings' interactions with nature must be understood in the contexts of particular kinds of society. The reproduction of the human species over time and the production of their means of subsistence has led to a continuing and massive expansion of human populations and human needs. These in turn have been associated with increased divisions of labour. The different tasks within the processes of production and the jobs of biological and cultural *re*production have rapidly proliferated with the development of modernity. Most important has been the rise of what Marx called the 'mental division of labour', particularly with certain kinds of conceptualising tasks being devolved to specific persons. The result has been a series of social

104

polarisations between those harnessing scientific knowledge in the labour process and those conducting boring production processes.

A particularly good example comes from the bioengineering industry that we will be studying shortly. Like the old industries, these emergent forms of production still attempt to manage workers' skills and orient them towards mass-production. Divisions of labour are established, often at the expense of over-riding people's skills. Skilled and knowledgeable subordinates put up a fight and the end-form of the division of labour is by no means pre-determined. Nevertheless, the long-term tendency is towards a harnessing of individuals' skills and knowledge towards the mass-production process. An early indication of these processes in the field of work with which we are concerned arose when Beckwith and Shapiro, two biotechnology scientists who were the first to isolate a gene, left their jobs in 1970. Their concerns partly centred on what they saw as the possibly malign purposes to which their science could be put. But they also left because they could not see how scientists could resist being made into de-skilled operatives. 'Scientists are workers', Beckwith argued. Their position is no different to that of 'the guys on the assembly line' (Glasman 1970).

But again we must ask whether such processes are only the product of capitalism. Would not the management of highly complex mass-production processes, and attendant alienation of large sections of the labour force, not be a central feature of any kind of modern society?

The increasing social and technical division of labour (the separation between different forms of abstract work on the one hand and lay and tacit knowledges on the other) has had a profound effect on people's understanding of, and interaction with, nature. People necessarily have to relate with others during their interaction with nature in the labour process. Such interaction becomes even more necessary and intense as the division of labour becomes more extensive. Such interaction has meant that human subjects have become on the one hand exposed to dominant abstract ideas. These forms of science and their application in the process of social and industrial innovation have of course made great progress. And they have strongly influenced their views as to what nature actually is. On the other hand, as we saw in the last chapter, they are by no means fully shared by those who do not participate in their creation and use. They live alongside the knowledge gained through practical experience.

The net effect on people's relations with nature has thus been contradictory. On the one hand, the mental labourers have certainly gained greater insights into the causal powers of nature. On the other hand, this knowledge has not been democratised. It remains not only rigidly defined within disciplinary constraints but controlled by those powerful minorities who commission, manage and use the making of knowledge. And of course there is a very important sense in which such divisions are necessary in a modern society. How, after all, could one mind grasp all these types of knowledge? The inevitable result of the growth and fragmentation of knowledge, as we found the Kogi saying in this book's introductory chapter, is that while information has increased real understanding has decreased.

Similarly, the harnessing of abstract knowledge by dominant elites and the modification of nature to human ends has brought, and can still bring, undoubted benefits in terms of human well-being and the realisation of previously recognised human potentials. On the other hand, these advances have been bought, often quite literally, both at the expense of other species and a range of unintended consequences. For human beings the gains have been made at the expense of an understanding of how lay and tacit knowledge relate to abstract scientific ideas. This has led to a tragic contradiction. Human beings are probably the species which is potentially the best able to understand the world (including the worlds of other species) and how to change it for the better. But the way in which they have actually worked on nature and understood it is destructive and denies the realisation of this very possibility. They have therefore managed to turn the very advantage they have over other animals against themselves and other living beings. In this way, and despite their remarkable potential for good, humans have joined the viruses they so much despise in wiping out whole species and sets of species.

Before going on to develop these themes in relation to current developments, one particular development within modern capitalism needs special mention. This is the tendency for capitalism and the market to penetrate civil society, the sphere of social life which is not part of the formal economy. This process was recognised in passing by Marx, and quite remarkably, in the early 1860s. As part of a discussion about servants, and whether they have a major role in the creation of surplus value, he refers to an emergent process whereby:

> capital conquers the whole of production, and therefore the home and petty form of industry – in short industry intended for self-consumption, not producing commodities – disappears.
>
> (1969: 159)

This process has continued apace in the modern day. As we will see, it includes not only the various forms of self-provisioning in the home but now even the biological production of future generations.

THE FRAGMENTATION OF NATURE

A recurrent theme in much of contemporary environmental philosophy is the fragmentation of modern society. Capra (1976: 28), for example, bemoans the fact that 'each individual has been split up into a large number of separate compartments' and 'the natural environment is treated as if it consisted of separate parts to be exploited by different interest groups'. Similarly Bohm (1980: 1) writes that 'fragmentation is now widespread, not only through society but also in each individual'. And this, as will be discussed in the next chapter in more detail, leads key elements in environmental philosophy to promote various kinds of 'holism'. In advancing the values of Hinduism, for example, Capra (1976: 101) insists that 'as long as our view of the world is fragmented, as long as we are under the spell of *maya* and think that we are separated from our environment and can act independently, we are bound by *karma*.

But such analyses are profoundly misleading. Their insistence that changing our thought alone is sufficient to stop fragmentation and create an emancipated society misses the core underlying processes which cause the fragmentations with which they are concerned. Similarly, it is not adequate to refer to the failings of Cartesian thinking. In separating mind from body (and thereby promoting one form of fragmentation) Descartes may have helped make an intellectual climate for the ways in which modern society was to fragment human beings and their relations to the environment. But once more the divisions in modern society are not simply through people having the wrong fragmenting Cartesian *ideas*.

We need to resist the idealism within much contemporary environmental thinking by constantly reminding ourselves that the separation of human beings from nature is not simply the result of people having the wrong ideas about nature. Loss of biodiversity, the thinning of the ozone layer and so on are not occurring simply because we have the wrong ideas. Rather, they are results of how human societies have worked on nature and how such work has led to, and been assisted by, wrong ideas.

Harvey (1992) refers to 'capitalism: the factory of fragmentation' (see also Harvey 1989). Capitalism, as we will shortly see, certainly has a great deal to do with fragmentation. But, as suggested above, separations of many kinds are also a product of modernity. The experience of the previously communist societies suggests that modernity has a dynamic of its own independent of capitalism. In practice, of course, it is difficult to distinguish between the two. The fragmentations between mind and body, between intellectual and manual labour, and between different branches of intellectual labour are a central feature of modernity, though they have been much exacerbated by capitalism. Similarly, the split between humans and the product of their labour, between humans and other humans and between different branches of intellectual labour are all features of the way in which modern life is organised. But these forms of alienation have been much extended by capitalist development.

LABOURING ON INTERNAL NATURE

The labour process, and the relations made in the reconstruction of nature, are at the very core of these fragmentations. In short, we must turn to the very opposite of what many people would see as 'the environment' if we are going to understand society's highly problematic relations with nature. This chapter will develop this theme in relation to some of the very dramatic contemporary ways in which modern society is transforming nature.

As much green philosophy would agree, a dominant image of nature in modern society is one in which nature is envisaged as some kind of rational mechanism, one composed of a number of linked but separable parts, each working in conjunction with the other. Yoxen, in his study of genetic engineering, puts it like this.

> The dominant image of nature in the second half of the twentieth century, deepened by the insights of genetics, is less reverential than that of the eighteenth, and places less emphasis on struggle and competition than that of the nineteenth. Nature is a system of systems. Organisms function, reproduce and evolve as systems ordered by their genes, 'managed' by the programme in their DNA. Life is the processing of information.
>
> (1986: 30)

Genetic structure offers one way of describing nature as a set of interacting parts. Perhaps it is now even the dominant way. If, however, we turn to emergent developments in the manipulation of nature, other fragmentations are being actively made. Eggs, sperm, fetuses, embryos, wombs are amongst the many other manipulable, even detachable, 'subsystems' which are now held to compose the system of 'the person'. And it is at this point, of course, that the new science and the language starts to assume massive social significance. More accurately we should say it starts to assume an *old* massive significance. In short, we are again witnessing an alienation of people's natural and species being. On the one hand the naturally inherited powers and capacities of people are being used. On the other hand, their well-developed capacities to understand their own situations are being marginalised. As Patricia Spallone points out, in the new definitions used by genetics and reproductive technology,

> there are no women mentioned as the subject of human reproduction . . . . This lack of recognising women's active presence in reproduction recurs in medical textbooks, in scientific articles and in government reports on the issues. They inevitably speak in terms of body parts, such as 'man's eggs' or 'human placenta' or 'human reproduction' when expressly describing distinctly female physiology and biochemistry.
>
> (1989: 16)

It is surely right to give a gender to this person. A key and long-standing image of nature is that it is feminine and, conversely, that women are part of nature. Women have long been conceptualised in this way; with men being associated with (or associating themselves with) 'culture' (Merchant 1980, Sydie 1987). Whether we are talking of the new reproductive technologies in the West or the 'family planning' programmes in certain Third World countries, it is predominantly women who are being made part of an industrialised assembly line: parts of them being components of this machinery, and manipulated to produce either more or fewer children (Corea 1985,

Koval 1990, Mies and Shiva 1993). Furthermore, women are actively participating in these processes, presumably believing that they will benefit.

In the case of *in vitro* fertilisation (IVF) and related technologies, such fragmentation, and the manipulation of separate parts, enables the possibility of exchanging and selling elements of the body between subjects (Brown *et al.* 1990). Eggs can be taken from a woman's body, mixed with sperm in a petri-dish and fertilised in a glass dish, or *in vitro*. The resulting embryo is then transferred back to the woman's uterus, or to that of another woman. An alternative technique involves the sperm's being artificially introduced into a woman's uterus to fertilise the ovum *in vivo*. A related technology entails the 'flushing' of a fertilised ovum from the uterus of one woman and placing the ovum into the womb of another female. More startling still, as will be discussed later, are prospects for making good any genetic flaws in the ovum or the embryo with genes which are not associated with certain diseases. The same principles of disassembly and replacement apply to other key elements of modern medicine. These include the transfer of kidneys and hearts.

All this can be seen as analogous to the kinds of fragmentation and alienation outlined by Marx in relation to industrial workers (Martin 1993). What was once theirs is being removed, changed and possibly used by others. But perhaps the most important form of alienation (and, as discussed earlier, the aspect of Marx's theory which has received so little attention) is again that deriving from failure to *understand* the processes involved. This takes us back to some of the issues about subordinated peoples' relation to knowledge raised earlier in this study. As Martin puts it:

> Women are not only fragmented into body parts by the practices of scientific medicine, as men are; they are also profoundly alienated from science itself.
>
> (1993: 21)

But the failure to understand what is occurring is even more complicated by the fact that humans, as knowing beings, seem to be actively participating in their own oppression. Women are surely not dupes or pawns and something is taking place which is leading them to participate. Modern institutions are not just associated with male domination but with persuading both genders that these are progressive ways forward (New 1995b). And the women engaging in these new reproductive technologies are presumably persuaded that, for all their disadvantages and despite the fact that they may not fully understand them, these technologies do offer the prospect of real gains. To attribute such an understanding to false consciousness comes close to being patronising. The lesson here seems to be not that of simply rejecting science but questioning the particular type of fragmenting forms in which science is constructed and used. The alternative is to insist that, while these technologies may offer benefits, bodies and their relations with the environment need to be considered as a whole, as composed of many interacting causal mechanisms as well as, of course, interacting with one another. And, as we will shortly discuss, there are now forms of biological science which are offering just such an understanding.

Such fragmentation is not confined to humans. Other kinds of animal have been subjected to the same processes. They too are whole organisms but they too are increasingly conceptualised as, treated as, eaten as and experimented on as kits of parts each serving a different function. Conceptualisation as systems of parts is a preliminary to domination. In much the same way as women do not feature in such narratives neither do whole animals. As Birke (1994: 120) puts it, 'there is no "naturalistic animal" here, only an "animal" stripped of its literal and metaphoric existence'.

This brings us to the question of why all this fragmentation is occurring. If we are looking for a key underlying mechanism in modern societies we should again be looking at the industrial labour-process on nature (a term which takes on a whole new meaning when applied to the new reproductive technologies) and its organisation in modern society. Nature, whether it is that of humans or other species, is divided up so that it can be worked on and manipulated. There are three interlocking reasons for this. In any modern society there is likely to be a tendency towards a division of work which simplifies tasks while enabling the human capacities of the workers involved to be used to best advantage. As Adam Smith wrote in 1776,

> the greatest improvement in the productive powers of labour, and the greater part of the skill, dexterity, and judgement which it is anywhere directed, or applied, seem to have been the effects of the division of labour.
>
> (1970: 109)

Such divisions allow planning and, through the concentration of individuals into particular tasks, the cheapening of the labour process.

But this brings us to the second great advantage. The division of labour, and especially the division between those charged with development and use of scientific knowledge and those predominantly reliant on lay and tacit knowledge, operates as a powerful means of control. Marx was writing about the division of labour as a means of controlling de-skilled workers in a capitalist factory. But feminist writers assessing the new reproductive technologies are concerned with a similar process in the social division of labour, one in which 'the workers' are not only being controlled by people with scientific knowledge but are having a labour process conducted on their very bodies with the benefit of this knowledge.

But this only brings us to the third and perhaps the most important reason for fragmentation. This is the penetration of market exchange into nature (Kimbrell 1995). Let us take the new reproductive technologies first. As many feminist writers are pointing out, a body which is divided up into parts is far more amenable to a system of commercialisation whereby each part is worth a certain amount and can be traded for money. Similarly, if a child is born by a surrogate mother, this too is highly compatible with commodification. The result is the child as also a saleable item, the result (more appropriately, 'the product') of a great deal of financial investment. These are all the result, as Gimenez (1991) has pointed out, of the emergence of 'a mode of procreation'. The new reproductive technologies mean that physical reproduction which takes place in households (and which can be regulated by the individuals concerned in the procreation of children) can now be subjected to a form of control (by an industrial manager or by some other authority such as the state) in some wider public interest.

In short, the biological reproduction of life is itself being increasingly made into a process of commodity production. And we are concerned with a complex division of labour in which not only capital but men and dominant races are in control. Civil society is being increasingly capitalised, as Marx predicted. The use of women's bodies and their packaging as commercial products is a familiar part of contemporary life. But IVF and related technologies are carrying this a stage further. As Rowland (1992: 4) puts it:

> With the new reproductive technologies women are further objectified and fragmented, dismembered into ovaries and eggs for exchange and wombs for rent. The commodity 'woman' or a part of woman can be used to produce the commodity 'child'.

The investment in the new reproductive technologies is not only a product of commercialisation but can also be seen as necessary to the very expansion of the market. These technologies are necessary to replace the old, worn-out technologies associated with earlier phases of capitalism. Middle-class groups in particular (those best able to exercise the consumer 'right' to have a child of their own) are being targeted. But, according to Mies, this technology is oppressive. Like many others before it, a particular form of science, and a technology based on this form, finishes up by relegating subordinate people still more firmly in their place. As Mies puts it in relation to women and the new reproductive technologies:

> It is an historical fact that technological innovations within exploitative relationships of domination lead only to an intensification of the exploitation of the groups oppressed. This applies in particular for the new reproductive technologies, the technology of the industrial production of human beings.
>
> (1986b: 553–60)

BIOTECHNOLOGY: WORKING ON EXTERNAL NATURE

As indeed Mies implies, there is another dynamic at work here besides the control of women by men. It is again that outlined earlier: the introduction of

111

capital into processes of reproduction. These same processes can be seen even more clearly if we turn from the propagation of people to the ways in which 'external nature' (the distinction between internal and external nature is increasingly difficult to maintain) is being modified. As Brown *et al.* (1990: 77) put it: 'the breeding of "better" plants and "better" animals for marketing purposes is an old story'.

Referring to contemporary developments in plant biotechnology, Goodman *et al.* (1987) deploy the concepts of *appropriationism* and *substitutionism*. The former refers to discrete elements of the production process's being taken over by industry: for example, 'broadcast sowing by the seed drill, the horse by the tractor, manure by synthetic chemicals' (p. 2). (See also Lawrence 1989, Goodman and Redclift 1991.) The latter refers to the increasing penetration of industry into food provision and the replacement of conventional agriculture by various forms of industrial input. Agriculture thus becomes 'trivialised' as production takes place in the factory rather than the farm (Goodman and Redclift 1991).

The division of the agricultural process into discrete elements looks at first sight like a process familiar in all industries, one in which the division of labour makes production more efficient, profitable and subject to detailed management. In the case of agriculture, however, a distinct additional process is taking place. The biology of plants (and indeed other organisms) represents a distinct challenge to commerce. Plants have in-built powers, capacities, 'lives of their own', all of which are part of their 'species being' and their 'natural being'. Their growth and development are also, of course, subject to the constraints of climate and other features of external nature. All this means that they cannot be considered as machines. There is no way in which they can be considered as mere aggregates of their genetic components. As Benton (1989: 169) writes,

> Organisms are not mere aggregate expressions of contingently connected and freely manipulable genetic particles.

All this means that capital has necessarily become much exercised in the management of organisms. How can they be harnessed, incorporated into the market and industrially managed as 'normal' commodities? Modern industry persists in attempting to manage and control organisms as sets of 'freely manipulable' elements. This despite the fact that such strategies often bring costs or 'revenges'. Some genetically modified organisms, for example, have certainly brought about extra yields. But such achievements have resulted in standardised monocultures and a declining resistance to disease. Despite such real and potential 'revenges', the process of fragmenting organisms continues, 'the problem' being divided up into its smallest possible components and then re-made into a manageable and more profitable entity. And this is the importance of bioengineering. Referring to genetic technology in plants, Goodman and Redclift (1991: 10) point out that

Only with the recent emergence of modern biotechnologies, notably recombinant DNA methods, has it become possible realistically to entertain the prospect that the process of biological transformation eventually may fall under direct industrial control.

The production of cheese and margarine, and the canning of processed meat and vegetables are old ways in which capital has drawn processes out of the farm and into the factory. New ways of manufacturing food

> seek to 'decompose' natural products (corn, wheat flour, sugar) into substrates which can be reformulated as manufactured or reconstituted products. When reduced to their basic ingredients and transformed with chemical additives, preservatives, flavourings and flavour enhancers, or when substrates can be converted to new products (or more cheaply produced products) by genetically engineered micro-organisms, food production can take place in the factory rather than on the farm.
>
> (Lawrence 1989: 4)

This process of breaking down of nature is aimed at transcending its biological limits and making it more amenable to conventional forms of industrial control and consequent productivity increases. The process is not, however, limited to the production of seeds. We will return shortly to the production of plants but, since the parallels between the treatment of human and non-human animals are very striking, let us take the making of 'better animals' first.

The new reproductive technologies outlined earlier were first developed to outdo nature by creating high-quality genetic stock (Brown *et al.* 1990). There is in fact quite a long history of 'better' animals being used to ensure that their progeny multiplied. Bulls of good genetic stock, for example, have long been sold as breeders and their sperm has long attracted high prices. By the mid 1970s, however, the manipulation of parts of animals was fully under way, ewes and cows being the main species in use. Eggs of high-quality breeding stock were taken out of the bodies of animals, fertilised and placed back into the less good stock. Similarly, around the 1970s, eggs started to be fertilised inside animals, then extracted and inserted into the bodies of animals with 'inferior' pedigrees. These surrogate mothers then gave birth to and nurtured the 'better' lambs and calves. This was a highly profitable operation. As the British Medical Association (1992: 100) puts it:

> Applied to dairy stock, this technique enables a top quality cow to produce as many as 20, rather than an average of 3.5, daughters per lifetime.

The genetic engineering of animals, however, takes this outdoing of nature a step further. The manipulation of an animal's innate capacities for growth and development is now becoming, thanks to genetic engineering, a relatively

113

routine aspect of animal production. One of the most contentious interventions concerns the used of genetically engineered growth hormones to manipulate the growth of pigs or the lactation of dairy cows. Leaving aside the central fact that surplus milk is not wanted by consumers in the developed societies and cannot be sold to the poor in developing countries, these developments are severely testing the limits of these organisms. As Webster (1990: 27) writes:

> My main objection to the use of BST is that the dairy cow, like the broiler chicken, is already at her metabolic limit.

A more thorough-going use of animals' 'natural being' and naturally inherited capacities is likely to be the manipulation of their reproductive capacities. Here we find genetic engineering being combined with reproductive technologies (Wheale and McNally 1988). Egg donation, IVF and surrogacy all combine to enable the industry to maximise the number of offspring of livestock which have the most desirable genetic traits. In the so-called MOET (multiple ovulation with embryo transfer) system, eggs are removed from a beef cow after it has been slaughtered. These are fertilised in a test-tube with semen from a beef bull, sexed, and the fertilised embryos are then implanted into a recipient cow. The over-riding imperative to these manipulations in the agricultural industry is again profit. As Webster (1990: 28) puts it:

> The commercial advantages of this are clear. A dairy cow may be implanted with one or two of the beef-type calves of superior genetic merit to herself.

In all these instances, therefore, the fragmentation of biological processes is taking place. It is again intended to enable the introduction of regulated industrial processes into biological life. Until relatively recently such natural life was hardly amenable to conventional forms of industrial management; it had, so to say, 'a life of its own' which left it insubordinate to such control. Whether it is women or non-human animals, the processes of appropriationism and substitutionism are rife. As we will discuss later, these processes bring some advantages, but one key result is an increase in the attack on what Marx called 'species being' and 'natural being'. Genetically inherited capacities and potential are being increasingly modified, regulated and used by powerful outside forces.

Let us now turn from animals to the ways in which the seeds of useful plants reproduce themselves. Here, as Goodman and Redclift (1991) point out, we again find capital intervening to regulate the way in which such reproduction takes place. If ways can be found of regulating the way in which these seeds simply reproduce themselves (or, more accurately, stopping farmers from using this capacity of plants) it can be a major boon to capital. As Kloppenburg (1988: 37) succinctly puts it:

114

The seed presents capital with a simple biological obstacle: Given appropriate conditions the seed will reproduce itself manyfold. This simple yet ineluctable biological fact poses significant difficulties for commercial interests that would engage in the development of new plant varieties for profit.

The most basic form of capitalism, what Marx called 'primitive accumulation', entails the separation of the worker from the means of production and the extension of the commodity form to new spheres of social life. Primitive accumulation in farming consists of the conventional circuit of capital in which the farmer combines the means of production (equipment as well as seeds) with labour power to set in train a production process which results in the commodity 'grain'. The farmer can save some of the seed for a new cycle in the following year's production. But this is a significant problem for companies' continued profit-making. It means that seeds are not being sold. The 'trick' for fully industrialised farming is to find or make a seed which is economically superior to that being used by the farmer, one which (perhaps given suitable advertising) the farmer would buy and become dependent on. (See, for example, Mies 1986a, Kloppenburg 1988, Mies and Shiva 1993, Shiva 1995.) Her or his tacit skills and local knowledge are allowed to decay and once more become subjugated. The danger is that they will be lost for ever.

Plant breeding, like animal breeding, is also of course not a new phenomenon. The method of crossing existing varieties to produce better plants has a very long history. And combining selected varieties and varying them with the aid of improvements in fertilisers, pesticides and herbicides are at the basis of the Green Revolution of the 1950s and 1960s. The problem with these latter techniques, however, has been their reliance on the whole of a genome, this being the whole of a sex cell or gamete. 'Desirable' genes may thus be inherited with 'undesirable' ones as new mutants are fashioned. The process of sorting and selecting genetically stable new varieties is also very slow, and the mutations leading to significant plant improvement can occur only gradually, even when the process is being artificially induced.

Access to, and manipulation of, plant genes allows these technical problems to be overcome, even if (as we will see shortly) it entails that new problems are invoked. Special seeds are produced and marketed by companies which, since they bring real benefits, cannot be easily resisted by the farmer. Transgenic plants, for example, are given enhanced resistance to pests such as butterflies and moths. Similarly, plants can now be genetically modified in such a way as to make them resistant to the herbicides used to eradicate weeds, and tomatoes can be modified to reduce their tendency to become mushy and rotten. Other possibilities include the creation of plants with enhanced nitrogen-fixing capacities and the introduction of genes from other species.

The application of genetic science in such ways also means that the social

115

relations and divisions of labour associated with primitive accumulation become transformed. Farmers lose control over, even understanding of, the very seed they use. They and their knowledge are in the hands of the companies that own and control the seeds. Not only has the farmer been separated from the reproduction of the seed but the commodification of a previously uncommodified process means that conventional farming is being made into a declining part of the food-producing process. The broad process is the one identified earlier. It is one in which fragmentation has occurred as part of the incorporation of the natural world into industry. Biotechnology is the latest instalment of a long-standing attempt to industrialise nature, to capture and isolate it from the vagaries of the non-human world and to render it compatible with the mass-production and consumption of commodities. This despite the fact that the causal powers and mechanisms affecting the development and growth of organisms, and their interaction with the environment, are left to their own devices. In practice, control is far from complete.

Parallel strategies include the electronic control of heating and ventilation in greenhouses and the use of faster refrigerated forms of transport to bring plants and vegetables immediately to the consumer before they rot. Virtually all forms of industrialisation have seen the gradual displacement of labour by technology and an attempted tighter control over the regulation of nature's powers. In the case of the industrialisation of agriculture we are, according to Eisenberg, witnessing a rationale whose objective is

> to change the production of certain crops from an agricultural operation subject to the whims of nature to a controllable, predictable and repeatable industrial process offering maximum yields.
>
> (Cited in Goodman *et al.* 1987)

This rationale is now being applied to all forms of nature, human nature as well as 'external' nature. As feminist analysis implies, women's capacity to give birth is also being turned into a 'controllable, predictable industrial process offering maximum yields'. But we must again remain alive to the possibility that the industrial modernisation of nature might be used towards more humane and less alienating ends. The risk otherwise is that resistance to new technologies will be seen as wholly negative and defensive. This is a matter to which we will shortly return.

LAY KNOWLEDGE, TACIT KNOWLEDGE AND THE DIVISION OF LABOUR

We can now relate some of the above themes with earlier discussions in this study. Most feminist analysis suggests that the technologies discussed above entail not only the subjugation of lay and tacit knowledge and the harnessing of modern science to the market but the further domination of women. As we saw in Chapter 2, these are all recurring themes within the feminist analysis of modernity. They return when we come to the impacts of the new reproductive technologies and the introduction of biotechnology into farming.

Historically there has been a long-term shift from a general recognition of women's own reproductive capacities (whereby women monitor their *own* well-being and movements within their body) to a system today in which they depend on technology: on, for example, a test result or a digital sonogram image to confirm that they are expecting a child (Duden 1993). As argued earlier, what was once a private experience has now become a public experience: monitored, interpreted and controlled by a predominantly male profession in a high-technology environment. Again, women's own tacit knowledges are undervalued and subjected to a highly managed industrialised and capitalised process which does not recognise understandings which are felt and cannot be easily expressed in modern and impersonal terms. Duden refers, for example, to a pre-modern (pre-mid-nineteenth-century Western) era when women referred to:

> an 'ebbing' and 'flowing'; and 'curdling' and 'hardening' and, above all, on an interior orientation of their being that is mysterious today but which in their own time was immediately understandable, not only to other women, but also to the physician.
>
> (1993: 8)

Similar arguments are made by a number of feminists writing of the present day. They too are alluding to and specifying in detail the kinds of alienation discussed earlier in Chapters 1 to 4 of this study. Mies (1986b) argues, for example, that such marginalisation of self-knowledge by modern science still leads directly to the loss of a woman's identity. Such tacit self-knowledge is a social product. It is created in the social world: passed on, for example, from women to their daughters. Yet such knowledge again largely fails to make contact with dominant 'scientific' ways of thinking, the latter being claimed to be detached or beyond society. Women's experiential knowledge therefore remains relegated as 'unscientific' and therefore not recognised as credible by dominant, male-dominated institutions. Rowland found similar feelings amongst the women she interviewed who had received IVF treatment and who claimed to know their bodies better than their doctors.

> I said 'Look, I know my body. I am feeling that I am about to ovulate . . . .' They didn't believe me and I had the laparoscopy only hours later. When I woke up I didn't even need to ask. I knew there were no eggs – and there weren't.
>
> (Rowland 1992: 75)

Another infertile woman made a similar point in the following way.

> I know my body really well. Always had very regular periods, always knew exactly when I would be ovulating. So I told them I wouldn't need a

hormone injection to release my eggs. (I didn't want any more hormones in my body!) They ignored me and insisted on the injection. I felt angry – and powerless.

(Rowland 1992: 75)

It would be difficult to imagine a better illustration of alienation. Such estrangement is primarily to do with power relations, commodification and the competing forms of knowledge associated with the separation of abstract knowledge from lay and tacit understandings.

The fragmentation of the reproductive process and its involvement in an increasingly controlled industrial process leads to particular problems with human surrogacy. There are now a number of instances of women who initially undertake to become a 'baby machine' on behalf of an infertile woman. But the process can often lead to all kinds of emotional difficulties. The machine turns out to be a woman with emotions, and it is extremely difficult to relinquish the child. As one surrogate mother has written after contacting the biological father: 'although the baby was biologically his, it was also mine' (McFadden 1990: 74).

These feelings of separation, isolation and alienation cannot be seen in isolation from the fact that, as Gimenez (1991) puts it; 'the mode of reproduction is in transition'. Procreation, as linked to IVF and related technologies, now has a decreasing connection with couples in nuclear families. It is also becoming decoupled from other forms of social and biological reproduction such as domestic work and childcare. The sentiments recorded by feminist writers such as Rowland are, in large part, a product of the fragmentations that are emerging as procreation becomes a new form of industrialised production process, this alienation of people's natural and social identities being analogous to that identified by Marx in the sphere of paid work.

IVF allows a number of possible relations between a woman and her child, each involving a particular combination of genetic, gestational and social relations (Gimenez 1991). One is the 'normal' form in which genetic, gestational and social relations overlap. A second, in which the woman acts as a surrogate with artificial insemination by the genetic and social father, entails no social relation between mother and child. A third, in which a womb is 'leased' and an embryo transplanted, involves no gestational relation between mother and child. A fourth, in which eggs are purchased or received as gifts, involves no genetic relation between mother and child. A fifth, in which a woman allows her womb to be leased and an embryo transplanted, entails no social or genetic relation between mother and child. A sixth, in which a woman donates or sells eggs, involves a genetic but no social or gestational relation between mother and child. Finally a wholly social relation between mother and child is possible: one enabled by surrogacy, embryo donation or purchase, step-parenting or adoption). Adopting and step-parenting of course involve a further set of fragmentations.

The new reproductive technologies being enabled with the investment of capital in reproduction, and the resulting incorporation of nature into the market, are therefore resulting in an often severe disruption of old forms of biological reproduction. The resistances and emotional turmoil recorded by much feminist writing are a product of this engagement of industrial production into the previously 'natural' household and its fragmentation into a wide array of alternatives and divisions of labour, all of them centring on the use of women's capacities to give birth.

At the same time, however, this marketisation of nature is not all the explanation. This brings us back to our more general understanding of alienation as outlined earlier. First, the regulatory process is being conducted by a predominantly male medical profession. Second, as Mies and Shiva (1993) point out, it is being used in a racist way. It brings definite advantages to white (and mainly middle-class) women in the West while Third World women are often having their fertility controlled by contraception and sterilisation programmes. Finally, the knowledge involved is of a highly abstract form and remains far from most lay-people's experience and understanding.

The alienation underlying these women's experience is therefore a combination of a complex division of labour in which capital, male domination and, perhaps most important, a particular form of abstract knowledge combine and overlap. The result is again one in which lay and difficult-to-formulate tacit skills are over-ruled with the result that people are unable to understand their circumstances and themselves. And, paradoxically, this estrangement is a result of the very advances in knowledge made by modern society. The modern reproductive technologies may well offer emancipation for those women who have access to them and for whom they are successful. (As yet, however, they only work for about 3 out of 4 women seeking assistance.)

The sense of alienation in these circumstances as expressed by one 32-year-old woman closely parallels the lack of comprehension we have earlier witnessed amongst the Mass-Observation correspondents. She has had seven failed IVFs but she says 'the thought of giving up my dream is devastating. I'll ride any bandwagon, try any experiment.' But which bandwagon is she to ride? She has considered clinics that focus on immunological approaches, and on proteins that help the embryo latch onto the uterus. 'But my clinic says they're experimental. Though they say there's a doctor in Boston who is a firm believer in embryo toxicity factors as the wave of the future. Who knows?' (Begley 1995).

Similar issues and forms of estrangement and disempowerment result from the contemporary industrialisation of nature, and in particular the search for genes for the creation of new plants and drugs, as it affects the developing countries. With advances in biotechnology there is a renewed and heightened interest in the plants and microbes located in developing countries. This applies to the potential uses of plants for healing, and the erosion of biodiversity places a particular premium on their medicinal value (RAFI 1989). It also particularly applies to the exploitation of genetic resources to create a wide range of new agricultural products. These include plants tolerant of the damaging effects of herbicides, long-life and low-cost vegetable oils, vanilla production which eliminates the cultivation of vanilla beans, and a very wide range of agricultural inputs, including seeds, pesticides and fertilisers.

Capital in the form of small biotechnology companies and large transnational corporations alike are attempting to exploit the genetic resources of plants to gain control over future agricultural markets. As Yoxen (1986: 147) puts it:

> The developing ability to design, create and patent specific kinds of plants will confer upon the suppliers of plant varieties a greater degree of control over what is grown, over what substances are bought to protect or increase yields, over the price at which seeds are sold and over the purpose for which crops are grown. Through the design of new plants a new structure of dependence on agri-business firms is being planned, in return for which some us will get food.

One irony of all this is that many of the genes used to create the new plants will have been taken from societies where food is short. The new genetically engineered products are likely to be offered back at prices that only a minority can afford.

Farmers in developing countries are under particular threat. Their own tacit knowledge, in this case knowledge they have developed for themselves in working on the land, is again in danger of being marginalised. As we have seen earlier, the commoditisation of nature entails a massive shift in the division of labour as they become increasingly dependent on packages of chemical inputs and technical advice. Their knowledge of local plants and ecosystems is attributed decreasing significance or converted into concerns which are somehow 'backward' relative to the values of modernity. Manor (1994) refers, for example, to a trend whereby indigenous knowledge is 'robbed of its own autonomous consciousness and a global consciousness is imposed on it'. He refers to recent research on Africa which shows local environmental knowledge being damned with faint praise. This is achieved through outside experts' ascribing local knowledge with a conservation objective or ethic which is laudable enough but which, at least according to the experts, is 'at odds with the present "unsustainable" livelihood strategies and aspirations of the people' (Manor 1994: 19).

Meanwhile, the increasing separation of production from consumption entails that it is not only food producers who are having their tacit knowledge marginalised. Consumers, and their tacit knowledge, are also progressively de-skilled. Few of us have much understanding of the processes leading to the creation of what we are buying. A striking example comes from the genetic engineering of plants. Extra genes can now be implanted in, for instance, tomatoes. The object is to stop the rotting and improve their flavour. Furthermore, genetically engineered vegetables do not have to be labelled. Margaret Mellon, of the US-based National Wildlife Federation, expresses the estrangement of consumers as a reductionist abstract science is linked to production, hidden behind closed doors and disconnected from their tacit knowledge:

> In the past we really knew what makes a tomato into a tomato. That trust is now about to be shattered by a technology that can put a human gene, a pig gene, a carrot gene, a bacterial gene into this tomato. We're not going to be able to trust the tomato of the future in the same way.
>
> (British Broadcasting Corporation 1993)

THE IMPOSITION OF A REDUCTIONIST ABSTRACT SCIENCE

These various forms of alienation are largely a result of the process noted earlier in this study: the domination of abstract ideas over lay, tacit and unarticulated knowledges. The problem is not abstract knowledge itself but the forms it takes and its failure to connect to people's experience. Much of this science involved in the above technologies still makes exaggerated claims for the effects of the manipulation of particular parts of an organism such as its genetic structure. As such, it is highly reductionist. In particular, science of this kind emphasises the manipulation of genes here or there without recognising the potentials and capacities of organisms as a whole and their relationships with their environments. Organisms are being created with genetic information and characteristics which they did not previously possess. But there is an extremely important methodological point here. Genes and genetic manipulation do not in themselves provide an understanding of an organism's underlying causal powers and the ways in which organisms (including human organisms) grow and have grown in the past. Genes in bioengineering are much reified as the secret of life. They are sold, bought and used as magic fetishised things when in practice they should be seen as carrying-codes for the *potentials* and *capacities* of organisms (Waddington 1961).

So the organism, the complex mechanisms and interactions of which it is composed and its relation with other organisms, have again gone missing with the great reification of genes in much of modern science. Needless to say, this includes the human organism. All this brings us back to abstract science. It is the absence of the organism which is fundamentally wrong about abstract theory as it affects people, animals, plants and their inter-relations. And it would be a re-focusing on the organism, the mechanisms giving rise to its innate capacity to grow and develop, which would be the most obvious meeting-point for abstract and tacit skills and understandings developed

121

during people's everyday work and experience. The idea of an organism with *qualities*; with potentials which may or may not be realised, is the starting point of a new concept of nature which is beginning to arise in modern biology. (See, for example, Kauffman 1994, Lewontin 1993, Wesson 1991, Goodwin 1994.) It is emerging out of the mechanistic metaphors of nature which have so far dominated the life sciences. As we saw in Chapter 1, there are still difficulties with this metaphor. But while a lay person cannot hope to understand the details of this modern biology, it is at least a metaphor or model which is immediately understandable to 'lay' people, or those uninitiated into modern science.

Failure by abstract science to recognise the organism as a whole not only mystifies lay-people's understandings, it is actually dangerous. As some scientists themselves are now arguing (see, for example, Kollek 1995) there are several latent dangers in not recognising the whole organism. One is the deliberate or accidental release of new forms of life into a nature which has not evolved in a way which is able to resist such release. A second example relates to the genetic engineering of animals, either by altering sequences of DNA and putting them back or introducing them to different species. Such strategies are now forming an increasingly important part of animal-breeding. Natural selection can in effect be overtaken by developing key characteristics, especially those likely to lead to increased profitability. Israeli researchers, for example, have recently used genetic manipulation to produce 'naked neck' broilers with 40 per cent fewer feathers. Their lower body temperature means they eat more, put on weight faster and go for slaughter sooner. Australian scientists have produced 'self-shearing' sheep which shed their own wool (Ryan 1995). Such innovations cut down on the labour required and, perhaps most important, speed up the process by which capital is invested in the circuit of capital and profits are realised.

This technology, however, can violently interfere with an animal's 'species being'. Turkeys, for example, are now of such broad meaty conformation that they cannot even mate naturally (Perlas 1994). Such intensive breeding is also bringing about a range of 'production diseases', the unanticipated result of other features of the organism's changing at the same time. Pigs, for example, are experiencing leg weaknesses and respiratory diseases. All such unintended consequences are a result of selecting a particular aspect of an animal's development (one that can be modified by genetic engineering and artificial insemination) rather than considering the organism as a whole, conducting the process of variation much too quickly and without reference to the organism's environment. Biotechnology here, as in the case of plants, is being presented as 'a clean surgical strike' (Levidow 1994b), one in which a wholly technical solution is created through the deft manipulation of genes involving no wider ramifications. Such a picture not only underestimates the unintended consequences of singling out genes as parts of whole organisms and ecosystems but such 'scientising' also means that the underlying social relations impacting on animals, humans and other organisms are omitted from consideration.

Finally, such breeding techniques are again leading to a depletion in the richness of genetic variability that accumulated in an evolutionary process which included adaptations to the particular circumstances of relatively stable natural environments. Animals, as a result, are left vulnerable to changing physical and social environments. Examples of such dangers can also be pointed to. In the mid 1980s, for example, poultry farmers in New Jersey, Virginia and Maryland lost 12 million poultry animals. This was the direct result of a flu virus's being able to spread rapidly as a result of the relative genetic uniformity of the breeds in question. The Council for Agricultural Science and Technology is now warning of serious potential problems amongst dairy cattle in the United States (Perlas 1994).

THE NEW TECHNOLOGIES: CONSTRAINING OR ENABLING?

As with the new reproductive technologies, therefore, these forms of separation in biotechnology are the result of a complex combination and interaction between commodification and the harnessing of often misleading forms of abstract knowledge to dominant sources of power. And yet power relations and the combination of this science with previously subordinated forms of understanding should be the central concern with these modernisations of nature. And these apply to the new reproductive technologies as well as to the genetic engineering of the environment. New combinations between the market and the powers of nature are obviously developing apace. But there remains a danger of maintaining that tacit, lay and local knowledges are on their own a necessarily wonderful thing, that indigenous peoples and women are wholly passive or powerless pawns, that the new technologies bring no advantages and that lay members of the public want nothing to do with them.

First, lay knowledge is complex. It involves the active and reflexive incorporation of modern scientific discourse and its combination with lay understandings. Furthermore, it is not as though the market is an exactly strange phenomenon to, say, a dispossessed Third World farmer. Rather, the issue is the incorporation of the market into what Amanor calls 'commercial agricultural input markets'.

There seem to be two broad options. One is to reject biotechnology and to press forward along completely alternative lines. 'Sustainable' agriculture, which resists commercial fertilisers and attempts to create and maintain ecologically self-sustaining, low-input production systems is one radical alternative (Amanor 1994). Practices here include permaculture and 'biodynamic agriculture' which takes heed of the natural rhythms of the seasons. The United States Department of Agriculture is actively supporting some of these developments: showing, for example, that they sometimes use only 40 per cent of the energy of conventional methods and give as much profit for the farmers (Perlas 1994). Such strategies will no doubt continue and develop. But the genetic genie is now, so to say, 'out of the bottle' and in the hands of the dominant institutions affecting contemporary agriculture. While remaining sympathetic to the alternatives, therefore, it seems as well to remain open to strategies for developing this biotechnology in different directions.

And it is easy to overlook the potential benefits which might result from the industrialisation and commodification of nature. Hobbelink (1991) is also critical of biotechnology and its application to farming in developing countries but, as he puts it, 'this is not to say that traditional farming practices could not use a helping hand from modern science'.

> They can, and in specific cases, urgently need it. Peruvian farmers would very much welcome frost- and disease-tolerant potato varieties. The Sahelians could very well use better drought-tolerant millets, while Filipino upland rice farmers certainly would not mind having improved dry-land rice varieties at their disposal.
>
> (Hobbelink 1991: 143)

There are two main problems here. The first is not so much the technology itself, but the rest of the 'package' that comes with it. The second is again the reductionist nature of the science in question and whether, as a result, it can deliver what it promises.

The 'chemical fix' of the Green Revolution brought with it a massive dependence on agricultural pesticides and fertilisers. Similarly, the 'genetic fix' now offered by biotechnology also brings a new range of problems and commitments. The way biotechnology has so been far introduced has, for example, reduced biodiversity, and this leads to considerable crop vulnerability. Precedents for the potentially disastrous effects of monoculture are clear. In the 1970s, for example, 15 per cent of the US maize harvest was lost to a fungus, and this is directly ascribable to genetic uniformity (Hobbelink 1991). Avoiding disasters of this kind often entails a ratcheting-up effect whereby manufacturers invent new ways to overcome the problems which the new technologies have precipitated in the first place. Biotechnologies, which provide techniques to move germplasm between organisms which do not naturally exchange, could in principle be used to *in*crease diversity. They could also be used to enable better storage of genetic resources and the creation of new variants in both plants and animals. As Kloppenburg (1988: 244) puts it:

> Though the capacity to move genetic material between species is a means for introducing additional variation, it is also a means for engineering genetic uniformity across species.

As things currently stand, however, increased uniformity and monoculture farming (with geographical regions becoming increasingly specialised in what they produce) is likely to be the continuing tendency. Regaining diversity and resisting monoculture would itself involve a number of diverse strategies (Fowler and Mooney 1990). These would include restoring farmers as part of the food chain and resisting the process whereby food production simply becomes another form of factory-based production process. In developing countries in particular it would entail consulting a diverse array of people in particular regions and localities: farmers, fishermen and women, medicine makers and so on. What are their local knowledges and priorities for genetic conservation? Finally, it would also mean actively and continuously using this diversity. It is only through using diversity that it can be maintained and further developed.

Thus, making a change towards biodiversity and local farmers would entail a large-scale shift in economic and political power towards small-scale farming. Some indications of this are perhaps present in the European Union's policies of set-aside and support of family farms. In the case of the developing countries it would mean a large-scale shift in economic and political power away from the large corporations' providing the seeds and other genetically modified commodities and again towards small-scale farming. But as Juma (1989) argued some time ago in relation to the African countries, it is not beyond the bounds of possibility. Such strategies would entail African countries' enhancing their own technological and scientific base. The best alternative way ahead, according to Juma, is state-led strategies using the same science, but applying it to labour-intensive forms of production. 'Biotechnology', Juma argues,

> is one of the few techniques that are amenable to popular participation. They can be applied to decentralized production systems and thus render themselves amenable to local control.
>
> (1989: 218)

Therefore, these technologies can be used to resist the concentration of economic and political power in the international division of labour. Microbiological Resources Centres in a number of developing countries are now using biotechnology for a number of locally generated projects. These involve the increasing of soil fertility, the creation of energy from agro-industrial waste and the degradation of persistent pollution.

Similar issues arise when we return to the new reproductive technologies. A recurrent feminist argument is that they should be completely abandoned. Mies and Shiva (1993) insist, for example, that they are inherently oppressive. They were developed in a patriarchal society and are used to control women by regulating their fertility. For them, therefore, the technology is not neutral and should be abandoned *in toto*.

It is difficult to deny, however, that science and technologies can bring real gains, even if they developed within particular power relations (Mitter 1994, Jackson 1994). The new reproductive technologies can bring real benefits, even if these are currently to the more affluent white households. Infertile women seek help from them and, despite the still low success-rate of the technology, many actually receive it. It can of course be argued that the demand for children from women is a result of a wholly social imposition, the barren or childless woman being made to feel abnormal. We are on very debatable ground here, but such an argument would deny that there are biologically inherited dispositions to reproduce amongst humans, something which would make us unique amongst all living species. A denial of this process would surely be another unhelpful triumph by culture over nature. As Soper (1995: 138) puts it 'to take all conditioning away from nature and to hand it all to culture is to risk re-trapping ourselves in a new form of determinism'.

Only the most extreme Luddite would deny the gains that the new reproductive technologies can bring to women who want children. Similarly, for both humans and plants, the addition of genes that would confer resistance to disease is surely a gain, as is the possibility of monitoring embryos for genetically inherited diseases, and replacing the embryo in the womb if it is healthy.

But against this it can be argued that such processes again lead to a denial of organisms and ecosystems as a whole. Furthermore, the standardisation of the human species means that those with any disease which is deemed socially unacceptable (such as achondroplasia, or dwarfism) being aborted. By contrast, genetic engineering could be used to produce wholly trivial variations in children. Blue eyes and blonde hair could be specified. Designer-children could be run off a 'post-fordist' production line, with parents increasingly envisaging their children as fashion accessories whose nature can in principle be specified in advance of their birth. Meanwhile, as Hayry (1994) fantasises, genetic engineering could also be used to design sub-human beings who would carry out the work that is too dangerous or too disagreeable for the privileged minority. Recent claims that a 'gay gene' or 'a gene for aggression' exist raise the stakes further. Assuming such genetic links to behavioural predispositions are established (something which at the moment seems quite unlikely) these characteristics could also be repaired out of the organism before he or she is born.

Perhaps more seriously, the possible genetic manipulation of future children could divert attention away from the possible *social* causes of disease. Technical fixes to environmental and social causes could be the order of the day. Meanwhile, the genetic management of the organism could also serve to reinforce existing discrimination towards certain groups of people, such as the disabled (Rowland 1992). And again, a monoculture of human beings could presumably lead to their vulnerability to disease.

But all these arguments against the manipulation of genes can seem exceptionally purist views in the light of the immediate sufferings directly attributable to genetically inherited diseases. These include cystic fibrosis, a common disease affecting the lungs which can now be treated. Other genetically treatable diseases include Huntington's chorea, a very distressing neuro-degenerative condition which does not appear until people approach middle age. The isolation of the gene responsible for this disease has not been achieved at the time of writing but this could be another candidate for some form of gene therapy, perhaps in conjunction with IVF. But again it is important not to exaggerate the benefits of these 'technical fixes'. Such therapies by no means guarantee a return to a normal life for the sufferers involved.

Once more, the problem probably lies less in the science itself than in the form of the science and the power relations surrounding it. As long ago as 1979 Firestone urged women to embrace the new technologies on the grounds that it could be liberating for women, releasing them from the tyranny of the 'natural' childbirth. 'Childbirth is at best necessary and tolerable. It is not fun' (p.189). On the other hand, she argued,

> Artificial reproduction is not inherently dehumanizing. At the very least, development of the option should make possible an honest re-examination of the ancient value of 'motherhood'.
>
> (Firestone 1979: 188)

Many feminist writers and activists would now take issue with this view, arguing that the actual way in which the new reproductive technologies are used perpetuates women's subordinate position. But the question originally raised by Firestone remains. Is the technology the problem or is it the oppressive and reductionist way it is used which is the cause of the oppression? A dialectical position, one which searches for emancipatory prospects with the aid of modern technologies, seems a better strategy than out-and-out resistance.

Some feminists continue to argue that, although the new technologies may have developed within a patriarchal society, it does not follow that they could not be subverted to emancipatory ends. The problem is patriarchy itself, rather than the technology. Murphy (1989: 68), for example, writing of techniques for removing women's eggs, storing them, genetically manipulating them, fertilising them in laboratories and returning them to women's bodies, writes:

> Scientific advances in egg research could be exciting, even liberating for women in non-patriarchal cultures. In patriarchy, however, we have so little control of our lives that such reproductive techniques threaten our very survival.

Similarly, Breeze (1989) pursues Firestone's original position in arguing, with the assistance of Marge Piercy's *Woman on the Edge of Time*, that the new reproductive technologies could have liberatory prospects. They could, for example, be the basis for new kinds of living arrangements, with a range of parents looking after a range of babies 'of non-womb procreation'. Similarly, each child would choose their own 'significant adult'. Perhaps the most significant recent development is self-help donor insemination. This is now seen as a new reproductive choice for some women, some of whom use 'low tech' methods of self-insemination as a way of developing new, more collective, relations between adults and children (Hornstein 1989, Klein 1989). So far, however, 'self-help biotechnology' (on a par with that suggested by Juma for local production of plants) has not found an equivalent in human reproduction.

CONCLUSION: ALIENATION AND THE NATURE INDUSTRY

Biotechnology is often said to be *the* industry of the twenty-first century. Another, and in some ways more startling, candidate is nanotechnology (Drexler 1990, Pearson 1995). This will enable the rearrangement of atoms, the very building-blocks of the natural world. Reducing items to the very smallest component will enable the assembly of any commodity whatsoever. Nanotechnology could therefore be the ultimate in the humanisation of nature. Nature, now including all human-made products, would be produced to order and without the inconvenience of an evolutionary process. Everlasting life could be guaranteed.

> Pure and perfect diamonds could be created out of coal in a matter of minutes, steak synthesised out of grass and water, cancerous cells repaired by minute robotic surgeons injected into the blood stream. Entire products like cars or computers could be built from scratch, one atom at a time. Even death itself might no longer be inevitable, since nanotechnology's atomic-scale dexterity would include the capability to repair cells damaged by the ageing process.
>
> (Pearson 1995: 32)

Whether or not this technology sees the light of day and whether it is exploited as a modern industry in the same way as biotechnology and the new reproductive technologies remain to be seen. The point here, however, is that this is yet another instance of contemporary industry's intervening in the workings of nature in a particular way – albeit one which will further humanise nature, to render it compatible with human needs. It could also, incidentally, do much to upset contemporary value-systems. What might be the implications of, for example, industrially made diamonds? This would join synthesised chemicals as a 'nature' that is no longer dug out of the ground but which is made entirely in a laboratory in a matter of minutes.

As we have seen, modern societies create commodities (for example, 'perfect' babies or manufactured diamonds) by first of all breaking nature down into a large number of components. Each of these components has the potential to be owned and to be commercially exploited. In modern society a labour process is organised around these components, dividing societies into classes but re-combining them in various ways in order to produce further commodities. Nature, or more accurately nature's powers, are thereby reconstructed. In the case of nanotechnology, the element concerned is atoms. The hope is that if

128

ways can be found to manipulate and move atoms into whatever patterns and structures are wanted, literally anything can be synthesised. Any product can be made at a negligible financial and possibly even environmental cost. Nanotechnology therefore proceeds by disassembling into the smallest components. But the basic strategy of disassembling and reconstructing remains the same as that adopted in other industries.

However, if the argument of this chapter is along the right lines, the separation of nature into components and its reconstruction into a human-made 'nature' are not the only important (and probably not even the most important) outcomes of modernity's interventions into the natural world. It is important to re-stress here that such refashioning of nature does not actually entail changing the laws of nature. In this sense it is quite wrong to refer to 'the end of nature'. The causal powers and relations involved in nature are not themselves changed as a result of this 'refashioning'. They are left intact. The structures and processes causing an organism to grow and develop, for example, are not changed as a result of, for example, genetic engineering. Genetic engineering and associated practices such as *in vitro* fertilisation still wholly depend on these general causal mechanisms. Such practices are affecting precisely *how* an organism grows and develops, but they are not changing the underlying processes themselves. Similarly, should nanotechnology ever be put in place, these technologies will not alter the laws of atomic physics. Rather, these laws will be depended on and exploited. In both these cases, therefore, nature has not been 'conquered' in the sense of put to rest. Rather, it has been broken down into constituent components and its powers deployed towards increasingly human ends. This even applies to the most advanced and fragmenting forms of biotechnology such as those involved in the making of 'biomass'. Bacteria, with their powers to replicate themselves millions of times over, are now being combined with selected genes. One end-result is massive quantities of amino acid, a material which can then be used to make food in large amounts and of many kinds (Perlas 1994). Thus even here the degrading and synthesising powers of living organisms are still being actively depended on. Once more, nature has in no sense been 'conquered'. Rather, its powers are being discovered and industrialised to human ends.

The question remains, however, whether the isolation and manipulation of parts may not yet have unforeseen consequences. Modernity is characterised by the attempt to rationalise all aspects of life, to organise production processes and forms of administration in such a way that their results are predictable. And yet, as Murphy (1994: 144) points out,

> Calculation and prediction of consequences have hitherto been limited to prices, movement of capital, of labor, and consumer desires. They have not been extended to the environmental impact of commodities and their production.

Nevertheless, as Murphy implies but does not fully spell out, these forms of rationalisation are in place for a key underlying purpose. That is the organisation of production in such a way that the materials and powers of nature are converted into commodities. The main problem as regards production in such forms as genetic engineering and the new reproductive technologies is that they are founded on myopic forms of abstraction which deny the importance of organisms as a whole and their wider social and ecological connections. And, as production proceeds, such denials run the real risk of further unanticipated 'revenges'. But again, one of the most important revenges may be on human beings themselves. The new biotechnologies based on 'biomass' move production out of agriculture and wholly into factories. In this way, industrial production not only becomes insulated from the vagaries of the weather but further separated from human labour and public accountability. These processes may bring some real gains. They could even begin, for example, to replace those forms of bioengineering which create unexpected effects on ecosystems. But, by the same token, they risk further obscuring the ways in which human beings relate to the environmental and ecological systems of which they are still part. 'Man' becomes further estranged from nature, 'his inorganic body'.

6

CIVIL SOCIETY
The recovery of wholeness?

Many of what we call 'environmental problems' can be ascribed to the labour process, to the technical division of labour, to the multiple ways in which knowledge is constructed and used and to the ways in which modern societies manipulate nature to produce commodities. All this is not to say that the labour process, including such processes within the home and outside the formal economy, offers a total understanding of modern societies' relations with nature. But it is a good starting point, and it is a sphere of social life which has gone almost entirely missing in contemporary environmental analysis. However, people's alienated relations to nature, to one another and to the products of their work cannot be wholly appreciated through a narrow concentration on the labour process. It is certainly with this process that many social and environmental problems start. But to develop the argument we need to take it a stage further, examining not just the division of labour in general but its spatial and temporal forms.

This chapter is primarily concerned with civil society, defined here as social life outside the place of employment and not immediately involved with the state. It links this concern with the spatial division of labour. It first tries to clarify what civil society actually is, with reference to recent debates on the subject. It argues that the concept cannot be allowed to include and conflate the sphere of industrial production on the one hand and that of the purchase and consumption of commodities on the other. This is because, as should be clear by now, the set of relationships with nature which are contained within the sphere of production are especially important in terms of explaining people's alienation from nature and their consequent lack of concern with the non-human world. Also important, however, are the relations formed within consumption, or the purchasing of commodities. This is all the more reason to break ranks with most analyses of civil society and to consider production separately from consumption.

The chapter goes on to link civil society to the ways in which the technical and social divisions of labour are now spatially manifesting themselves. Bringing together changes in the spatial division of labour with forms of civil society means that we can further develop our understanding of alienation and

131

environmental problems. This discussion then forms a basis for the subsequent chapter on new social movements and environmental politics.

ASPECTS OF THE CIVIL SOCIETY DEBATE

In the environmental literature frequent appeal is made to 'community'. It is here where collections of people are seen as coming together to share experiences, relate to the local natural environments and assemble to protest against threats. It is a rallying cry, and one which contains all kinds of resonances about past and future societies which are wholly good and which must be recovered and retained. This study will, however, be mounting something of a campaign against the use of the term 'community'. In the end the notion is too vacuous. Appeal to arcadian pasts and futures does little or no justice to the often vicious and exploitative relations which persist in neighbourly relations.

Durkheim is well known for suggesting that the increase in the division of labour would lead to new forms of community. This is because these same divisions of labour necessarily lead to greater interdependence between the different roles carved out by modernity. As Sayer and Walker (1992) argue, there is more than an element of wishful thinking in this: 'Specialization divides people experientially, organizationally, and ideologically' (p. 17). As many sociological commentators have pointed out, the word 'community' brushes under the carpet often exploitative and unequal relations between classes, genders, races and age groups. More importantly still, it ignores the fact that such relations are more the rule than the exception.

All this, however, is not to deny the fact that face-to-face association does not have real personal value and that people, especially when they are in some way oppressed, do not feel the value of combining as a community of equals against such oppression. But 'community' is not a helpful way of understanding the sphere of social life outside employment and outside the state. Rather, this chapter will go for 'civil society' as a more helpful concept. Nevertheless, an adequate understanding of people's problematic relations with their environments needs to consider civil society in relation to the sphere of industrial production.

The concept of 'civil society' is in fact now receiving a great deal of attention. As Cohen and Arato (1992: 29) have put it, 'phrases involving the resurrection, re-emergence, rebirth, reconstruction or renaissance of civil society are heard repeatedly today'. The concept is used very differently by different authors, and this is largely a result of the different political purposes to which it is being put. One reason for the widespread discussion of the concept is the downfall of the communist regimes in the Soviet Union and Eastern Europe. Here 'civil society' was defined in relation to the state. It became a rallying cry and a site for the expansion of democracy in opposition to state bureaucracies (Stammers 1995). The Soviet and East European party-state regimes were 'totalising' in the sense that their ambition was to abolish the distinction between state and civil society by absorbing the latter sphere into the former. This attempt was an apparent way of resolving the dichotomy between state and civil society against which Marx railed when he was attacking liberal thinking. It was never completely successful and the way in which it was conducted was, to say the very least, ham-fisted and undemocratic in almost every way.

In this context civil society became defined as the area of social life outside such bureaucracies and a sphere of social life within which individual and social identity can be re-formed. And, as will be discussed in the next chapter, it is seen by some as a setting for wholly new forms of politics, outside the 'old' politics of production and class. A second reason for the outburst of interest in civil society has been the crisis of the welfare state in many Western capitalist societies. Here civil society is again advanced as an alternative to oppressive state apparatuses. It is envisaged as a context within which family life, voluntary association, public communication and new forms of social movement can thrive.

This seems to be a particular feature of 'the new communitarianism' (Etzioni 1993). Here again, it is envisaged as a sphere of beneficial autonomy, a realm of social life which self-constitution and self-mobilisation can develop. Interestingly, however, the use of the concept for the understanding of capitalist societies tends to exclude 'the economy'. For Cohen and Arato (1992) civil society is 'a sphere between the economy and the state' (p. ix). It is a cipher for 'community', those institutions and practices outside of the market and the state which people construct for themselves.

It would not be appropriate here to enter current debates on civil society in great detail. But three features deriving from the above brief discussion should be apparent. First, there is a great deal of muddle about the relationship between civil society and the economy. As Seligman (1992: 3) puts it in his comprehensive study of civil society, 'contemporary uses of the term tend to be broad and often lack intellectual rigour'. For those advancing the cause of civil society in the previously communist societies it was initially a political anti-state strategy. It was later on that it became specified as concerned with the relations between states and markets. Meanwhile for the New Right advancing alternatives to the welfare state under capitalism, it excludes the production of commodities (and the classes and processes formed in such production) but includes the buying and selling of such commodities. For both such understandings, the sphere of production again remains something of a black box. The danger for both perspectives is that, while they have to recognise the sphere of production, they do not see it in relation to civil society generally and the market exchange more specifically.

Second, and despite the conceptual differences between these approaches, there is some common recognition that 'civil society' (whatever it is!) represents a sphere of relative freedom for human beings and the possibility for the active creation of personal identity. And this reflects much mainstream sociological thinking, especially that in North America. Gouldner, for example, writes that:

> Sociology conceives of civil society as a haven and support for individual persons, i.e. as de-atomizing; as a medium through which they can pursue their own projects in the course of their everyday lives; and as ways of avoiding dependence on the domination by the state.
>
> (Quoted in Kumar 1993: 3)

More recently, however, and especially with the arrival of the so-called 'new communitarianism', the concept has come to denote a process of not only individual development, but of individuals developing within some kind of social collective. Seligman's review of the concept argues that the concept has long encapsulated a notion of like-minded individuals held together by a strong set of moral beliefs. Contemporary enthusiasts for civil society pursue this notion, using it to affirm community as well as individuality.

> In our analysis of the civil society tradition a number of themes have emerged as central concerns to those writers who joined the debate over civil society. One of those themes was the perduring need to articulate some vision of the individual that would both uphold his (and ever so much later, her) autonomy and agentic nature and at the same time present a vision of a 'public' – that is, a group of individuals sharing core ideas, ideals, and values.
>
> (Seligman 1992: 60)

Interestingly, perspectives on civil society from radically different political positions converge on the notion of civil society's being a 'good', one which allows the unfolding of human capacities but which is simultaneously under threat. Habermas's discussion of the lifeworld is particularly relevant here (Habermas 1987, 1989, Outhwaite 1994). He argues on the one hand that everyday life is being de-coupled from the wider social system. The business of practical living is being detached from the political and economic order despite the fact that the sustained reproduction of this order needs a continuing attachment to practical and everyday life. At the same time, however, Habermas echoes Marx in suggesting that the 'lifeworld' is increasingly penetrated by the market and by state bureaucracies. Public opinion is no longer a product of rational discussion and debate and is increasingly subject to 'opinion research', 'public relations', 'publicity' and so on. Furthermore, day-to-day existence is being systematically robbed of its symbolic and normative content. It has decreasing meaning.

Habermas can thus be seen as referring to a type of alienation, although it is of course of a type some way removed from the specific forms (such as the alienation of industrial workers from the products of their labours) originally outlined by Marx. Out of such tensions, he argues, there are now emerging new forms of politics. The environmental movement and feminism are examples of how people are attempting to resist and overcome the colonisation of the lifeworld and at the same time link up the social system as a whole to the day-to-day practicalities of everyday life. Habermas argues that these are political movements which are not class or production based. They are emerging from civil society. Again, this is a key point made by a number of civil society theorists and it is one to which we will return in the next chapter.

Third, there is very little discussion of environmental matters in these debates on civil society. The analytical work relating civil society to the environment remains to be done. Etzioni (1994: 266), in discussing the importance of transmitting values to future generations, does argue that 'social environments, like natural environments, cannot be taken for granted'. But this hardly constitutes a wide-ranging discussion of the relations between humans and nature. Habermas's view is also not a great advance. His notion of everyday life and the 'lifeworld' makes no sustained reference to lives or worlds other than those of the human variety.

All of this implies that a revised understanding of civil society is needed, one with greater analytical value and one which links to society's relations to nature. This is another expression of the general problem of disciplinary boundaries. As a starting point, and one which is broadly compatible with the analysis here, we should turn to those writers who have been developing the Marxian tradition. Marx himself seems to have identified civil society with 'the economy' (Kumar 1993). But such a link again does not take the discussion much further. As argued above, a key distinction if we are to adequately understand the relation between societies and nature is between industrial production (and the technical division of labour which this incorporates) and the circulation of commodities. So what is needed is a distinction between industrial production and that sector of 'the economy' involving the circulation of money through the buying and selling of commodities.

Urry some time ago (1981) promoted an understanding of civil society which permits such a distinction. It is one which has some parallels with the writings of Gramsci and Althusser. Civil society, according to Urry's analysis, has three main dimensions. First, the circulation of capital (the realm Marx called 'Freedom, Equality, Property and Bentham'). This is the sphere in which buyers and sellers freely engage in these processes. No-one is forcing them to do so at a particular time and place. Such a definition of 'the economic' thus deliberately excludes the sphere of production and refers, again, to the selling and buying of commodities. Second, it refers to the sphere of reproduction: the reproduction of labour power in the biological, economic and cultural senses. This again, therefore, explicitly excludes the sphere of production. It does refer, however, to the reproduction of the conditions necessary for such production: the production of new generations of people and ideas, with particular reference to the role of the household. Third, civil society, according to this definition, refers to a range of struggles which cannot be reduced to those at the workplace. Many would argue that environmental struggles are good examples of such struggles within civil society, though this is an issue to which we will return. Finally, Urry argued (and here he is more in line with conventional sociological thinking as outlined above) that civil society is especially important in the constitution of subjectivity, in the creation of 'autonomous, whole and independent subjects' (1981: 72).

We have here, then, an understanding of 'civil society' which is compatible with the theoretical perspective adopted in this study. It refers to the circulation of commodities, various forms of reproduction including cultural reproduction and a range of struggles. It is also a definition which allows a systematic understanding of the important processes that take place within industrial production. But having separated civil society from the sphere of production, it is important to conduct our enquiries by exploring the connections between these two spheres of social life. People's lives and politics are of course the product of a combination of their experiences in *both* spheres of social life. How do they combine with one another? More specifically, how do they combine with one another in particular times and places? It is at this point that we need to briefly revisit the sphere of industrial production and examine its changing links with civil society and with people's relations with nature.

CIVIL SOCIETY AND THE CHANGING SPATIAL DIVISION OF LABOUR

Nearly one hundred years ago the anarchist writer Peter Kropotkin was referring to an important way in which the division of labour was manifesting itself. He referred to the growing 'specialisation' of nations and regions. In addition to promoting the division of labour in the workplace celebrated by Adam Smith, he argued, industrialists and politicians were now creating the *spatial* division of labour.

> Dazzled with the results obtained by a century of marvellous inventions, especially in England, our economists and political men went still farther in their dreams of the division of labour. They proclaimed the necessity of dividing the whole of humanity into national workshops having each of them its own speciality. We were taught, for instance, that Hungary and Russia are predestined by nature to grow corn in order to feed the manufacturing countries; that Britain had to provide the world-market with cottons, iron goods, and coal; Belgium with woollen cloth; and so on. Nay, within each nation, each region had to have its own speciality.
>
> (Kropotkin 1985: 24)

And yet, Kropotkin argued, these specialisations were in no way based on the characteristics of the local people or the land. An imposition of the spatial division of labour on the landscape was as bad as the imposition of the technical division of labour on the working population.

136

Each nation is a compound aggregate of tastes and inclinations, of wants and resources, of capacities and inventive powers. The territory occupied by each nation is in its turn a most varied texture of soil and climates, of hills and valleys, of slopes leading to a still greater variety of territories and races. Variety is the distinctive feature, both of the territory and its inhabitants.

(1985: 25)

Kropotkin was pointing in a very far-sighted way to the way in which the division of labour impacts on landscapes. And the process of making 'national workshops' (out of regions as well as countries) has continued to develop since the time he was writing.

The contemporary global division of labour is one in which production-processes have been fragmented and industrial production can take place in a number of societies, including of course the newly industrialising societies offering relatively cheap or 'flexible' labour. This is of course quite distinct from the pattern described by Kropotkin in which the older industrial countries produced the manufactured goods and the non-industrialised societies provided raw materials, agricultural products and acted as markets for some of the finished items.

But it is even more different from the kind of society represented by the Kogi. In modern societies the relationships with nature which were once visible have been drastically displaced to other parts of the globe. They are now invisible. Multiple labours needing many features of a local ecosystem have been steadily replaced by a single kind of labour. The result has been to discourage agricultural diversity and a reliance on imported natural resources. Ignatieff, writing of former colonies says:

Where once their agriculture was sufficiently diversified to feed their populations, now their economies depend dangerously on monocultures, on the export of cash crops or basic resources in return for international currency.

(1990: 128)

Needed resources now come from an environment in which the user does not have to live and on which she or he is not directly dependent. This is because there are usually alternative sources of materials in other places.

All this means that local civil society, the sphere of life outside industrial production, comes to have a particular significance in terms of people's physical, social and environmental well-being. It becomes an important setting within which people attempt to make or remake identities, politics, social relations and relations with nature. In short, shifts in the global division of labour place a particular premium on other relations outside the sphere of industrial production. Let us now take the different elements of civil society, exploring their relationships with nature.

137

CIVIL SOCIETY AND THE COMMODITY 'NATURE'

If modern and capitalist production spends much of its time disassembling social life and relations between humans and nature, civil society represents the obverse of this. It offers a whole vision of society, one in which the relations between societies and nature are treated as wholes and even one in which people are considered as wholes. And yet such visions are contradictory. They choose to largely ignore the sphere of modern production, a myopia which is potentially disastrous. At the same time it will become clear that such visions are important in prefiguring new ways of life and in discovering mechanisms and causal powers within human beings and within external nature which could have important emancipatory prospects.

Civil society presents purchasable commodities, images, spectacles and ways of life which, although definitely still only concerned with parts of nature and parts of human social and economic systems, offer at least a sense or semblance of wholeness. This recovered wholeness is increasingly constituted by symbols. As Lash and Urry (1994: 4) put it, 'what is increasingly produced are not material objects, but signs'. The wholeness represented in this way is to a large extent spurious, but lives are nevertheless made and identities formed through the acquisition of such symbols. This applies as much to people's relations with nature as any other form of association.

Furthermore, as Marx in particular argued, people's lives and thoughts in modern societies can easily start to revolve around one particular aspect of civil society, the purchase and consumption of such commodities. The fragments and partial visions start to become things in their own right; items to be consumed, worshipped or 'fetishised'. Referring back to our concerns in the last chapter, for example, Franklin (1988) has argued that in television documentaries genes are held up as 'fetish objects', their discovery and use being separated from the social and historical origins and from 'the genetic commodity fetishism evident in contemporary society' (p. 100).

The result of such fetishisation is that isolated items are abstracted away from the harsh world of social relations, divisions of labour, regulation of knowledge, production processes and links between all these items and the causal powers of nature. They are considered as things; their relationships to people, to nature and to processes involved in their production becoming neglected and even forgotten. In modern societies a sense of connectedness between people, commodities and nature revolves largely around the market. As neo-classical economists fondly point out, the market is the means by which supply and demand are coordinated. It is a means by which dispersed and individualised choices are linked to production. This is, of course, an overly idyllic and harmonious picture. It chooses to ignore the effects of distancing people from the environment. It also systematically overlooks social and power relations and the degree of havoc caused by industrial restructuring. It is again therefore most important to unpack what is meant here by 'the market'. It is used in this study to refer specifically to the selling and buying of commodities. This does not refer to the buying and selling of the commodity 'labour power' and it specifically excludes the production of things. The consumption of commodities can now be seen as all-pervading and all-consuming. As Plant has recently emphasised, it is the 'whole' around which people's lives are organised.

> It is not just that the relationship to commodities is now plain to see. Commodities are now all there is to see; the world we see is the world *of* the commodity. And this vision of a united, completed and natural social whole is a representation which compensates for the increasing fragmentation and alienation of daily life and belies the existence of all discontinuity and contradiction.
>
> (1992: 12, Plant's emphasis)

Turning to the more specific question of the relation between civil society and nature, this idea of the naturalness and wholeness of the market is now being extended to incorporate the physical and biological environment. The dominant process is the increasing extent to which the global environment is being bound up with the wholeness represented by the global market. In particular it is being integrated into the wholeness represented by a particular *aspect* of the civil society: the buying and selling of commodities. So while avoiding an analysis and understanding of wholeness in terms of the multiple mechanisms affecting concrete events, modernity simultaneously provides a substitute in civil society, albeit one which tends to be passively chosen and consumed rather than actively made or constructed. In this sense alienation thus seems to be complete. People are systematically removed from an understanding of their own lives and from their relations of nature by one sphere of society only to be offered an apparent replacement in another.

But there are several *caveats* to be made here. People are only *offered* emancipation through the purchase of symbols as commodities. They may be treated as spectators and consumers (including consumers of a resurrected 'nature'). Furthermore, as Plant and others have argued, in escaping from the mundanity and dullness of everyday life, 'we run blindly towards the promises of wholeness, fulfilment, and unity implicit in the world of the abundant commodity' (Plant 1992: 64).

But of course none of this by any means guarantees emancipated lives. People do not necessarily engage in the wholesale fetishisation of commodities. They maintain a need to understand and control their lives despite, perhaps indeed because of, such fetishisation and reification. And, as we saw earlier in Chapter 4, they simultaneously retain many knowledges – including of course scientific knowledge of how they and their understandings simultaneously have come to be marginalised.

Perhaps even more important than any of the above considerations is, again, the fact that nature is not actually subjugated even though it is increasingly penetrated, fragmented, reconstructed and formed into commodities. Once more, natural objects, including human beings, retain their structures and ways of acting in virtue of these structures. These structures and resulting powers may be modified and used in new ways, but the idea that nature has been finally subjugated by modernity is misleading and of course dangerous to all concerned. Furthermore, as Alvater (1993, 1994) has pointed out, all-encompassing market relations (this again refers to the sphere of commodity-exchange rather than their production) tend to be at odds with the variety of ecological and environmental systems. Commodity fetishism and spectacle, including the spectacle of a highly planned 'nature' in which tourists and others can indulge, leaves the powers of nature intact and may be combining with them in ecologically disastrous ways. This arises from the collision between the global market and local diversity.

> The heterogeneity of physical transformation in real space and time – that is, the particularity of materials, place, and ecology – is at odds with the axiom of general comparability in the world marketplace imposed by capitalism.
>
> (Alvater 1994: 79–80)

On the one hand this particular kind of consumption offers a seductive array of apparently 'natural' experiences. MacNaghten and Urry (1995: 213) refer to the contemporary seduction of the marketplace through

> the mix of feelings and emotions by seeing, holding, hearing, testing, smelling, and moving through the extraordinary array of goods and services, places and environments, that characterise contemporary consumerism organised around a particular 'culture of nature'.

At the same time, as Alvater suggests, such experiences can be highly disruptive for global and local environments. Arguably tourism is 'the peak experience' of this process, offering all the semblances and excitements of cultures and natures while at the same time doing its best to undermine these same phenomena.

There are, therefore, a number of contradictions between the market and the environment and these are by no means necessarily overcome by any amount of commodity-fetishism and re-constructed 'natures' in civil society. Perhaps the most important contradiction, and the one particularly stressed by Alvater, is the creation of entropy (or various forms of 'waste') by production processes. An increase of entropy in the production of use-values is inevitable. It is a necessary outcome of materials' and energy's being transformed. But the actual rate of entropy-maximisation is socially produced. It is a result of, and is shaped by, social and political organisation (Alvater 1993). And it is 'waste' in its many forms which threatens to overwhelm the systems of production which are creating it.

Alienated knowledge, as we have discussed earlier, has been removed from the material and social ways in which the powers of nature combine with each other and which are being refashioned by various forms of human intervention. It is knowledge which is attributed a life of its own, an understanding which is comparable with fetishised commodities which are considered separate from the processes underlying their production. As argued before, modern commodity-based societies are surely more likely to 'trade' in generalised and abstract knowledge rather than the knowledges generated by people in their everyday lives.

Newton's laws of physics or Darwin's laws of natural selection would not be different in, say, a socialist society. They are not, seen in isolation, 'wrong'. But, assuming 'socialism' implies some reversal of commodity fetishism and a shift in the generation of knowledge towards those lay-people carrying out various forms of practical and manual work, such particular forms of abstract knowledge would no longer be treated as separate things in themselves. Nor would knowledge be treated as an abstract quantity in itself. Its characteristic as a generalised and saleable commodity would be far less significant. Other forms of knowledge would become important. These would incorporate, for example, nature's qualities (including its aesthetic qualities), the individual subject's understandings of nature and its multiple connections to different parts of nature and to human society.

It is true to say that the separation of abstract knowledge from the kinds of fragmented knowledge developed in everyday life also has a long history, one which can be traced back as far as Ancient Greece. The point is, however, that a separated abstract knowledge has particularly thrived in a society where the things made for human use actually are abstract in the sense that they are reconstituted as a set of quantities ready to be sold on a global market. Most people learn of nature, for example, through television programmes, books and compact discs which are available on the mass market. There would be no necessary problem with this if such information were couched in a way which allowed connections to be made between such abstract science and knowledge of particular contingent circumstances of local areas. This would mean specifying the general underlying mechanisms that operate at different strata within the natural and social worlds but allowing for people to feed in their own understandings of how these mechanisms work out in practice.

Arguably much 'green' theory is alienated or separated knowledge. This is of course ironic considering the extent to which science and society are subjected to criticism by such theory. A large part of this understanding, including the philosophy of bioregionalists, deep greens and authors such as Lovelock and Sheldrake belong to what Martell (1994: 51) calls 'the lessons from nature school of environmentalism'. An unadorned 'nature' is an example of fetishised and alienated knowledge. On its own it may (or may not) be right. But, since it marginalises the ways in which modern societies actively disassemble nature, it offers few clues as to how such a society should in future be organised. This is because the formation of knowledge by dominant orders (and especially those associated with the sphere of industrial production) remain hidden and barely considered. Green theory is very frequently, therefore, an instance of alienated and reified knowledge.

A similar problem persists with virtually all understandings. Each academic discipline seems to offer a whole understanding. This is partly understandable since each discipline is indeed associated with particular causal powers. But at the same time it offers a restricted vision. Great authority and respect are attributed to the experts representing each isolated fragment but, as Vaneigem puts it, each expert is:

> alienated in being out of place with the others; he [sic] knows the whole of one fragment and knows no realisation.

(Quoted in Plant 1992)

Expecially important is mainstream economics, including so-called 'environmental economics' (see, for example, Pearce *et al.* 1989 and Barde and Pearce 1991). This insists, quite rightly, that the resources which societies have previously considered to be free should be charged for. Such costs would eventually find their way into, for example, lower dividends, higher prices or technical innovations which reduced environmental degradation. This represents an extremely important intervention. Who would seriously question a strategy which charges people for using previously costless resources? On the other hand, this approach systematically ignores divisions of labour and forms of alienation between people and nature in production processes. It is another good, and highly influential, example of an abstract and alienated knowledge, one which fetishises this particular part of social reality without reference to the manipulation of nature in the sphere of production. But does this necessarily mean it should be resisted?

Environmental economists argue persuasively, and in line with much contemporary environmental thinking, that economic development must be made sustainable. It must offer to future generations the same or greater levels of well-being as are now being enjoyed by the existing population. This inevitably involves, they argue, systems of valuation. Hard decisions need making between, for example, roads for mountains or housing developments for wild areas. Conventional economics, they argue, has failed the environment. Conventional economic development has operated against the environment. It has favoured traditional forms of development (roads and housing developments) and systematically prejudiced the environment. The answer, according to Pearce and his colleagues, is to change market signals in such a way that prices and quantities reflect human populations' environmental preferences. This is to be achieved through manipulating what environmental economists refer to as 'the market'. Environmental economics can thereby be seen as another form of fetishism, again attaching monetary value to environmental systems (or, more accurately, very limited parts of such systems) and abstracting them away from the processes involved in their production: not only the social and political processes involved but knowledge of the relations with the

142

causal powers of nature engaged during their production. Systems and relations that produce things (including environmental things) remain ignored and the things themselves become the object of attention and admiration. Their value is equated wholly with their cost. Again, however, it is certainly very difficult to oppose such thinking in a wholesale way. The risks of not valuing environments and resources are surely also very considerable. The further encouragement of waste might be one important result of not carrying out such interventions.

The problem here is that environmental economics is concentrating myopically on surface appearances and attributing new commodities with thing-like qualities. (Martinez Allier's survey (1987) seems to largely confirm this.) Environmental economics may indeed be the best that can be achieved within a modern economy. Furthermore, rejecting money and commodities would mean returning to a very primitive level of living to which few people would in practice wish to return. But at the same time, constant reminders need to be made to the effect that this style of analysis is still merely playing with the parts rather than with the key relationships and causal powers involved. Alvater (1993: 208) mounts an effective attack along these lines when he writes that:

> If an attempt is made to base ecological calculation upon monetary values, it will inevitably erect into a principle the characteristics of the commodity form: reification and the screening out of the natural constraints of production and consumption. If, on the other hand, that principle is discarded, the possibility of economic calculation based upon commodification and monetization will be curtailed.

And yet there is a certain inevitability about ecological destruction under modern conditions. This is not simply a result of an abstract 'capitalism' wrecking the environment, although this is certainly a part of the problem. It has as much if not more to do with the advanced division of labour under modernity. It has a great deal to do with divisions between different firms or capitals. Each producer understandably focuses on the particular inputs it requires for its production process. It has little or no sense of the inputs required by other producers. It has even less sense of its impacts on complex ecological systems as a whole and how modernity is impacting on these systems.

So environmental economics in its predominant if varying forms falls prey to reifying and fetishising processes which render understanding and management of the environment into another exercise in the manipulation of surface appearances. The market system (defined in terms of the buying and selling of commodities) can certainly be seen as much like ecosystems themselves. In the same way as the market continually adapts to changing circumstances without a centralised, conscious control, ecological systems also contain their own feedback mechanisms, adapting to form a new 'balance'. Indeed, the logic of environmental economics is to eventually fuse these two

143

systems, to humanise ecological systems to the extent of making their adaptations increasingly subject to how much humans are prepared to pay for the parts they most value. There are two central difficulties with such a fusion between the ecological system and the market. First, the sphere of production is omitted. This sphere may be able to provide the 'environmentally friendly' products that consumers need, but this still says little about the environmental degradation and use of resources caused in the process of such production. But second, and in the longer term perhaps more important, such a 'solution' provides even less understanding of the causal powers of nature and how humans are affecting them.

So how do we account for the popularity of such a vision? The relationship between knowledge and power is again central. Some commentators (for example, Barde and Pearce 1991) seem genuinely surprised, for example, that the most influential decision-makers are enthusiastic about environmental economics. But anyone (and particularly influential advisors to governments such as these authors) should be able to see that it is easier and politically less contentious to focus on individual preferences regarding the purchase of environmental commodities rather than ask difficult questions about the power relations surrounding knowledge and the relations and processes involved in the making of these commodities.

Much the same can be said about so-called green consumerism. Most of us who engage in such practices have little understanding of what we are doing and of the processes which lead to the production of 'green' products. Green consumers are in a state of permanent tension and beset by high degrees of anxiety over which form of consumption is more correct and whether they should be doing so much consuming anyway. Should we buy organic coffee from Mexico which has travelled thousands of miles or local produce which has been sprayed by insecticides? Similarly,

> Now, even if you've actually been an environmentalist for a decade or more, you find yourself standing in the supermarket aisles racking your brains over whether you should be buying straight recycled toilet paper, or searching vainly for non-chlorine bleached recycled toilet paper, or rejecting the otherwise perfect recycled, non-chlorine bleached toilet paper because it was trucked in from two thousand miles away.
>
> (Plant and Plant 1991: 2)

A characteristic feature of modernity and of the global markets connecting local social systems is that no-one knows the answers to such questions. On the one hand, green purchasing is likely to offer only a partial solution to the problem. Consumption's role in destroying or protecting the environment is a poorly understood process. But thinking which extends beyond the fetishisation of the market strongly suggests, as Plant and Plant put it, that 'we can hardly hope for societal transformation from recycled toilet paper'. If, for example, everyone in the United States recycles 100 per cent of *personal* solid waste, 99 per cent of the *country's* solid waste would remain: industry and the military accounting for the latter. In Britain the situation seems marginally 'better'. Even here, however, agriculture, industry and mining are by far the largest contributors (Gandy 1994).

Again, no-one in their right minds would wish to stop green consumption, but the idea that solutions can easily be found through changes in individual lifestyles is illusory. And yet it is easy to imagine that solutions are indeed to be found this way. This is again the result of commodity fetishism with extensive support from industry itself.

> Because the commodity spectacle is so all-engaging, 'light' green business tends to merely perpetuate the colonization of the mind, sapping our visions of an alternative and giving the idea that our salvation can be gained through shopping rather than through social struggle and transformation. In this respect, green business at worst is a danger and a trap.
>
> (Plant and Plant 1991: 7)

On the other hand, the above does not sufficiently recognise the extent to which commodity fetishism is a double-edged sword. 'The colonization of the mind' is surely always an incomplete and contradictory project, engendering as it often does some form of anti-consumption, pro-green consciousness. Much of what we call 'green' social and economic theory is celebrating surface appearances. But there is certainly a value in doing so since it is touching on and perhaps transforming people's consciousness of themselves and their relations with nature. But it remains illusory if the relatively permanent structures, causal powers and processes behind the surface appearances remain neglected or even wholly ignored.

However, it is possible to be far more positive and up-beat about it if we see it as a form of prefigurative politics, one which could eventually lead to an understanding of causal processes and relations. Any emancipatory form of politics must continue to engage first with how the world is physically organised. As Collier puts it,

> Freedom must be 'in gear' rather than 'out of gear' freedom; it is not a matter of disengaging ourselves from the world so that it gets no grip on us – for by the same token we would get no grip on it. We do not escape from necessity in that what we do we do in ways governed by causal laws.
>
> (1994: 192–3)

Developments such as environmental economics and green consumerism can still be seen positively if they are seen as a way of getting 'in gear' or purchasing some grip on the causal processes underlying concrete reality. A similar point can be made about cultural reproduction, with reference to the concept of 'nature'.

145

ALIENATION, SELF-PROVISIONING AND CULTURES OF NATURE

The second feature of civil society to be discussed here concerns reproduction as distinct from production. We will be looking here first at forms of production in the home and community all of which are means by which individuals and households reproduce themselves. We will then explore cultural reproduction with special reference to the environment.

It is very easy to neglect the various forms of self-provisioning and self-help in which people engage. Examples are the small-scale production of food by lay-people or even the production of houses in the form of so-called 'community architecture'. In Britain and other advanced industrial countries such forms of production were a central feature of life during the nineteenth century. They were an important part of a tradition of working-class self-help and mutual aid. But the extension of wage labour, combined with the growth of the welfare state and the commoditisation of most products, means that this form of production has become increasingly marginalised. Nevertheless, it is easy to assume that such forms of production have entirely disappeared. Such an assumption is almost certainly wrong (Pahl 1984, Mingione 1985, Ward 1985). Self-provisioning is alive and kicking even if not on the scale of the mid nineteenth century. Furthermore, the difficulties now being experienced in many governments as regards the public financing of welfare could even mean a possible growth in this form of production. Should this be welcomed?

The fact that such forms of production continue to be assumed away as small-scale and unimportant is part of the general process we identified earlier whereby practices and knowledges developed outside industrial production have been consistently down-graded or even ignored in academic analysis and politics. Similarly, the skills and knowledge developed outside the formal economy and mass-consumption go unrecognised and largely unrewarded. And yet these forms of production should be illuminated since they contain within them important sources of understanding of the self and of a person's relations with nature.

Growing your own vegetables or raising a few animals on a small patch of rented ground, preparing and cooking them may well be more expensive than buying frozen food from a supermarket. Similarly, building your own home at weekends and in the evenings may well be, depending on how the self-producer's time is costed, a more expensive enterprise than buying a house. But such activities do provide some kind of understanding of how what we consume is actually produced. They also offer a degree of control over personal and collective life. Writing of allotments, Crouch and Ward (1988: 14) write:

> It is possible to buy a packet of frozen food and cook it instantly without knowing where or how or by whom it was produced. And this is less expensive than seeding, nurturing and harvesting the food yourself. Why, then, does the allotment garden continue to flourish? The answer

must lie in its image, in the role of communal effort, in the feelings growers have in feeding a family through their own efforts. Our image of the allotment turns out not to be, not a matter of the way we glimpse its landscape from the train, but a reflection of our image of the world as a whole and the social relationships we make in our small patch of it.

But the above offers only part of the answer to Crouch and Ward's question. Seeding, nurturing and harvesting your own peas as distinct from buying them in a supermarket also offers a better understanding of the powers of organisms in their environmental setting and the processes whereby the thing you eat has been produced.

In short, self-provisioning starts to overcome the kinds of alienation which we have been identifying earlier. Its possible extension, examples of which we will encounter in Chapter 8, must again be welcomed as possibly prefiguring forms of more emancipated society, this incorporating new kinds of social relations and more direct relations with the causal powers of nature. Nevertheless, we must of course be careful not to over-romanticise these developments. Three considerations come to mind.

In some cases it is the better-off working classes (those who are able to afford the tools) who are most likely to engage in these informal forms of production (Pahl 1984). Presumably the same problems apply when it comes to renting or owning ground for the self-production of food. Research in Southern Italy strongly suggests, however, that in some instances such self-provisioning should be seen as 'survival strategies' rather than forms of emancipatory work in which people engage by choice (Mingione 1985, 1988). Finally, there is of course the central question of the gender relations surrounding these practices. There is a long tradition of self-provisioning outside the home's being carried out by men, while the cooking and preparation is conducted by women in the home. The self-provisioning by men on small patches of land joins watching football and the pub as a refuge not only from the conditions of wage labour but work within the home (Crouch and Ward 1988). In other words, the social division of labour implied by such developments could still leave intact the marginalisation of women, their skills and knowledge while ensuring that men's skills are developed. So such developments are contradictory. They may be prefiguring important new forms of less alienated relations with society and nature but they are still associated with frugality, with 'making do' under conditions of poverty and with very oppressive and long-standing social relations. Like many 'prefiguring' developments, they offer mixed messages.

We now turn to cultural reproduction, specifically 'cultures of nature'. This refers to ideas about nature, to different types of ideas. We saw in Chapter 3 that there is an important distinction to be made between two types of concept. On the one hand, we have knowledge describing real causal powers and tendencies in society and nature and their combination to produce material events. On the other hand, we have relatively simple symbols and images used on an everyday basis to make these complexities coherent. But how do these two types of concept relate to each other?

Raymond Williams (1973) long ago explored some of these links. He still provides important insights into what is taking place. Williams argued that the literature surrounding the concept of nature constantly refers back to an arcadian golden past in which people at one time not only lived in closer harmony with the natural world but with one another. He refers to an 'escalator' of pastoral writing in which, however far back the relations between people and the land is traced, there is always a yearning for an older, more organic or natural way of life, one which has apparently just been lost. (See also Soper 1995.) Eventually we reach the Garden of Eden, from which of course humanity was expelled.

But, at the same time, Williams traces an alternative image, that of the city. This in many respects is the opposite of the lost arcadian, rural world. It is an image of modernity, development, progress and the future, one to which people can look in attempting to resolve the difficulties in which they are presently engaged. Taking both these constructs together, then,

> in what is then a tension, a present experienced as tension, we use the contrast of country and city to ratify an unresolved division and conflict of impulses, which it might be better to face in its own terms.
>
> (Williams 1973: 297)

But what actually are these conflicts 'in their own terms'? What are the real material processes to which they are a response and which they are partially interpreting?

> Most obviously since the Industrial Revolution, but in my view also since the beginning of the capitalist agrarian mode of production, our powerful images of country and city have been ways of responding to a whole social development. This is why, in the end, we must not limit ourselves to their contrast but go on to see their interrelations and through these the real shape of the underlying crisis.
>
> (Williams 1973: 296–7)

In short, these kinds of social construction, what we have earlier referred to as 'strong' social constructions, are often a response to some kind of crisis. The underlying problem is one in which the real or material relations between people and nature are being substantially re-forged. These relations and processes are extremely complex and difficult for anyone to understand. The knowledges currently available are not, to a coin a phrase, 'man for the job' in terms of offering an understanding of what is taking place. But most of us can understand simple versions of these material realities, versions which maintain some reference to what is actually taking place.

How does such a perspective help in interpreting contemporary constructions of nature, especially those 'strong' social constructions used by environmentalists and others? Again, we must be careful to stress that these social constructions are often, perhaps even usually, made by theoretically well-informed people. If there is a criticism of Williams it is that the images to which he refers are primarily, and perhaps necessarily, those of intellectuals or at least of the more articulate and well informed. But since these are amongst the most socially and politically influential, we can assume that other less dominant classes of people endorse and use at least parts of these discourses.

Williams's perspective is useful in locating many of the 'strong' social constructions now used by contemporary environmentalists. On the one hand, as this study has emphasised a number of times, contemporary environmentalism is characterised by a profound failure to understand their relations with nature. This has primarily to do with the division of labour in modernity in its social and spatial sense. This in no way means that humanity has lost a relation with nature. Indeed, precisely the reverse. Again, we are talking primarily of a crisis of understanding.

Given such an underlying crisis, it comes as no surprise to find the 'strong' social constructions deployed by the contemporary environmental movement taking two main forms. One is the return to community, face-to-face association and close integration with nature in a Garden of Eden. These are partly historical reconstructions of ways of life which are supposed to have taken place in the past. Archaic societies operate as a powerful impulse in this respect. But at the same time they are offering guidelines to more ecologically sane futures. As Dobson (1995) argues and as Pepper (1993) shows in detail, many of these environmental reconstructions are re-worked versions of much older forms of politics, especially communitarian anarchism.

One version comes from Goldsmith. He, like many environmentalists, argues that ecology itself offers the guidelines necessary for the making of a new form of social life. Note his sensitivity to the charge that such communities are introspective and his demands for establishing links between modern, decentralised, society. The over-riding demand, however, remains that of small-scale community.

> Although we believe that the small community should be the basic unit of society and that each community should be as self-sufficient and self-regulating as possible, we would like to stress that we are not proposing that they be inward-looking and self-obsessed or in any way closed to the rest of the world. Basic precepts of ecology such as the interrelatedness of all things and the far-reaching effects of ecological processes and their disruption, should influence community decision-making and therefore must be an efficient and sensitive communications network between all communities.... We emphasize that our goal should be to create

149

community feeling and global awareness, rather than that dangerous and sterile compromise which is nationalism.

(Quoted in Martell 1994: 56)

'Bioregionalists' such as Sale, who argue for 'dwelling in the land', represent a more extreme form of this vision. Again, the emphasis is on essentially small-scale, locally based, self-governing units which are close to, and learning from, the workings of the natural world.

We must somehow live as close to it as possible, be in touch with its particular soils, its waters, its winds; we must learn its ways, its capacities, its limits. We must make its rhythms our patterns, its laws our guide, its fruits our bounty.

(Quoted in Martell 1994: 52)

Again, however, this type of communitarian thinking recognises that modernity must entail connections. While the small scale is seen as increasing a sense of citizenship and supporting the development of the individual through close association with other people and with nature, a future society (and indeed more conscious of global environmental problems) is envisaged as a federation of such communities. A future modern way of life is therefore envisaged as a kind of up-dated version of older ways of life. Nevertheless, we are still firmly on Raymond Williams's 'escalator'. The response to the crisis of understanding generated by modernity is again that of trying to restore and renovate older arcadian ways of life which are now missing, assumed dead.

But there is a second image (or 'strong social construction') of nature which parallels Williams's second idea of a future which embraces modernity. There are many examples of a 'nature' which, supposedly at least, has been made to submit to rationality and technology (see, for example, Wilson 1994). A current and highly influential instance is that offered by Haraway (1992a,b). But before coming to this image, we should briefly discuss Haraway's theoretical position. Although she seems somewhat ambivalent about the matter, she does quite consistently argue against a notion that there can be a real underlying nature.

Like the human sciences, the natural sciences are culturally and historically specific, modified, involved. They matter to real people. It makes sense to ask what stakes, methods and kinds of authority are involved in natural scientific accounts, how they differ, for example, from religion or ethnography.

(1992a: 12)

Unlike many 'strong' social constructionists, she is not arguing that the view of natural scientists is wholly without value. She is saying that no-one, natural or social scientist alike, can afford to stand outside the 'facts' being observed. These facts are always subject to change in the light of the society in which the

150

observer is living. Haraway would be at best very cautious about recognising the possibility of an independent nature, one composed of mechanisms operating at different strata and of course existing independently of values and discourse. Her constructionism is still of the 'strong' variety. 'The detached eye of objective science' is, she argues,

> an ideological fiction and a powerful one. But it is a fiction that hides – and is designed to hide – how the powerful discourses of the natural sciences really work.

> (1992a: 13)

A passage such as that above suggests that there is indeed nothing other than social construction when we come to consider the non-human world. It is again solely a matter of power plays and language. Once more there is no independent reality 'out there', one which is (inevitably) constructed in human societies but which has any special independent status as a result of theorising and concepts which have stood the test of time. Rather, as her book *Primate Visions* (1992a) in particular argues, notions of nature merely reflect dominant divisions of labour and social relations. Primate behaviour, for example, is seen as simply having projected on to it ideas and relationships which are characteristic of human life. The effect, according to Haraway, is to naturalise the inequities of class, gender and race, making them seem like inevitable features of nature rather than the product of hard-fought battles between classes, races, men and women.

Haraway offers important accounts of how nature is being constructed in contemporary thinking and discourse. This includes her influential image of women constructed as 'cyborgs': half humans, half machines. This latter is an example of a forward-looking futuristic vision, and that vision is of a nature which has been largely rationalised and conquered. Furthermore, such an image offers an at least partly adequate account of the ways in which the naturally inherited powers of *inner* nature (especially of course that of women) are being modified. For some feminists these interventions are for good, for others, ill (Stabile 1994). Contemporary assisted reproduction can indeed be seen as involved in the creation of embryos which are 'cyborg entities', organic entities assisted by technology.

But, reflecting back on the actual processes involved as outlined in the last chapter, such images are, to say the least, massive over-simplifications. Again, it is actually difficult to assess the extent to which this particular image is indeed shared by people other than the social constructionists themselves ('cyborgs' are hardly an image summoned up by the Mass-Observation participants) but this does not seem to be of major import to Haraway herself.

Strong social constructionism of this kind therefore tends to miss out half the necessary analysis. The overlapping and difficult-to-understand causal powers, social relations, processes and interventions in nature to which these images refer are real and yet they have somehow gone largely missing from the

151

analysis. In such circumstances simple images such as 'communities' and 'cyborgs' both reflect the real causal mechanisms and material processes involved while (and this is the important point) much simplifying them and expressing deep concerns about what is taking place. These latter are a result of not knowing much about these processes and yet remaining very often anxious about the unexpected consequences of meddling with nature.

As argued earlier, no-one would argue that scientific knowledge is other than socially constructed. Furthermore, no-one would argue that scientific knowledge is sometimes used to legitimate the *status quo*, sociobiology being perhaps the most recent prize example. But if the argument says that all scientific knowledge is *only* the product of power play and language this becomes far too sociologising and dismissive. Further, it is by no means clear why disciplines such as politics, sociology and social anthropology should claim to have any more of a monopoly of understanding than subjects such as biology and ecology. At best strong social constructionism is a celebration of the inventive capacities of human minds. At worst it is yet another case of special pleading, another form of disciplinary imperialism.

In this connection Kate Soper (1995) argues, acutely, that the hole in the ozone layer is not a hole in language. It is a hole in the ozone layer. Similarly, the birth, development and death of organisms (including even that of a human organism!) is not the same thing as the birth, growth and death of society's discourses. All theory is socially constructed (how could it be anything else?) and social relations and languages of course affect how we understand and describe nature. But they are not identical with it. A realist analysis insists that the structures and causal powers of nature have a life of their own, albeit one which is certainly amenable to revision and improvement by the on-going revision by physical and natural scientists.

The central task, as we have seen Williams arguing, is to see the *relationships* between these images of nature on the one hand and the material processes by which the powers of nature are being transformed on the other. As he argues, a shift in image, and the construction of a new image of 'nature', usually betrays a major problem in understanding how real social relations and processes are combining with the real processes of the natural world.

In our own era the crisis is not just a product of capitalism but above all about understanding modernity more generally. The questions 'what is nature?' and 'what is human?' are being asked under circumstances in which we are increasingly humanising nature, in which nature seems to be increasingly modifying us and in which we as a natural species are realising new powers we never knew we had. Williams's view of the images of country and city in literature could be applied directly to the images of nature that are produced in our current period of high uncertainty or lack of understanding. The underlying problems lie elsewhere, with the division of labour having a central role.

The division and opposition of city and country, industry and agriculture, in their modern forms, are the critical culmination of the division and specialisation of labour which, though it did not begin with capitalism, was developed under it to an extraordinary and transforming degree. Other forms of the fundamental division are the separation between mental and manual labour, between administration and operation, between politics and social life.

(1973: 304)

CIVIL SOCIETY AS STRUGGLE

So far the implication of this chapter has been that civil society offers a particular kind of relation to nature: one which offers or seems to offer a revived form of wholeness and connection but which often does so at the expense of a fetishised version of nature. It thereby finishes by celebrating surface appearances.

We now turn to environmental struggle. There are many types of green politics. For this reason alone it is quite wrong for neo-liberals to lump them all together. Some forms, while recognising the reality of ecological problems, would not argue for any general level of causation. These people, sometimes labelled 'technocentrists' (O'Riordan 1981) or 'environmentalists' (Dobson 1995), would not see any need for fundamental social and political change. A second form offers some general, sometimes radical, explanation of what is occurring. What Dobson calls 'ecologism' recognises that some major change will have to occur within society and between humans and nature. As will be discussed in the next chapter, this group tends to be more 'political' in the sense that it either engages with, or deliberately resists, state power. A third type of green politics also offers a radical analysis, but it is less concerned with substantial social or economic change and more with changing forms of consciousness. This is a form of intervention which operates largely within the market and within civil society. For this reason it is given particular prominence here.

A central feature of such a politics is its dissatisfaction with mainstream science. In particular it argues that science as used by modern medicine is largely ineffective when it comes to dealing with modern-day problems such as psycho-social complaints (Keulartz et al. 1985). Approaches which were once effective in detecting and conquering such diseases as cholera and smallpox, typhoid and diphtheria are no longer appropriate for dealing with problems which are to do with self-realisation and with restoring the connections between mind, body and the environment.

For people in this sphere of environmental activity the priority is consciousness raising, with particular emphasis on the notion that humans are subordinate to nature and that environmental laws should therefore be allowed to operate. At its most extreme, this type of politics merges into 'environmental fascism', with the survival of the fittest's being actively promoted and no cure for a disease such as AIDS being sought. This chapter will not be considering this variant, however. Rather, it is concerned with those people and groups who see themselves as working largely from within civil society to steadily improve on the existing social order.

It is initially tempting to suggest that this type of environmental politics remains wholly superficial. Its emphasis on consciousness and spirituality is doing little more than celebrating appearances. The parts and the fragments resulting from modernity's disassembly of nature are again becoming fetishised as things without connections to modernity and its spatial and social divisions of labour. As such, struggles of this type within civil society can offer an appearance of understanding and ways forward, but one which is at best partial. Writing of the 'fiction, fragmentation, collage and eclecticism' of modern architecture and urban design, Harvey asks us to explore how such sensibilities take the form they do.

> To answer that question with any power requires that we first take stock of the mundane realities of capitalist modernity and postmodernity, and see what clues might lie there as to the possible functions of such fictions and fragmentations in the reproduction of social life.
>
> (1989: 98)

The discussion so far has been largely in line with Harvey's approach, though with the important difference that such 'fictions and fragmentations' may be associated as much with modernity and its divisions of labour as with capitalism *per se*.

But in one key respect this might be a rushed judgement. Even if the forms of knowledge arising from civil society remain partial, they are still important in generating new forms of knowledge which will eventually inform the social relations of capitalism and modernity. We can assess this argument by looking at some of the new 'alternative' cultures and networks alluded to above. More specifically, we should by no means dismiss such developments in civil society as complementary medicine, environmental movements and networks that stress the aesthetic and spiritual dimensions of human life. They are exploring and developing our understanding of the causal powers, potential and capacities of human beings and indeed other natural forms. They are also once again giving credence to what we have earlier termed 'tacit knowledge', the uncodified and personally embodied forms of knowledge of self and environment which have long been denied by a rationalising modern Western culture. As such, they should again not be dismissed because they are not considering the relations between nature and industrial production. This is still a problem but they can be seen, as can other interventions in civil society, as prefiguring new kinds of knowledge, social relations and relations with the powers of nature.

The historical origins of these cultural forms are complex but they are instructive in this context. Alternative medicine is a good example. Innovations such as the Alexander Technique and Lindlahr's work on therapeutics and vegetarianism stretch at least as far back as the late nineteenth and early twentieth centuries (Lindlahr 1975). But their real growth and development occurred in California in the 1960s (Grossinger 1985). It was in this particular context that ideas that were already in evidence started to be developed in the context of heightened political awareness and resistance to the dominant values of capitalist modernity. They became allied with an overtly 'political' programme.

Thus the significance of these developments to this study is indicated by the fact that their intellectual leaders included writers such as Fromm and Marcuse. Basing their analysis on a heady mixture of Marx and Freud, they offered a sustained critique of capitalist society. They tried to put most aspects of contemporary modernity to the sword, including commodity fetishism, culture, mechanisation, rationalisation and bureaucracy. The search for the new values specifically alluded to Marx's ideas of humans' 'species being', their qualities as social and biological or sexual beings. The new cultural networks were an explicit attempt to recover what had been lost during the process of alienation. Furthermore, people's aesthetic and spiritual capacities were brought to the fore by these alternative movements. This was in line with the Frankfurt School of Sociology which argued, *inter alia*, that such capacities had been systematically suppressed or repressed by the forces of monopoly capitalism. In his early *Economic and Philosophical Manuscripts* Marx had argued that the effect of capitalism was to undermine human beings' aesthetic appreciation.

> The man who is burdened with worries and needs has no sense for the finest of plays.
>
> (1975: 353)

Writers such as Fromm and Marcuse were to develop such insights, even arguing that a recovery of human beings' aesthetic sense was a royal route to human emancipation.

Last, but by no means least, these new networks and cultural forms were seen as an attempt to regain what Marx referred to as humans' 'natural being'. If species being alluded for Marx to characteristics specific (or supposedly specific) to human beings, 'natural being' referred to the characteristics shared with other species. Sexuality is part of such natural being and, for Californian culture of the 1960s, this became a further route to emancipation.

These new cultural developments such as psychotherapy, alternative medicine and the ending of repressed sexuality were inspired by Marx and were quite explicitly intended as a point of opposition to modernity. As such they represented a radical alternative, one again emerging from civil society but eventually changing the social order more fundamentally. They can be summed up around the linked themes of holism, community and spiritual values, each

155

of which seems to counter the fragmentations and forms of alienation represented by modern life.

One of the most important recurrent themes in the new cultural networks is 'holism'. This refers first to the attempted abolition of the mind/body distinction. But it also refers to a consideration of the links between the body and nature as a whole; between what Marx called 'man' and 'his inorganic body'. New holistic health models work at over-riding this fragmentation between mind and body. In conventional medicine 'mind' tends to be associated with ideas, visualisations, images, fantasies and neuroses while body is seen as concerned with organs, skeletal structure, circulating fluids and so on. Holistic health typically works to overcome this duality, insisting on the necessary *connections* between mind and body and working to overcome the divisions of labour over the body, each portion of the body in conventional medicine being 'patrolled by different professionals' (Donnelly 1994).

Holism, and its application through such techniques as acupuncture, is not simply or only concerned with re-spiritualising and consciousness-raising. As part of such practices it can be seen very positively as offering alternative insights into the causal powers of bodies and their interactions with environments. Their potential is that of illuminating the structures and processes underlying their growth and development. Furthermore, these practices recognise the importance of not only lay but the tacit judgements, feelings and skills which people create for themselves. Herein lie the major contributions of such alternative cultural movements. They work with the whole patient, he or she being composed of three connected elements: mind, body and spirit.

One way in which holism is attempted is through the rediscovery of 'the inner child'. Psychosynthesis and the Alexander Technique, for example, attempt to overcome the forms of repression and guilt to which children are subjected by their teachers and parents. The Alexander Technique is very specifically aimed at 'body balancing' which aims to affect the entire personality and state of the organism (Grossinger 1985). In all such treatments and therapies, there remains a strong sense of a 'natural being' within each person, one composed of potentials waiting to be discovered and restored.

Another version of holism comes from Chinese medicine. The philosophy of The Dao ('The Way' or 'The Way of Life') insists that people should balance their lives (Mole 1992). They should, for example, combine activity with rest, excitement with reflection. Furthermore (and this is a feature of holism more generally) they should live in a close relation to nature, seeing themselves as not only natural beings but beings with a necessarily close relation to the non-human world. Personal energy should, for example, be conserved in the autumn and winter in order to balance increased activity in the spring and summer.

Holistic medicine and therapy therefore address, whether consciously or otherwise, many of the forms of fragmentation and alienation associated with modernity. It treats the entire patient, paying attention to all disorders, whether the origins are internal or external. Buddhism is also influential in this respect, this again having significant impacts not only on alternative medicine but on branches of the environmental movement, including the so-called 'deep greens' (Naess 1989). For Buddhism too the emphasis is one which insists that everything is connected: mind, body, person, environment. The world view emerging from Taoist China also has some startling parallels with the young Marx, 'man' again be considered an integral part of nature.

He is not against nature; he cannot be separated from it – he is in nature, and nature in him.

(Boldt 1993: 4)

Gandhi's philosophy of the relation between the individual and society is also worth recalling here. His views also seem to counter many of the fragmentations associated with daily life under modernity. And certainly they provide a major inspiration for many associated with the new alternative or complementary therapies. Within modern society it is easy to see the attraction of his vision of a community of equals, one in which any division of labour has been voluntarily negotiated. His view was again that of a social whole in which people are an integral part of a closely connected system. 'I believe', he wrote, 'in the essential unity of all people and for that matter, of all that lives. Therefore, I believe that if one person gains spiritually, the whole world gains, and if one person falls, the whole world falls to that extent' (quoted in Dass and Bush 1992).

A related theme to these alternative cultural movements is 'tradition': the antidote (or apparent antidote) to modernity, alienation and social isolation. Tradition is an important concept to these alternative therapies and lifestyles. They are, after all, remedies towards the person which have been used for exceptionally long time-periods, perhaps even thousands of years. Furthermore, they have been tried and tested by millions of other people, so they seem worth adopting on this basis alone. The recovery of tradition by these alternative movements is therefore resistance to a number of contemporary processes. These latter include antagonism towards handed-down tacit knowledge and the overthrow of the knowledge offered by earlier generations.

Tradition also brings to the practitioner an aura which conventional doctors do not have. Acupuncturists, homeopaths, osteopaths, naturopaths and herbalists, for example, are all able to offer a body of well-established knowledge. Unlike conventional doctors, these alternative practitioners are not subject to continued innovation, some of which may be forced on them by, say, governments or drug companies. Alternative practitioners therefore offer continuity, a set of practices handed down through the generations. This means that they and their patients are not subject to changing fads of science and their manipulation by contemporary social forces.

Taking a remedy that has been used for generations gives a small but
perceptible sense of community with other patients and of belonging,
even though the association is with nameless and faceless people who have
been down the same path.

(Buckman and Sabbagh 1993)

The fact that the practitioners involved may have had relatively little
formal training and have developed their skills through practice rather than
through abstract study has the effect of actually recommending them to their
participants. 'The exotic', 'the unfamiliar', 'the unscientific' and the admis-
sion of lay-persons' tacit knowledge of themselves become of value in their
own right. 'Community' enters into these considerations in yet another way.
Its relatively unhierarchical networks, non-competitive relations and local
informal networks offer an alternative to the social relations, enforced
divisions of labour and globalisation of social life which are central features
of modernity.

The final aspect of these alternative cultures and networks which needs
special mention is the significance of aesthetic values and spirituality. They can
be seen as religions or philosophies which are attempting to recover the values
of joy, beauty and happiness: values which are under threat by contemporary
modernity's attempt to equate happiness with possession and spending of
money. And these alternative values link back to community, since they are
associated by their participants with collective, communal and 'sharing'
practices.

The attempt to recover lost symbolic and spiritual values must partly once
more account for contemporary interest in archaic or native societies. In these
instances, as in Eastern forms of spirituality, belief-systems are seen as less
systematised and formalised than is the case with religions in the West. Social
relations and relations with nature are again caught up in the philosophies of
indigenous peoples. Social events, for example moral transgressions, are
sometimes seen as triggering natural disasters. In short, the boundaries
between work, spiritual life, medicine, sexuality, politics and healing seem
(at least to the outside observer) relatively more permeable. More general
understanding on the one hand and practical, tacit and lay knowledges on the
other start to be combined. All this leads to their endorsement by contemporary forms of spiritual healing and therapy as a way of both achieving holism
and recovering a sense of meaning in modern society. They are again offering, to
those who are suffering, a sense of a whole and a mending of the divisions
characteristic of modernity. For example, in promoting Shamanism to contemporary society, Money (1994) argues that what appears to be mental disease
may in fact be the product of

a deeper malaise – of the loss of meaning in the life of the individual. This
loss of meaning may result from the progressive devaluation and
destruction of a mythic and symbolic component to consciousness, with

its consequent anomie and internal loss. The shamanic view of the cosmos is in direct opposition to such an impoverished view of the self, and can function as an antidote to it.

Somewhat similarly, Hay (1995), writing in a magazine for 'engaged Buddhists' describes the attraction of all forms of religion to people who have become physically and emotionally estranged from other people and from their environment.

> They feel enriched because they discover that they are not alienated from the rest of reality, but very close to it. Awareness of the presence of God engenders a realisation of having common cause with all of creation, or, if the experience is non-theistic, of being at one with all of reality. It is as if the psychological distance between the individual and environment is reduced or disappears. Once we realise that we are totally bound up in our environment, we also understand that damage to any part of it is, implicitly, damage to ourselves.

(p. 21)

Archaic societies, Buddhism and Indian philosophies therefore all represent radically alternative cultures and values to those adopted under modernity. They all go some way to addressing the forms of alienation originally outlined by Marx, although they do remain largely contained within civil society. Much the same can be said of less explicit forms of nature-religion such as the Goddess spirituality associated with Gaia philosophy and certain forms of ecofeminism. It is fairly easy to see, therefore, the attractions of these traditions to the alienated peoples of modern Western societies. Furthermore, as suggested earlier, they may be offering very important new insights into the structures and causal powers of human and other organisms.

But the problem is, of course, that the kinds of 'whole' to which these alternative philosophies and therapies appeal bear precious little relationship to the 'whole' of a complex modern economic, social and political system. The social relations of modernity and the labour processes at the core of modern economic systems are, for example, a million miles away from the thinking represented by these alternative philosophies. The danger is that of reverting to the kinds of mystical holism which we encountered in Chapter 1 when discussing the misleading ways in which modern physics is being applied to an understanding of both society and nature. Douglas (1966) refers to the ways in which humanity's relation to the environment can itself easily become held up as a kind of omnipotent religion, a kind of court of appeal which obviates any need to turn to how societies actually work.

Potentially important as the restoration of these old philosophies is, the result can be an uncomfortable mix between traditional or archaic philosophies on the one hand and Western-style individualism on the other. Those who espouse these supposedly radical alternatives can easily finish up

159

endorsing and bolstering the very values they have set out to resist. Adopting alternative ways of thinking does rather little to counter the material processes actively undermining relations between people and nature and causing the very unhappinesses which these alternative cultures are trying to overcome.

More problematic still, many of these erstwhile oppositional cultures have now lost much of their radical political impulse and come quite close to the forms of unalloyed individualism associated with modern bourgeois society. They are further means by which the individual can improve themselves by giving that extra ('alternative') tug at their own bootstraps. To put it in Habermasian terms, the 'lifeworld' represented by these forms of resistance is again in danger of being 'colonised'. Coward, in her study of health foods and alternative medicine, put the matter thus:

> The health of the body achieved through (these) healing processes is presented as the vital front line by which the individual can counter the excesses of 'modernity', of industrialization and impersonality. Becoming healthy has become synonymous with finding 'nature' and 'a natural life style' and this is to be the route by which advanced industrial society will be resisted. The resistance does not rest on an analysis of social structures, of social divisions, of unequal control of resources. Instead it is a vision of personal resistance, of making oneself 'immune' to modern life.
>
> (1989: 203)

The appeal of alternative philosophies to individualism again comes through from the following quotation from a Zen career consultant based in San Francisco. This is a relatively unusual example of how the social relations of industrial production might learn from this form of green politics. He denies that this way of thinking implies conformity to social rules and structures but it is not difficult to imagine such 'alternative' ways of thinking as being largely acceptable to the captains of industry with their new-found concern to promote human resources.

> 'Going with the flow' requires that you be here now, that you allow yourself to drift automatically into a lackadaisical conformity to structure. It also requires respecting your humanity and holding it inviolate. Work doesn't have to be a dehumanizing experience, and should not be accepted as such. One of the main tenets of Mahatma Gandhi's theory and practice of nonviolence is non-cooperation with anything that diminishes human dignity. Of course, non-cooperation means not engaging in anything that is blatantly oppressive or abusive to others. It also means avoiding that which is oppressive to one's own soul – to one's innate sense of humanity.
>
> (Boldt 1993: 11)

Somewhat similarly, the new forms of therapy deriving from these alternative philosophies are increasingly finding incorporation into 'official' medicine (Benor 1994, Keenan 1994). This is another instance of an erstwhile 'alternative' cultural form's being incorporated into dominant social relations, divisions of labour and practices. The contradictions are considerable: not least the endorsement and use by mainstream medical experts of oppositional knowledge and 'self-help'. Perhaps even more important, self-help again not only legitimises a particular kind of neo-liberal philosophy but appears to provide a respectable way out of crises within welfare states. Furthermore, there are continuing tensions between the proponents of alternative medicine and those of mainstream treatment. These include arguments over what the 'testing' of the alternatives actually entails and whether the 'curing' of 'disease' should remain the priority of medicine at all. Many in the so-called alternative movement argue, for example, that 'pain, disease and death are essential experiences with which each of us shall have to learn to live' (Keulartz *et al.* 1985).

So the original radical impulse leading to the adoption of these philosophies and forms of therapy is now being transformed and at least part-incorporated into the very beast which they were designed to attack. As with environmental economics and green consumerism, however, their implications are again contradictory. The alternatives being hammered out in civil society may again be presaging new, more emancipated, ways of life.

A recent survey from the USA shows that one-third of the population is using complementary medicine (Eisenberg *et al.* 1993, cited in Ernst 1994). They are spending 12 billion US dollars, excluding medicines, literature and technologies. The figures in Britain are equivalent. This must surely mean that they are helping people. Presumably their attraction lies in the prospect that they once more offer self-knowledge, self-organisation, knowledge of people–environment relations and in their relatively democratic forms of organisation (Ernst 1994). Their incorporation of new understandings of the human and animal body into mainstream culture, and indeed into 'establish-ment medicine' can be seen as a major gain, despite the difficulties. It would therefore be quite wrong to say that they are undesirable and have made no difference to dominant institutions. It would also be wrong to say that they are no more than a simple backward-looking response to the forms of alienation and estrangement which are characteristic of modernity. On the one hand they do offer individuals and groups some degree of control and understanding over their lives. Furthermore, they offer an understanding of people's relations with the natural world. In this sense they may well be prefiguring new kinds of relations which are emancipatory for humans and for other species. On the other hand, their promotion of individual significance could well leave intact most of the underlying social relations, structures of power, divisions of labour, global markets and labour processes which in the first place gave rise to estrangement and the need for coping. Once more, their message is contradictory.

CIVIL SOCIETY: THE RECOVERY OF WHOLENESS?

We now proceed to the more overtly political forms of environmental struggles by which oppositional cultures become focused into mass-movements. Many of these are seen as a new form of politics associated with civil society. The analysis offered by this study throws some light on these developments.

7

KNOWLEDGE, STATE AUTHORITY AND THE DIVISION OF LABOUR

In late summer 1995 the French government started to detonate a series of atomic explosions in the mid-Pacific. Clearly there were a number of reasons for these events, not least the assertion of nuclear independence by the French authorities. But the reasons surrounding the technology of nuclear devices are also instructive. For all the computer-modelling of whether and how nuclear devices will operate, scientists still depend greatly on tacit knowledge in predicting whether they will work. Designers of nuclear weapons know full well that computer predictions are only approximations of the reality that will ensue when a detonation takes place (McKenzie and Spinardi 1995). They know, for example, that contingent factors such as ambient temperatures, the ages of the weapons and irregularities in the production of weapons, cannot be accommodated in their computer-based modelling. These factors have be taken into account by judgements and skills accumulated over long periods and in different places. To an increasing extent such tacit knowledge can be built into the more abstract and quantitative modelling of the processes and relations involved. But such qualitative and unformulated judgements still have to be made. Note, incidentally, that tacit knowledge cannot be equated with 'lay' understandings. A scientific prediction as to how the causal powers of nature combine with one another also depends on unformulated tacit judgements. Everyone uses tacit knowledge all the time, but some forms of this knowledge are consistently neglected and allowed to decay while others, such as those of the designers of nuclear weapons, remain relied upon for the development of scientific authority.

Scientific activity underplays the extent to which tacit knowledge is used to develop understanding. In practice, however, tacit skills are an important part of the scientific process. Even when nuclear explosions have taken place, for example, judgements based on tacit knowledge still come into play in assessing what the impacts have been. Furthermore, judgements based on past events are by no means a good guide to what will occur in new contingent conditions. Some scientists advising the French government about their series of detonations maintained that any resulting radiation would be contained within an area under the sea which would be vitrified by the explosions. Against this, other scientists argued that glass created by the tests would become unstable at low temperatures and nuclear waste would leak out. Yet other scientists argued that explosions of this sort would set off a series of underwater landslides and that resulting tidal waves would threaten many well-populated areas such as towns in Australia. Meanwhile, the tests set off a latent independence movement in Tahiti, the main island in French Polynesia.

The debates over the French atomic tests are just one instance of the theme under study here. Conflicts between different types of knowledge can have profoundly de-stabilising effects on state authority. In many respects an analysis of the relations between society and nature culminates with the question of state power. National states remain the cockpits of societies, mediating between different types of knowledge and power, attempting to ensure profitable economies and at the same time promoting forms of knowledge which are intended to ensure a degree of social harmony. In approaching environmental questions, however, we come back again both to the social and technical division of labour and to its spatial manifestations. Uncertainties over the relations between types of knowledge pose a large number of difficulties for nation states. These divisions and uncertainties are the product of a complex division of labour. The result is a potential and sometimes actual delegitimation of government.

State power of course takes a number of forms, but one of the key and less coercive ways is through the imposition of general and abstract ideas on people's lay, local and tacit knowledges. Of course there is absolutely no guarantee that this process will be successful. Indeed, as we will see later, there are important reasons why this should not be so. Nevertheless, dominant ideas are often mediated through, and legitimated by, states and this is why state power should have a central position in a study of this kind.

This chapter is divided into three main sections. It first elaborates on the above arguments, developing the notion of state institutions acting as an 'alienated community', apparently operating on behalf of all its citizens. It then turns to the specific question of states and environmental knowledge, further arguing that the promotion of a general knowledge is a key but highly unstable way in which social relations are managed by state bureaucracies. Finally, this chapter turns to the demands made by people of these state institutions. Specifically, it addresses the theory of New Social Movements. It argues that this theory as it stands is inadequate and that the assertion of popular, lay and tacit knowledge is a key feature of 'old' as well as 'new' social movements.

THE STATE AS ALIENATED COMMUNITY

About one hundred and fifty years ago Marx argued that there is a central distinction to be made in capitalist societies between the political realm and civil society. Indeed, he saw the separation of the state from civil society as the key characteristic of modern politics. Referring to the French Revolution, Marx referred approvingly to a process whereby 'the class distinctions in civil society became mere social differences in private life of no significance in political life' (1975: 146).

The separation between the state and civil society or 'private life' had immense consequences. It meant that political life now had an apparent existence of its own, one operating independently of how the rest of society operated. Marx argued that such state structures forming an alienated political realm of social life had to be abolished. And it was the Paris Commune which he envisaged as the model for a non-alienated form of state for the future (Schechter 1994). He saw production as the principal part of what he called 'civil society'. In the Paris Commune this part was successfully linked to the state.

> The Parisian Communards set up a system of 'recall on demand': representatives of the people could be relieved of office *from the moment* a majority of electors deemed that their views were no longer being accurately defended. Executive and legislative activities were fused, such that those who made the laws also had to carry them out.
> (Schechter 1994: 8, original author's emphasis)

Such a solution then creatively linked civil society to politics. Each individual became, in some sense, a legislator. The bureaucratic nature of lawmaking was abolished since the days of the professional political class supposedly operating in a 'universal interest' were numbered. Also abolished were endless and useless parliamentary debates. It was the ideal solution for a 'self-government of the producers'. It was in essence 'the political form at last discovered to work out the economic emancipation of labour' (quoted in Schechter 1994: 8).

But the political sphere with a separated 'life of its own' of course persists as a central feature of modern politics. Its components are quite varied. Perhaps best known are the rights of citizens. They have, for example, the right to vote at elections. They also have rights which, before a court of law, mean that in principle at least we are all equal. In some countries such rights (including rights to certain levels of welfare) are encapsulated in bills and charters.

These citizens' rights have been fought for and are certainly worth having (Thompson 1979). But they come as part of a package in which societies are atomised into individual citizens, each with her or his own rights. Meanwhile there of course remains a parallel real social world, one constituted by massive inequalities and processes (such as labour processes on nature) dependent on such inequalities. The analogy between citizenship and heaven is not a common one in our own time, but Marx made the parallel in describing the emergence of modern social democracy thus:

Just as the Christians are equal in heaven though unequal on earth, the individual members of the people became equal in the heaven of their political world, though unequal in their earthly existence in society.

(1975: 146)

One way of summarising this view of the state is that it is an 'alienated community'. While people have been systematically alienated from nature, from their fellow human beings, from nature and from their own naturally endowed capacities in the real social world, they have these relations apparently restored in 'the heaven of their political world'. The state and its equality of equal citizens is therefore a pretended recovery of what has been lost, but at the same time it is a community which remains very partial and estranged from people's 'earthly existence'. Importantly, the same basic issue has arisen recently in relation to animals' rights (Benton 1992, 1993). Many writers in this area (for example, Regan 1990, Singer 1990) are implicitly arguing for rights which remain enshrined in the heaven of the political world. Again, to get animals protected even at this level would certainly be a fine first step. But the danger is that the form of such rights is not extended to include the necessary fundamental *social* changes to the ways in which animals are treated in their 'earthly existence' in modern society. As is now increasingly recognised, this includes various forms of factory farming and the exploitation of animals in laboratories. Important as they are, the discourses of unequal and equal rights could again be thoroughly inadequate in dealing with such abuses.

'WHAT THE HELL ARE THESE BLOKES TALKING ABOUT?' KNOWLEDGE AND THE STATE AS ALIENATED COMMUNITY

Any understanding of knowledge, alienation and state power must also give special attention to government bureaucracy. For generalised and abstract knowledge is the currency of bureaucracies. And it is simultaneously a key way in which they legitimate their own existence. At the same time, however, state authority is itself of course bound up with this knowledge. It largely depends on it for its legitimacy.

When it comes to environmental questions, central planning by state bureaucracies can be disastrous. The large-scale mining, construction and nuclear power projects under the old East European and Soviet regimes are well-known cases in point (O'Connor 1989). Powerful bureaucracies of this kind, whether of the Western or old Communist varieties are therefore a central part of the social division of labour. Furthermore, they tend to work separately, the workers in each having little or no overview of the economic and environmental system as a whole. Extreme as the experience of the old state socialist societies may be, this suggests that there is one more key element to the links between the division of labour, knowledge and alienation in modern society. This is bureaucracy and state power in relation to citizens.

How does a political class manage, with state authority depending on such management, to hold on to such a powerful position in the division of labour? It is again precisely through claiming to operate in some general good and creating social relations which treat, or at least apparently treat, all citizens as equals. Abstract knowledge, and in particular certain *kinds* of abstract knowledge, has a central role in this. Governments of all kinds depend on what Haas (1992) call 'epistemic communities', groups of scientists and experts who are responsible for the production of scientific knowledge. And yet the form of this knowledge rarely if ever demonstrates that any one particular strategy is 'correct'. Many interpretations of the same knowledge can be made (Haas 1992). This leaves governments in a set of continuous contradictions.

Before coming to such overt measures as legal and parliamentary structures, production and civil society are managed through the attempted imposition of certain forms of universal ideas onto tacit and lay knowledge. Such abstract knowledge may indeed have some general application to the population at large, though it inevitably runs into difficulties when applied to particular places at particular times.

A local and national illustration of the problematic link between knowledge and the state in environmental politics comes from the ways in which the British state attempted to manage farming interests in North West England following the Chernobyl disaster when large amounts of radioactive caesium were deposited over the countryside (Wynne 1989, 1991). The main citizens affected in this case were the farmers raising sheep. Their concerns were, of course, with the radioactivity affecting their sheep and lambs and the acquisition of compensation from the British state. Their knowledge was, and is, of a mainly tacit, local and practical kind. They knew, for example, about local variations in radioactive fallout, about the optimum times for selling sheep in the light of breeding-cycles, about the local geological and vegetal conditions which affected how the radioactivity impacted on the landscape. And, through years of experience, they knew that the herding of sheep needs quite complex reciprocal activities between farmers.

Against all this was aligned the central British state, with politicians working in close harmony with their own official scientists or 'epistemic communities'. The knowledge of the latter contrasted dramatically with that of the farmers. It was of an almost wholly abstract kind. Furthermore, it was of an abstract kind which had little relevance to local conditions. Again, their credibility, and that of the government, depended on their holding this type of universal and abstract knowledge. Needless to say, their practical knowledge of farming in the Lake District was virtually nil. It was in practice ignored. The result was a thorough non-meeting of minds.

Many local practices and judgements important to hill farming were unknown to the experts, who assumed that scientific knowledge could be applied without adjusting to local circumstances.

(Wynne 1989: 34).

Thus government experts armed with predominantly abstract knowledge, and without an understanding of how such knowledge combined with local contingent factors, could do little to reassure farmers about the actual spatial spread of the radioactivity. Furthermore, their advice to the farmers as to how to proceed was well out of line with the practices which were both necessary and familiar for sheep-farming. The farmers constantly found themselves confronted by a bureaucratic way of working. Whereas the farmers needed to respond flexibly and autonomously in relation to local and changing conditions, the 'universal class' required them to do everything by the book. The selling of lambs as proposed by the universal class was a bureaucratised and formalised process while the farmers needed to take a great range of local conditions into consideration simultaneously.

This particular episode therefore illustrates our main theme, the marginalisation of lay and ill-formulated tacit environmental-cum-social knowledge and its separation from abstract ideas. It is again a picture in which people have their understandings (as well as their control) over their own lives removed. This time, however, the process was a result of the division of labour represented by the state as alienated community on the one hand and the citizens on the other. Paradoxically, the original cause of the problem (the Chernobyl accident) was itself a result of a highly centralised and non-democratised form of state decision-making.

The most important thing to emerge from this story, however, is that the management of production by the political or universal class is by no means guaranteed. It constantly needs re-making. The British experts eventually emerged from this episode as wholly lacking in credibility as far as the farmers were concerned. Their indiscriminate application of abstract knowledge led not only to flawed advice but, quite rapidly, a thorough-going disrespect for state officialdom itself. One low point in the proceedings seems to have been a suggestion from one of the experts that the sheep would register clean as soon as they were fed imported straw. As one farmer put it:

I've never heard of a sheep that would even look at straw as fodder. When you hear things like that it makes your hair stand on end. You just wonder what are these blokes talking about?

(Wynne 1989, p. 34)

STATES AND THE CONTRADICTIONS OF ENVIRONMENTAL KNOWLEDGE

As the above example then illustrates, the imposition of general or abstract knowledge on local and particular populations with their own tacit and lay knowledges is in practice fraught with many difficulties. And this brings us back to the division of labour, especially in its many spatial manifestations. No matter how general or indeed 'national' the knowledge and science promoted by states is, there is no convincing possibility of it being directly applicable across particular and diverse regions, localities and circumstances. This is the Achilles' heel of national and cross-national state institutions and their attempts to manage knowledge and develop strategies which are actually universally applicable (Duncan and Goodwin 1988).

It can of course be argued that local or regional governments are there precisely to deal with this issue, to create their own strategies based on local social and environmental conditions or to adapt national or cross-national strategy towards their own ends. This is of course true, but the necessary outcome is that there will be a permanent tension between these different levels of government, each responding to the particular social relations and divisions of labour for which they are responsible.

Similarly, strategies developed at the international scale (especially the so-called International Environmental Agreements) keep coming up against the virtual impossibility of developing plans which are in practice universally applicable (Glover 1994). Attempts to develop such plans have consistently run into trouble. Examples are the Law of the Sea, the Vienna/Montreal agreements on substances that deplete the ozone layer and negotiations to reduce practices believed to be causing global warming. National, regional and local variability, and more particularly variability in different countries' own political strategies to manage such variability, have consistently weakened attempts to impose global solutions. The Less Developed Countries (LDCs) often see the environmental strategies imposed by the developed countries as particularly damaging. The former are, for example, frequently committed to market-oriented use of their own natural resources. Interventions by quasi-government agencies represent a block to such strategies, and the LDCs often demand compensation for not intervening in their preferred ways. The result at the international scale has been little concrete success. Meanwhile the shifting and unclear state of the knowledge itself remains a continuing problem. 'There is', in Glover's words, 'sufficient disagreement to provide recalcitrant govern-ments with justification for inaction' (1994: 285).

In short, there is in an important sense a necessary conflict within and between state and quasi-state institutions which is generated by the uneven development of society and the spatial division of labour. All this, in combination with the social and technical divisions of labour more generally within a nation state, systematically undermines the possibility of general environmental knowledge's being imposed over lay populations at large and their understandings. The environmental question thereby joins the interna-tional economy as operating at a scale which bedevils intervention by any particular level of the state. In some ways national states are historically best-equipped to deal with environmental questions. But they are simultaneously too large to deal with local environmental matters and too small to deal with the growing number of global considerations (Hurrell 1995).

These problems pose a major problem for state legitimation by its own citizens. Hay (1994) has shown the kinds of difficulty into which governments get themselves with their own publics while attempting to operate in some general interest. Few governments are in practice likely to attack the systems of production on which their national economies depend. This is the case even if such systems can be held up as major contributions to environmental problems. The actual result tends to be the adoption by national governments of those policies, such as measures to protect the ozone layer, which are important but have few economic costs. 'Ozone diplomacy and the Montreal Protocol are', as Hay puts it, 'held up as the supreme example of concerted global action to avert ecological damage' (1995: 222). Meanwhile, measures which are expensive and could represent a serious threat to production and capital accumulation at the national level (such as those necessary to deal with global warming, deforestation and the degradation of environments in developing countries) become down-played and even marginalised. In other words, national states find themselves surrounded on all sides by competing forms of knowledge. And this again has potentially seriously destabilising effects on state authority itself. States become unable to deliver on their promises not only at home but abroad too.

RE-THINKING 'NEW SOCIAL MOVEMENTS'

How might the perspectives developed in this study contribute to an understanding of contemporary forms of politics, specifically the so-called 'New Social Movements'? Green politics is of course a central element of such movements. At this point we can bring together a number of the themes outlined earlier. These particularly include the divisions between different types of abstract knowledge, between abstract, lay and tacit knowledges, and the various forms of alienation in contemporary society. The last include the role of industrial production in fragmenting and recomposing nature, the role of civil society in fetishising wholeness but recovering aspects of people's 'species-being', and the state as a form of alienated community. Finally, the spatial division of labour has an important role in what Giddens (1990, 1991) calls the 'disembedding' of people from local social and ecological systems.

The type of alienation which we have been discussing, that of failure by people to adequately understand their circumstances, is a more or less permanent condition. The central point here is that a general theory of politics could be founded on the notion that such alienation lies behind political struggle of all types. The stakes to politics whether 'old' or 'new' are no less than a recovery of self, of meaning and identity in a society where lay, tacit and local knowledge are systematically denied. The increasing globalisation of society, and in particular the globalisation of the market and systems of production

170

adds an extra relatively recent twist to the above very long-standing forms of alienation.

Given all the above, how does such an understanding relate to green politics as an example of what are sometimes now called 'New Social Movements' (NSMs)? Before drawing some new conclusions we first need to briefly remind ourselves of what is usually meant by the concept. Foweraker (1995) in fact draws attention to the confusion over what social movements, both old and new, actually are. (For a similar discussion see Kumar 1993.) 'Despite the range of social movement theory', Foweraker argues, 'a satisfactory definition of social movements remains elusive' (1995: 23). Foweraker's frustration becomes clear when he complains (p. 4) that:

> a wide variety of disparate social phenomena have suddenly been certified by the new social movement label. In some accounts it appears that folk dancers, basket weavers and virtually any form of social or economic life may qualify. But not everything that moves may qualify.

These confusions are symptomatic of a more general problem. Not knowing what the item to be explained actually is must leave the theory to explain it in some difficulty. Despite the problems of definition, the concept seems to refer to forms of politics other than those of class (Miliband 1989). Thus 'old' protests and political strategies are seen as largely centred on the working class and the workplace. And these, it is argued, are giving way to 'new' forms. They include the environment but they also include, for example, the women's movement, the peace movement, anti-racism and the demand for human and animal rights. As such,

> 'old' movements are typically seen as class based whereas 'new move-ments encompass a cross-class constituency'.
>
> (Stammers 1995: 4)

What, in more detail, is said to be taking place? The literature is quite complex and of course contains its internal disagreements. But there are five important cross-cutting themes. One concerns, as mentioned above, the relation between the NSMs and 'old' forms of struggle. The second concerns human identity. The third concerns the notion of 'nature' contained within these movements. Fourth is the question of the leading participants in NSMs. Finally there is the central concern of this chapter, that of the state.

A first key idea is, then, that these new forms of politics cannot be reduced to the politics of class. They are seen as simply not expressing class characteristics, and therefore class analysis cannot be used to explain social reality in these new types of protest. Intellectuals and activists alike, therefore, are urged to stop fighting nineteenth-century battles of the kind analysed by Marx. Instead, they need to recognise a 'post-industrial' age, one in which profound shifts have occurred in social and economic life.

Central to these (although, as we will see, this is an issue given varying prominence by the commentators involved) is said to be a shift in material and structural conditions. Thus 'Fordist' mass-production economies are seen as moving towards new forms of 'post-Fordism' in which large sectors of the population are only spasmodically drawn into the production process (Scott 1992). And this means that paid work, and the struggles around it, have decreasing salience for large sections of the population. Similarly, the transition away from manufacturing to more knowledge-based and 'services' employment has done much to undermine old working-class solidarities (Touraine 1981). This too is said to lie behind the emergence of the New Social Movements outside the workplace. It is what might be called a 'hydraulic' view of politics. If protest and struggle declines or is blocked in one social sphere it emerges elsewhere, albeit in new forms.

Disenchanted young people in particular are said to be leaving behind the old working-class organisations, the result being what Offe (1987) calls 'a crisis of orientation in worker consciousness'.

> For a growing number of young workers, the union is no longer perceived as the primary representative of their interests – a development which is only reinforced by signs of a bureaucratic paralysis of labour union work with youth.
>
> (p. 152)

And, again adopting the hydraulic view of political movements, this is seen as associated with 'an increase in non-institutional political conflict', characterised by a rise in what Offe calls 'single issue movements', these focusing on environmental, urban and other issues such as disarmament. The result is, for Offe, the rise of polarised forms of politics. Some core workers remain within institutionalised forms of representation such as the trade union. But others, especially those only marginally part of the paid workforce, join more amorphous social movements and horizontal networks without autocratic leaderships. Indeed, those on the fringes of the workforce join these alternative forms of politics precisely because they see collaboration between unions and core workers as de-fusing outright conflict and marginalising those who are not central members of the workforce.

How does the perspective we have developed contribute to this analysis? As we have seen, production is increasingly organised at a global scale. This helps to put production-based 'old' forms of class struggle into perspective. Such struggles are of course still there latent and geographically spread. But organising less around them and turning to other sources of emancipation and understanding of the world is a wholly rational response to changing social and economic conditions. It goes without saying, however, that there is also a dialectical process at work here whereby capital investments on a global scale are themselves a response to the presence or absence of 'old' forms of political and trade union organisation.

Our second central and linked issue for the NSMs, according to the predominant commentators, is that of values and of personal-cum-social identity. Those engaging and making these movements are often said to be 'postmaterialists'. They are rejecting the 'old' values of material well-being and economic growth in favour of quality of life. This includes quality of the physical environment. Thus, according to Inglehart (1990) they are a result of becoming more aware or reflexive.

> The rise of the ecology movement is not simply due to the fact that the environment is in worse shape than it used to be. Partly this development has taken place because the public has become more sensitive to the quality of the environment than it was a generation ago.
>
> (pp. 44–5)

The 'postmaterialist' priorities of the NSMs are held to endorse and engage in less hierarchical, intimate and personal relations between people. In short, the 'new' values are said to be endorsing many of the old values of 'community'. But the difference between this and old community is diversity. The emphasis on individuality, on single-issue politics and on values inevitably leads to a considerable *range* and *diversity* of communities.

A pre-requisite of such identity formation and the making of a new 'post-material' society is held to be human agency. People, either as individuals or as social groups, are taking life into their own hands. Touraine places particular emphasis on the role of the subject in NSMs. He is counter-balancing those Marxist and other traditions which interpret the world solely in terms of structures. He is, in short, arguing for an approach which recognises the reality of the dialectical relations between actors on the one hand and structures on the other. People are not acting out pre-ordained roles in the inevitable transition to socialism. As Touraine most recently has argued:

> The idea of a social movement, which has so often been central to my work, is radically different to the idea of class struggle. The latter appeals to the logic of history, whereas the former appeals to the freedom of the Subject, even if that means rejecting the pseudo-laws of history.
>
> (1995: 370)

How can we assist this second set of arguments? The insistence by Touraine and others on the role of the actor and her or his identity is clearly very important. On the other hand, we can again be a bit more precise about this matter. Social scientists are understandably cautious about imputing anything regarding 'human nature'. But, as regards what Marx called 'man's species-being' we can insist that human beings do indeed have certain real, material, characteristics. They are conceptualising animals, blessed by remarkable potential for self-knowledge, knowledge-creation, communication and reflex-ivity. To the extent that these are blocked or distorted, human beings' potentials and capacities become stunted or unrealised. If the arguments of this study are accepted, it is this blocking-process which in large part accounts for political consciousness and various forms of green politics. Green politics is therefore above all part of what Wainwright (1994) calls 'the politics of knowledge'.

Human beings have in principle an enormous advantage over other animals in terms of their ability to form and communicate concepts. And yet the concepts they have actually formed have turned these advantages against them. The result is that their relationship with their environment is in many respects more impoverished than that of other animals. If the arguments in the foregoing sections of this study are correct, the NSMs are about alienation and knowledge, about the complex combinations of many different types of knowledge, about the failure of people to understand the stratified world of nature, their relations to it and the links between what they can observe, on the one hand, and the deep-lying structures and processes affecting the events they can experience, on the other. Thus lay understandings and tacit but difficult-to-articulate judgements or skills all consistently fail to link up with the abstract ideas with which they are confronted.

We should also give special attention to human beings' natural being; the capacities they share with other animals such as their inborn biologies enabling them to reproduce future generations. Many of the so-called NSMs (health and sexuality in addition to environmental concerns) seem particularly organised around the protection of such natural being. At the same time, however, they defend the fact that in the human case sexuality can take very particular forms. They are, in Soper's words, 'irredeemably symbolic, orchestrated through fantasy, self-reflexive and consciously pursued for interests other than procreation' (1995: 143). Human natural being, or biology, necessitates or prescribes some form of heterosexual relation for the reproduction of the species. But it does not prescribe or indeed prevent the persecution of homosexuals or celibates. Some understanding along these lines as to what does and does not constitute human nature helps us get a better grip on what NSMs are really about.

Let us now turn to the third theme in the NSM literature. What is the view of external nature (or 'the environment') in this theory? Similar remarks apply. As we have seen, theorists of NSMs view the ecological movement as very much part of the process by which contemporary society becomes 'disorganised' or decreasingly centred on employment. Melucci (1989, 1992) is important here. He first offers an understanding of NSMs which in some respects parallels writers such as Touraine and Offe. He places much less emphasis on structural shifts in the society and the economy and much more on how people are actively making social relations and social identities through the NSMs. Nevertheless, like Touraine, he sees the rise of 'the cultural dimension' as particularly important. This means that culture, symbols and means of communication acquire a special emphasis in modern society. And this, again, is said by Melucci to distinguish modern society from the old forms. Although Melucci may not be typical of all NSM theorists, his view of nature is an influential one.

For he argues that the exploitation of nature itself has now faded away as an issue. He pushes his argument about the central role of culture to its logical extreme to suggest that the real issue is again that of the formation of self-identity.

> The simple domination of nature and the transformation of raw materials into commodities is no longer central. Instead, society's capacity to produce information, communications and sociability depends upon an increasing level of self-reflexiveness and upon the self-production of action itself.
>
> (1989: 46)

According to Melucci, therefore, the rise of ecological issues is only partly to do with any real rise in environmental problems. The problems derive from within the individual and society rather from the way in which human societies are using, and as a result encountering, any natural powers and limits. The movements are arising from how people are viewing themselves, their relation to other people and the links between one society and another. They are as much a commentary on our society as on the state of nature itself. The reason for the rise in environmentalism therefore

> does not lie only in increasing pollution or the gradual worsening of environmental decay. The real reason is that we are beginning to perceive reality in different terms; our definition of individual and collective needs is changing.
>
> (1989: 95)

Let us now assess these arguments. The perspective under development in this study would in a limited respect support the argument of Melucci and others. Whilst they may be over-stressing the importance of the rise of personal identity, they are correct to suggest that the environmental crisis is only partly about the degradation of the environment itself. If the Mass-Observers in Chapter 4 are taken seriously, a central concern should be the insecurity and alienation deriving from people's inadequate *understanding* of their relationships with society and nature more generally. In this respect at least it is surely right to insist that an adequate appreciation of the environmental problem must look behind the deterioration of the environment.

Having said this, however, we must be very cautious about strong social constructionism as represented by Melucci. A very substantial part of the problem indeed lies in the problematic ways people understand, and communicate about, their environment. On the other hand, we must not lose sight of the fact that there are simultaneously *real* and potentially disastrous changes occurring to the physical and organic environment. These are a direct result of the work in which modern societies engage in transforming raw materials into the products they need or want. There are therefore real physical processes involved here, and strong social constructionists such as Melucci quite

175

explicitly play down their importance in the modern era. Melucci's ontology (one stemming from an over-socialised view of nature, as practised by many social scientists) seems to actively preclude consideration of the relations between people's labour processes and the causal powers of nature. Strong social constructionism is therefore potentially dangerous and eventually at odds with that adopted by this study.

A fourth important theme in NSM theory concerns social class participation. Who exactly, according to NSM theory, are all these 'subjects' fighting for identity, causing major social transformation and, as we will later see, rejecting state authority? They are the middle classes. They are not necessarily, of course, the only ones engaging in the contests and establishing 'alternative' lifestyles but they do set the terms for the argument. It is predominantly their values and cultures which are most significant. Thus, having thrown out class as an explanatory device, many theorists of the NSMs bring class back in. But this time it is in terms of middle-class cultures and values. Classes seen in this way are, in Eder's terms, 'the key for explaining social developments' (Eder 1993). The 'new middle class' are held to be the core group in this respect. It is, again, their view of human beings' relations to nature, rights to difference, lifestyle-choice and participation in decision-making which are having the key formative influence. As Eder puts it, 'the new middle class is the potential carrier of countercultural traditions'. And as regards the environment, it is the particular understandings of nature which they adopt which will come to serve for everyone else.

> The way the natural world is symbolised will become the new cultural model organizing class action in the emerging middle class society.
>
> (Eder 1993: 135)

Thus, it is often argued by the NSM literature, the middle classes are indeed prominent in green politics. How should this argument be evaluated? There is actually nothing very new about political struggle's having its agendas largely set by the middle classes. The 'old' forms of politics also had their priorities set by the middle classes; Marx, Engels, Trotsky and Lenin spring to mind. But there are two senses in which the NSM literature could be developed in this regard. First, the concept of 'the new middle classes' does not sufficiently recognise the fragmentations and divisions within this group. Recent work suggests that when it comes to environmental activism it tends to be well-educated and younger people who are particularly engaged, especially in the less struggle-oriented green politics as outlined in the foregoing chapter (Savage *et al.* 1992). But more significantly as regards the central arguments here, the middle classes in government and in civil society have a clear central role in articulating the type of *knowledge* used in 'green' political struggle. In this respect our argument that competing knowledges are the key source of alienation again needs to link back to the question of power relations and who is actually promoting and resisting such knowledges. Therefore the literature stressing the key role of the middle classes is important, especially if we relate it to the types of knowledge which they are promoting.

Finally, we come to the main concern of this chapter, the question of state power. Part of the redefinition of individual and collective needs as outlined in NSM theory is also said to concern the state. At one time, and not all that long ago, the state was envisaged by social democrats as a beneficent provider of welfare: to be on the right side, so to speak. Here we return to the state as 'alienated community' since NSM activists have followed earlier Marxists and anarchists in critiquing the bourgeois state itself, seeing it as not only impenetrable but, even more importantly, generating many of the problems itself and clearly acting on behalf of some interests and not others. They have therefore thoroughly seen through the notion of the state as a universal community, even if they remain dependent on it. Much the same can be said of related forms of politics such as the women's movement. Here again, strong, centralised, state-imposed 'solutions' are being recast as oppressive rather than emancipatory. Lash and Urry (1987), for example, argue that the contemporary women's movement is characterised by:

> a strong resistance to the central state which seems to have violated much of the trust placed in it (through, for example, failing to prevent wife-battering, rape etc.). The national state which was once seen by women as necessary to ensure that, for example, local councils were forced to provide decent welfare facilities, is now very much viewed as the problem rather than the solution and this has become more the case as 'the state, violence and sexuality' have become centrally salient issues in the contemporary movement.
>
> (p. 224)

The obvious implication for those contesting state oppression is to conduct politics independently of the state. This again makes 'civil society' into the main site of such struggles. We are once more back to the Habermasian idea of the private realm of social life having been colonised and rationalised by outside forces and the attempt to 'recolonise' by conducting the contests outside of formal politics. Social and political action therefore becomes a series of movements without reference or appeal to the state, and especially to bureau-cratic central government. Struggles over, for example, the environment, over sexuality, lifestyle and peace again become diffused in the form of horizontal networks. To the extent that they do relate to the state apparatus, they are addressed to the local level (Duncan and Goodwin 1988). But, more im-portantly, the struggles of these 'new movements' shift to cultural reproduction and the struggle for new and alternative ideas as much as for the attention and resources offered by government (Rucht 1990, Pieterse 1992).

How would the themes of this study contribute to this final area of NSM theory? Much of the foregoing analysis in this study would be in line with the analysis of NSM theory. In particular, the delicate balancing act of national states attempting to appear to be universal communities when they are acting in increasingly complex, local, national and cross-national negotiations with a number of warring interests is proving to be a virtually impossible act to accomplish. Furthermore, as we have seen, problems of their own legitimation occur when national governments bring their strategies back, as it were, 'home'. Conflicting knowledges consistently undermine and de-stabilise state authority and the claim to be socially disinterested.

Another good and particularly well-publicised recent example was the debate in June 1995 over how Shell's Brent Spar oil rig should be disposed of (Pearce 1995). Shell's marine biologists argued that the sea bed would not be damaged if the rig was sunk and that there was considerable potential danger to humans and the environment if it was dismantled on land. Greenpeace argued that the spreading of drilling waste and the hazard of sinking it would lead to a major disaster on the sea bed. The British government initially adopted the former position, supporting the company and disagreeing very publicly with the German political authorities. But after large-scale consumer-boycotts and a severe outburst of eco-terrorism in the form of fire-bombs and shootings in German petrol stations, the company abandoned their plans to sink the rig. The main point here, however, is that this change of strategy left the British authorities and their epistemic communities exposed to considerable ridicule. Shell's motto remained 'You Can be Sure of Shell'. But few people were left sure of the British government.

There are again, therefore, serious problems as regards the legitimacy of state authority as a result of the contradictory circumstances with which governments are surrounded and the often fragmented contradictory knowledges with which they are dealing. And it is indeed these which the NSMs are latching on to and exposing. There are, however, some problems with existing NSM analysis of state power. First, it is probably wrong to see the state in such unambiguous terms as those proposed by NSM theorists. The point about the state as an 'alienated community' is that it does offer *real* gains in the form of resources and rights. To say that state authority is now seen as an unmitigated disaster-area by the NSMs is therefore a one-sided exaggeration. This may be partly a result of putting all NSMs into the same category. In the case of green politics, the range of relations between institutions and the states is actually very diverse. Friends of the Earth, for example, can work quite closely (and sometimes indeed in a bureaucratic and hierarchical manner) with government. On the other hand the monkey-wrenchers of Earth First! would almost certainly resist working hand-in-glove with representatives of state power. Many forms of green politics presumably operate somewhere in between, perhaps accepting the real gains represented by resources and backing from government even if they have reservations about doing so.

There are two final points about NSM analysis, both of which argue for a re-drawing of NSM theory along the lines suggested here. First, the distinction between 'new' and 'old' does less than justice to important historical continuities. Tucker (1991) has shown, for example, that 'old' forms of socialism such as syndicalism went to great lengths to adopt what are now considered to be 'new' strategies. In many ways they prefigured NSMs.

> They opposed the bureaucratic organizations of the state and political parties with a decentralized, federalist and radically democratic structure.
>
> (p. 91)

Similarly, Stammers (1995) argues persuasively that much of green politics is not so much new as a continuation of quite old forms of struggle, especially that of early anarchism.

> What has been claimed and identified as the key descriptive characteristic of NSMs – which might be summed up as seeking to challenge and abolish all relations of domination – could then be re-cast as describing and identifying *radical currents within social movements.*
>
> (Stammers's emphasis)

Second, NSM theory tacitly only recognises what it sees as 'good' emancipatory practices. There is little attention given to, for example, eco-fascism and Not-In-My-Backyardism. And, outside the environmental sphere, little attention is given to the nationalisms, ethnic struggles and religious fundamentalisms now affecting many societies. This is a serious oversight and brings us back to the more general theory of politics which we have started to sketch out here. Politics of all kinds, whether 'old' or 'new', 'emancipatory' or 'backward' are again all ways in which people are trying to gain some kind of purchase on, or understanding of, their place in the social-cum-natural world. There are many different ways of attempting to achieve this at different times and at different places, some no doubt less desirable than others.

Thus on the one hand the so-called New Social Movements can be merged with the Old Social Movements within a broader context of alienation and continuing attempts at emancipatory politics under modernity. On the other hand, something new is indeed happening. NSMs do have new characteristics, and these are largely a product of a relatively new geo-political context. This is the emergence of a global market and, in particular, the globalisation of industrial production. NSMs are a product of, and a resistance to, these processes and their impacts on people's lives.

A revised understanding along the lines outlined above begins to answer some of the problems we encountered earlier over what exactly a 'New Social Movement' actually is. The issues surrounding the struggles referred to by NSM theorists become clearer once we have an understanding both of the alienated capacities of human beings and of the changing social, temporal and spatial contexts within which people are trying to emancipate themselves.

But perhaps the most important connecting theme of the NSMs is the relationship between society and nature. It is no accident that the central issues of the New Social Movements (the physical environment, gender, race, health, the human body and the rights of animals) are all on the society/nature divide. On the one hand, this boundary is being rapidly permeated. On the other hand, human societies with their divisions of labour and fragmented knowledges, have little understanding of what they are doing. The result is a failure by human beings to understand the very world they are making. This contradiction is central to the NSMs. It is one they are illuminating and indeed trying to overcome.

8

GREEN UTOPIAS AND THE DIVISION OF LABOUR

Recently arguing from a 'Red-Green' perspective, Benton (1995) says correctly that 'none but the most unthinking dogmatists can now believe that any of the existing radical traditions, unaided and unreformed has all the answers'. He is arguing against those few socialists who would attribute doctrinal status to the writings of Marx and other early writers on the Left. Their work clearly needs developing in relation to developments over the past century, not least the rise and fall of a range of states claiming to have been inspired by Marxist thinking.

Clearly this study has relied on Marx. But it has used Marx as a basis for a new set of themes. The reconstruction of nature to create commodities is a familiar part of Marxism, but the divisions of labour formed during the process are a new way of envisaging our relations to nature. The division of labour is a central element in our understanding, or rather failing to understand, our relations with nature. Giving this feature of modernity such prominence in attempting to explain why modern societies neglect and misuse their relations with nature may indeed lead to this approach's parting company with that of some 'Red-Greens'.

This chapter now starts to turn from this type of analysis to the question 'what is to be done?'. The Red-Green Study Group (1995) have aptly altered Lenin's question to 'what on earth is to be done?'. Clearly, having identified the division of labour as a key obstacle along with class and a range of other social relations, this has to be the main abiding theme here. This last chapter will first critically review some influential green utopias. Attention will be given to those schemes touching on the main themes of this study, especially the question of alienation stemming from the division of labour. It will then go on to discuss tendencies and forms of struggle which are now pointing ways towards combating the forms of alienation and estrangement stemming from the division of labour.

We will then turn to recent developments in electronic communications technologies and their role in the manipulation and transmission of knowledge. Again, if the problem of knowledge (and especially its fragmentation) is one of the key factors underlying forms of society which are ecologically unsustainable, then the question of how knowledge is now being manipulated and communicated is a matter of central concern. For this reason, therefore, this chapter gives special emphasis to recent and possibly far-reaching developments in communications technologies. Are they disempowering or emancipatory? What are their implications as regards knowledge and action affecting the relations between society and nature?

Finally, this conclusion will draw together the main themes of this book, specifying in more general terms the processes necessary for a re-integration between human society and nature.

GREEN UTOPIAS AND THE DIVISION OF LABOUR

It is not the intention here to suggest that existing green thinking is 'incorrect'. Indeed, one of the problems of much socialist and indeed sociological thinking has been the outright dismissal of environmental thinking rather than an active engagement with it. The result has been a ducking out of a potentially creative tension. Green utopian thought has much to offer. The issue is how to combine it with the kinds of analysis adopted by socialists (Benton 1995, Red-Green Study Group 1995). In the case of the present study, the issue is how to combine ecological analysis with an understanding of human society, and especially one which includes divisions of labour and the problem of knowledge as a central consideration.

The argument of this chapter is that, for all their value, ecological utopias have so far largely failed to deal adequately with the division of labour. They have indeed begun to answer some key questions. These include the simultaneous addressing of social *and* environmental questions. They have also addressed, albeit in different ways, the question of the bureaucratic state. This, as we have seen, is a prime source of alienation. They have also started to address the spatial division of labour, with decentralisation and 'community' having pride of place in the creation of a socially and environmentally satisfactory future. Tacitly or otherwise, such emphasis recognises one of the simplest relationships between the rise of the division of labour and alienation from nature. Such division changes local and multiple ties and dependencies on nature into selective and often dispensable links. It also entails increased reliance on distant, often unknown, ecosystems.

But the division of labour stemming from the division between abstract and concrete knowledge and between different types of abstract knowledge has so far been hardly addressed. This is, to say the least, unfortunate. As argued throughout this study, the division of labour is perhaps the central reason why modern societies so misuse their relations with nature.

Let us first take the work of Gorz. He does indeed address a number of themes already outlined in this study. For example, much of his work reaches the conclusion that labour under capitalism is virtually guaranteed to be alienating to human beings. Technology and standardisation of labour processes, he argues, will ensure that work remains unfulfilling to most human beings. Furthermore, according to Gorz, work in what he calls the 'hetero-nomous' sector, that associated with paid work, will always tend to be a means to an end. It is something to be got through in order to lead a civilised life afterwards. Improvements can be made, but the long-term prognosis is not good. Gorz says this is essentially because work remains tied to profit and the exchange of commodities for money. A further obstacle is the competition between firms. This militates against mutuality and cooperation. In sum,

> the success of workers' struggles for self-determination of working conditions and self-management of the technical production process must not be confused with the elimination of heteronomous work's inherent alienation. Oppressive hierarchies, laboriousness, monotony, boredom – all these can be eradicated, and the workplace can become a place of mutual exchange, co-operation and harmony. But such a liberation of work relations is not the same as autonomy of work itself or workers' self-determination (or self-management) of its overall purpose and content.
>
> (Gorz 1985: 52)

What is wrong with Gorz's view here? His opinion that there is no potential for change in the sphere of employment and paid work is in some respects dangerously dismissive of precisely the area which is causing such social and environmental degradation. It is also unnecessarily pessimistic about the potential for change in that area. Trade unions in Britain, for example, are now showing themselves quite capable of engaging with environmental questions. Presumably, similar changes are afoot in other countries. Besides, trade unions have long been amongst the leaders in insisting on health and safety at work. To some extent, at least, they have always been environmen-talists. But in other ways Gorz is not pessimistic enough. Much of his analysis centres on alienation stemming from capitalism. The social and technical division of labour in any modern society will present continuing problems of separation.

Gorz is not wholly downhearted about the future. Emancipation, he argues, is to be found largely in social life outside heteronomous work. It is to be restored in autonomous work outside the sphere of formal employment. A return to meaningful and active relations between people, what they produce and what they exchange is to be created beyond the grasp of capitalism. Cooperative work outside employment, what some would term 'community', is therefore seen as the main sphere of potential and actual self-management. This is where the effects of existing social, political and indeed spatial divisions of labour can be partly overcome. This is also where people can restore what Marx called their 'natural' and 'species-beings'. It is also outside employment that divisions of labour are more a product of inclination and skill rather than arising from enforcement by imposed structures and institutions. (See also Gorz 1988.)

The proposal to develop autonomous work and mobilise against hetero-nomous labour leads Gorz to the proposition that each citizen would have a lifetime guarantee of work in the heteronomous sector. This would be state-regulated. Human emancipation within this social sphere may be limited but such work has to be done.

Gorz is implying that modern societies should, as it were, 'take a deep breath' and get on with this relatively unpleasant sphere of social life (one dominated by de-skilled boredom and alienation) in order to acquire freedom outside it. This again seems at best a questionable strategy. It is largely writing off the very processes and relationships which are the cause not only of alienation but of despoilation of the environment. And, as mentioned earlier, it is also marginalising the importance of organised labour in resisting these processes and possibly, as we will later see, developing alternative practical steps as a way of countering them.

But in a key respect Gorz is correct about the potential of civil society, or of the sphere of social life outside work. He is definitely not suggesting that emancipation outside the heteronomous sphere simply consists of the passive consumption of fetishised commodities. Gorz is again looking to the sphere of social life outside employment as one of proactivity, self-management and the development of personality. In this sense his proposals recognise the potentials for emancipation outside paid work which we addressed in Chapter 6. (See also Gorz 1987.) It is predominantly a sphere of self-managed or autonomous *work*.

> Autonomous production is essentially handicraft production in which
> the individual or the 'convivial' group controls the means of production,
> the labour process and the nature and quality of the product itself.
>
> (1985: 68)

It is not, however, 'handicraft production' which is resorting to 'the spinning wheel, and the domestic or village economy'. Gorz envisages this autonomy's using to the full the new innovations such as computers as well as the old technologies such as bicycles. Like Marx over a century ago, he is not rejecting modernity but calling on it, in this case summoning the use of new technologies, to develop human capacities and autonomy. In this respect, Gorz is surely correct in insisting that a socialist perspective on the environment has to endorse science and technology. It does not, however, have to accept all that science says, nor does technology have to continue being used in oppressive, de-skilling, ways. Nevertheless, Gorz is a good corrective to much of green thinking on these matters. Much of contemporary ecological thinking is deeply contradictory insofar as it rejects science and rationality on the one hand and yet insists that a future ecologically sound society must be more scientific and rational. Hayward (1995: 4) points, for example, to the contra-dictory attitudes towards rationality within the work of Vandana Shiva, the ecofeminist writer.

GREEN UTOPIAS AND THE DIVISION OF LABOUR

What is especially noteworthy is that the grounds of the objection to enlightenment rationality, as stated by Shiva, are that it is precisely not *rational*, that it is not *enlightened*.

(Hayward's emphases)

Where, according to Gorz, would these technologies come from? Who would actually make them? This again leads Gorz back to the 'heteronomous' sphere, in which people (working again in production units with advanced divisions of labour) are creating such goods for a more fulfilled life in Gorz's 'sphere of autonomy'. So, although he is dismissing the world of paid employment from his utopia (and, with it, the kinds of opposition represented by trade unions) he still needs this world in order to create the utopia he is looking for.

There is surely a major problem here insofar as this perspective does not properly confront the schizophrenic division between work and play in modern society. In fact, it is doing much to reinforce it. Again, emancipatory strategies cannot afford to write off a whole sphere of social life as beyond repair. Ways are surely needed, using trades unions and other institutions such as more democratically organised companies and central and transnational states, to confront and modify 'the heteronomous sphere'.

As mentioned, Gorz proposes a contract between the state and the people which would guarantee a lifelong wage producing the goods that are necessary for survival. Gorz agrees that the state, and especially that in East European societies, has done much to exacerbate the division of labour and to further dominate people's lives. But he argues, perhaps over-optimistically, that a state need not be oppressive in these ways. A state-led strategy aimed at restructuring the relations between people, work and social life outside work could be liberating. And this, Gorz argues, indeed becomes possible with the development of new technologies. This means that there is no longer any need for everyone to be working full-time all their lives. Furthermore, an intervention of this kind would be simultaneously addressed to the large numbers of people who are unemployed. Many of these, he says, are suffering abysmally low standards of living because of very low income supplements. They too could be brought up to a reasonable lifestyle as they are introduced to the heteronomous sector.

Gorz also envisages an ecologically responsible state as recruiting the support of, and alliances with, groups other than the working class. Like many writers influenced by Marxism, he recognises the severe limitations of appealing to the unionised working class as a lone vanguard group for social emancipation. 'Today's working class', he argues,

is too highly differentiated for its unity to have an immediate material basis. Its unification will have to be constructed by systematically attacking the roots of division from a class perspective.

(1987: 135)

This brings us to the question of society's relations with nature. Gorz recognises that a rejuvenation of the Left entails that the unions would have to greatly widen out their concerns and make very conscious links with other key marginalised groups such as women, young people and pensioners. Although many of these latter are affected by the results of modern and capitalist labour processes, they are not directly involved in such processes. Their main political concerns may well be with other spheres of social life. This especially applies to ecological politics. In particular, a diverse set of groups of this kind would need to recognise that:

> the solution to this crisis cannot be found in the recovery of economic growth but only in an inversion of the logic of capitalism itself. This logic tends intrinsically towards maximization: creating the greatest possible amount of marketable goods and services in order to derive the greatest possible profit from the greatest possible flow of energy and resources.
>
> (1987: 27)

Gorz's views on the compatibility or otherwise between capitalism and nature seem to fluctuate. On the one hand he argues, as indeed do many other greens and certainly many 'reds', that the rationality of the market must give way to an alternative set of values: one in which rationality is defined in terms of the more sensible use of resources and the end of environmental degradation. Such a society, he argues, is largely incompatible with capitalism, a society based on generating maximum levels of consumption.

On the other hand, there are times when Gorz adopts a more managerial stance, one which argues that particular sectors of the capitalist economy are particularly destructive and can be dealt with independently of other industrial sectors within the market economy. An instance is below when he is responding to proposals made by the German Social Democrat Party. The tone is more that of a lofty state bureaucrat or at least that of a political elite proposing 'top-down' environmental and industrial strategies for everyone else.

> The ecological reshaping of the industrial system relates particularly to heavy and capital-intensive industries. The chemical industry, for example, will have to undergo a substantial fall in its sales as a result of the move towards an agriculture 'which respects natural balances'. This latter will spend only a fraction of what was spent by chemical agriculture on fertilizers and pest control. The development of urban and suburban public transport, the priority granted to rail over road in the carrying of goods and passengers, speed limits, and the use of durable means of transport that are easy to repair and 'ecologically sound' will lead to a fall in automobile production.
>
> (1994: 32)

A somewhat stratospheric view of this kind fails to consider some of the intractable difficulties we have spelt out earlier in this study. These particularly

include the incorporation of lay and tacit knowledges into the active management and control of 'companies'. Again, he seems to imply that such attempts
are a lost cause. Similarly, a top-down view of 'agriculture' runs the risk of not
considering local diversity and resistance to monocultures at the local level.

A second influential set of green utopias comes from an anarchist direction.
Peter Kropotkin's answer to the division of labour generally and to the spatial
division of labour in particular is:

> While all the benefits of the temporary division of labour must be
> maintained, it is high time to claim those of the *integration of labour*.
> Political economy has hitherto insisted chiefly upon division. We
> proclaim *integration*; and we maintain that the ideal of society – that is,
> the state towards which society is already marching – is a society of
> integrated, combined labour. A society where each individual is a worker,
> and where each worker works both in the field and the industrial
> workshop.
>
> (1985: 26, Kropotkin's emphases)

A reorganised society, Kropotkin argued, would have to abandon 'the fallacy of
nations specialised for the production of either agricultural or manufactured
produce'. Rather, it would have to be self-dependent, to rely mainly on its own
resources for food and production. Industry itself would become more directly
integrated into agriculture, and education would promote science as well as the
handicrafts. The division of labour within individual people would thereby be
overcome.

Murray Bookchin is in many respects the twentieth-century equivalent of
Kropotkin. He too has a great deal to say about the alienation created by
modern society and the role of locality or community in recovering human
potential. There are some similarities between him and Gorz but, as might be
expected from an anarchist writer, he has no faith whatsoever in the state, and
still less in a state-led environmental programme. Like Gorz, he is radically
opposed to hierarchy and oppressive bureaucracy. Many environmentalists,
Bookchin argues, miss the central problem underlying ecological decay and
human immiseration. This is the spirit of hierarchy and domination which he
sees as characterising and pervading human beings' attitudes and actions
towards nature. Environmentalism, he argues, 'is merely environmental
engineering'. The underlying human priorities of hierarchy and domination
are overlooked by an approach which seeks a technical fix.

> The very notions of hierarchy and domination are obscured by a technical
> emphasis on 'alternative' power sources, structural designs for 'conser-
> ving' energy, 'simple' lifestyles in the name of 'limits to growth' that now
> represent an enormous industry in its own right.
>
> (Bookchin 1980: 77)

Where do these priorities of hierarchy and domination towards nature come from? Unlike many environmental and ecological writers, Bookchin sees them as emerging from *human* society. Much thinking in this field, and especially from those who would identify themselves with the so-called 'deep greens', sees the exploitation of nature as the key problem to be addressed. But Bookchin sees the necessary starting-point as changed practices between human beings. Exploitative and hierarchical attitudes and actions toward nature are, as Bookchin sees it, a product of exploitative and hierarchical attitudes and actions in human society. The patriarchal family in particular, he argues, carries much of the blame. It is here where these attitudes have long been cultivated and remain dominant.

Nature itself, argues Bookchin, offers a model for human society. It offers 'the free interplay between species' (1970: 79), and it shows to the anarchist how such interaction could lead to the fulfilment of human beings' capacities. Darwinian thinking, he argues, demonstrates the value of self-sufficiency. This has enabled the non-human world to evolve while satisfactorily reproducing itself for millions of years. It is a lesson to humans who now seem bent on dominating other humans rather than living with them. Bookchin argues that such living with humans, and with other species, will lead to the fulfilment of human capacities. Nature again shows us that the development of diversity and complexity are a product of organisms living with one another in some kind of community. Thus *human* capacities, and *their* variation, are most likely to develop in a communal or collective setting whereby individuals relate to one another.

The priority for Bookchin is therefore that of creating small-scale communitarian settings which enable human potential to be fully realised. He gives little attention to the powerful tendencies operating in precisely the opposite direction and towards a global division of labour. For Bookchin, creating small-scale communities entails dispensing with those bureaucratic and alienating institutions, including in particular the state, which threatened such realisation of an individual's skill, abilities and potential. Bookchin is in many key respects antagonistic towards Marxism. He criticises the notion that class struggle (one based, as he sees it, on the politics of envy) will necessarily lead to emancipation. He finds Marxism lacking in terms of any realistic vision of the future. But, in the somewhat limited respect of the state, Bookchin remains firmly in line with much of Marx's thinking. Hierarchy and bureaucratic domination are his most general targets for attack. It is the state which is the most alienating feature of modern society for this anarchistic form of ecological thinking. It is the worst-case example of alienation resulting from the division of labour. In the light of the arguments outlined earlier in this study, it is perhaps here that Bookchin's critique of contemporary society and environmental degradation are at their most helpful. On the other hand, it is not clear why the state should be such a prime focus for attack. The main problems lie outside the state and within the sphere of production and the division of labour.

Political, social and spatial decentralisation are priorities for Bookchin and his colleagues promoting 'social ecology'. Community, therefore, makes a reappearance in Bookchin's utopia. Small-scale settings, in which the priority turns to face-to-face interaction are a priority. It is within such contexts that self-fulfilment, as well as collective well-being, are more likely to emerge.

> Anarchism is not only a stateless society but also a harmonised society which exposes man to the stimuli provided by both agrarian and urban life, to physical and mental activity, to unrepressed sensuality and self-directed spirituality, to communal solidarity and individual development, to regional uniqueness and worldwide brotherhood.
>
> (1970: 79)

Community, or 'communes' is therefore a central theme for many green utopians. It is an attractive proposition but, as we will later see, it is one which contains problems. Another instance comes from Rudolf Bahro. He argues, rather like Bookchin, that withdrawing from traditional state-based politics into 'A New Benedictine Order' organised in the form of 'a commune-type' network is the preferred way to a society which is in harmony with its environment (Bahro 1984). Community, for Bahro, has a strong spiritual quality. There can be no hope, he argues, of abolishing work. What is needed is a harnessing of work and social life both to achieve environmental sustainability and a new set of values. These would be largely about resisting consumerism and engaging in subsistence economies organised around basic human needs such as housing, shelter, health. Adapting lifestyles in this way would entail that communes had a central spiritual quality. The purpose of this social form is, therefore,

> not the production of means of subsistence – whether of the agrarian or industrial type, whether in the country or in the town – but the reproduction of the commune-type community. Economic efficiency is not negated, but subordinated to ecological demands and above all to the development of social relationships and the self-development and transformation of individuals. In the ideal case the commune network is so strong that all material and institutional infrastructure on any but the local levels remains dependent upon it, instead of the other way round as formerly.
>
> (Bahro 1986: 87)

COMMUNITY AND THE PROBLEM OF KNOWLEDGE

Decentralised localism, as we have seen, is therefore a strong theme in green utopian thinking. It is clearly advanced as one way of resisting the alienation stemming from the division of labour, and in particular, the division of labour represented by the central state's power over the people. It also represents, of course, a challenge to the spatial division of labour and the division of the globe

189

into what Kropotkin called 'national workshops'. There are, however, some major difficulties here.

Few people would want to deny that 'the local' can be an important starting-point for the development of people's environmental and social consciousness. Furthermore, it is often of course an important setting for all kinds of environmental and social politics. But an over-stressing of 'community' and 'communes' can easily become an exercise in wishful thinking, one which chooses to neglect the parochialism of community, often vicious and prying relationships and the important fact that the social and environmental world is if anything becoming more global. As we saw in Chapter 3, it is all too easy to construct and romanticise an arcadian 'community' as an easy way out of social environmental difficulties.

Localism, important as it is, needs constantly placing in the context of the wider social and environmental world. It would be no good pretending that a future ecologically sound and socially just society could be constituted by a fragmented array of small communities. Although locality and local, face-to-face experience may be important starting-points, other institutions would have to be created which operated at national and (increasingly international) scales to operate as coordinators, facilitators and enablers of local collective decision-making. Such institutions would be engaged in what the Red-Green Study Group (1995) calls 'enabling from above'. They would operate in a facilitating fashion towards the needs and demands of more autonomous small-scale localities.

It is also very important in this discussion to make the important distinction between 'the local' and concrete, lay and tacit understandings. As implied in our discussion in Chapter 2, localism is in danger of going off at a tangent here by eliding these categories. What green utopian thinking is often actually driving at in promoting localism is the idea that people's own knowledge should be recognised. This would give them an understanding of, and ultimately control over, their own lives. Furthermore, given that production systems and markets increasingly operate at a global scale, there is little advantage (and some very distinct disadvantages) in insisting on 'the local' as the sole or even the main setting of political action. Again, communes and communities may be missing some important, real, 'concrete' phenomena. And, as regards offering an understanding of daily life, global concrete information is just as important as data about the local level. Relationships between various levels of democratic government would have to be the order of the day, with perhaps different relationships according to the scale and form of the problem itself. Questions of information become particularly important at this point and this is an issue we will return to.

A final danger of localism is that the realm of abstract ideas becomes eased out altogether. If the central problem being addressed is the estrangement of people from themselves, from other people, from their work and from nature, then it makes little sense to promote localism or indeed concrete and practical information for their own sakes. The central problem, therefore, is not localism but knowledge and the power deriving from such knowledge. If, let us say, we are concerned with the alienation stemming from the workplace (Gorz's 'heteronomous' sphere) the aim is not just to promote 'the local' or even to acquire more concrete information. As, again, we were emphasising in Chapter 2, emancipation stems from linking more abstract 'textbook' information to practical knowledge and wisdom and eventually to action on the ground or at the workplace. Once more, localism (particularly if it is promoted as a necessarily good thing in its own right) could do very little to overcome people's estrangement unless it were seen more as a means to developing understanding than as an end in itself.

So, two cheers for 'community'. But again this is definitely not to say that locality or community are unimportant in developing a new form of society which is socially and environmentally more desirable. Rather, the priority must be to keep our eye on the social and environmental ball. As we have discussed at some length earlier, the ball in question is again the disconnections from knowledge and power which people of many kinds suffer. The labour process and the conversion of nature is a key element of this alienation in modern societies, with separated and fetishised forms of consumption doing much to exacerbate people's relations with the social and natural worlds. These forms of alienation extend to people not immediately engaged in the labour process. They are as affected as anyone else by the divisions between different forms of intellectual labour and between abstract and practical knowledge.

'SELF-GOVERNMENT OF THE PRODUCERS': SOME INNOVATIONS WITHIN MODERNITY

A central starting-point as regards the relations between society and nature would involve engagement with labour processes. This despite the fact, as stated often enough earlier, that these processes are by no means the only sources of alienation in modern society. Labour processes refer here to all the ways in which people convert nature into the things which people need. This applies firstly to labour processes in the formal economy. What can be achieved here? An alternative type of green utopia is one which starts with these processes and works outwards towards 'communities' and states. Further, it is again one which places great simultaneous emphasis on questions of social justice *and* the issue of environmental degradation. In other words, it would be quite possible to imagine a future society which is environmentally more acceptable but socially and politically disastrous. The perils of eco-fascism and eco-tyranny need to be constantly borne in mind.

Furthermore, environmental degradation and social justice are, in a number of complex ways, implicated with one another. Poor people in developing countries, for example, are often obliged to degrade their environment simply as a result of their social positions. Women and children, precisely those groups with least political power, are often amongst those hardest-hit by the environmental degradation. Similarly, the over-use of resources and wrecking of physical environments in the so-called 'Third World' is closely connected to consumption levels and industrial processes and, above all, the concentrations of economic power in the more affluent countries (Red-Green Study Group 1995).

So ways need to be found of developing strategies which are not only environmentally sound but which shift the balance of social and political power in favour of the threatened and those whose capacities and knowledge are not being properly realised. A key part of this process is the creation of what Irwin (1995) calls 'citizen science', knowledge which is not rejecting science but is using it to alternative ends. A good example in the British case was the initiative by trades unions in Lucas Aerospace during the 1970s. This prefigured important ways forward. And these were, to use Collier's (1994) phrase, 'in gear' with the ways in which society actually worked. Their importance was that they built, albeit in a subversive manner, on the way in which the world actually worked. They remained engaged even if they left some difficulties relatively untouched.

Their 'self-government' took the form of developing skills, new ways of working and new technologies which are socially and environmentally acceptable (Wainwright and Elliott 1982, Cooley 1987). Four thousand redundancies were proposed, and the Shop Stewards' Combine Committee at the company drew up an audit of the skills that were likely to be wasted. They asked local authorities, universities, other trades unions and institutions what a company like theirs should do. What should they be making? They asked the same question of their workers. One hundred and fifty ideas were proposed by the employees, the guiding theme being making and selling things which were socially useful and environmentally desirable. These included new forms of medical equipment, new energy-efficient heat pumps, the development of solar-cell and fuel-cell technologies and a lightweight coach which would run on both road and rail. At the same time, the Combine Committee created work teams which closely integrated the technical staff, with their more abstract scientific knowledge, with the shop-floor workers with their experience of how things were actually made. (See Wainwright and Elliott 1982 for further details.)

In short, this experiment, which was later to be taken up by the Greater London Council and by networks associated with different industrial sectors at a national and pan-European scale, threatened to be successful on a number of fronts at the same time. The products made promised to be environmentally less damaging. Second, the initiatives were aimed at marginalised or threatened groups. Third, these innovations challenged the very forms of alienation which we have been discussing throughout this study. They worked with Howard Rosenbrock, a scientist with a special interest in interactive computer-aided design. He developed new types of technology which recognised the distinctive capacities of human beings to recognise patterns, rapidly appraise complex situations and make intuitive leaps towards alternative solutions. The 'skills' of the computer, he argued, are complementary to the human being. It is good at numerical computation and analysis. The technologies developed by Rosenbrock allow a new relation between humans and machines, one which does not lose or degrade the skills of human beings. Science is therefore again used, this time to create human-centred technology.

Perhaps most important of all, it is used to challenge the alienation of a particular group of threatened people. It linked abstract or scientific knowledge with the knowledge gained on the job and operatives' own skills. Abstract and more subjective types of knowledge thereby became linked to action. Human assets, ingenuity, energy and creativity were retained, revived and used rather than wasted. 'Community' was helpful in defining what products should be made and in developing local and regional networks aimed at reorganising labour processes and defining objectives. 'Community' is also a key way of developing the necessary alliances between classes, men and women and between adults and young people, around liberatory projects of this kind. But it was not the inward-looking community to which many green utopians appeal.

The over-riding objective is one whereby dispossessed and marginalised people (industrial workers in this case) develop their own views and strategies in collaboration with others. Meanwhile they are working with outside sources and institutions, including 'communities', central governments and national governments overseas, to help them develop and extend their ideas. The extent of the challenge represented by this type of alternative can be measured by the hysterical reactions it engendered from the radical right-wing national government led by Margaret Thatcher. Such hostility led, of course, to the Greater London Council's being closed down. But the same type of thinking continues with the GLC's successors within Britain, such as the South East Economic Development Strategy (see, for example, SEEDS 1993) and networks within the European Community (Cooley 1987).

These interventions are not without their difficulties (Rustin 1986). Perhaps most important is the fact that they left workers in each enterprise knowing only about one narrow set of products. They came to know, for example, about the technical division of labour in their own enterprise but, despite their engagement with 'the community', could still not comprehend how their work related to that of other people. Hayek's 'catallaxy' of a vast range of unplanned and spontaneously organised activities which are not subject to control remains a serious block to a wider understanding.

Despite such difficulties these initiatives should be seen as just worked examples of a more general strategy with social as well as environmental objectives. It remains for them to be extended elsewhere, with emphases on other labour processes and technologies. It is not too difficult to imagine other types of industry, such as the biotechnology industries outlined in Chapter 5, being similarly re-deployed towards the use of other marginalised groups such as the small farmers of Africa.

But giving special emphasis to the sphere of industrial production should not blind us to important developments in civil society, the sphere of market exchange and social reproduction. Work involving not only relations between people but between people and nature is also taking place in this, Gorz's 'autonomous', sphere. And de-skilling has also been a feature of this area of social life as industry has once more tended to marginalise many human capacities and abilities.

In the case of the growing and cooking of food, for example, manufacturers, caterers, retailers and growers have turned many of us into passive consumers of food. Eating in everyday life becomes more a question of individualised 'eating on the run' rather than a social occasion in which good cooking is enjoyed. The process seems to be particularly marked in the North European countries, the so-called 'Slow Food' movement doing something in Italy and other Southern countries to resist high-speed eating in the form of pizzas and McDonalds burgers (Lang and Baker 1993).

The alternative is for people to be re-skilled or for them to re-skill themselves not only in the cooking but in the growing and preparation of food and, more generally, adopting lifestyles which are more desirable from an environmental viewpoint. There are signs of this occurring, with larger numbers of people (and especially the young) wanting to learn more about cooking (Lang and Baker 1993). There are now signs, in Britain and no doubt elsewhere, of local governments developing and encouraging these lost skills. At the same time they are able to introduce forms of local eco-agriculture which are self-sustaining and adapted to the particular environments in question.

Similarly, an important set of self-help initiatives in civil society are now emerging, all of which are in effect 'alternative local economies'. Examples are cooperatives, credit unions and Local Exchange Trading Schemes (LETSs). These have remarkable potential. But inevitably they contain tensions. LETSs, for example, demonstrate some of the gains and tensions arising from these self-help 'feasible utopias'. In operation in Britain, Canada and elsewhere, LETSs are examples of people's coming together to exchange, share, and thereby develop their skills (Gosling 1994, Lang 1994). Sometimes with the assistance of enabling, left-leaning, local authorities, the organisers of these schemes, rather like the Lucas Trade Union Combine, typically draw up an audit of skills in a local area. These become services which members trade using standard, non-cash units of exchange.

The range of such schemes is very diverse (Seyfang 1994). Some, such as that in my own rather middle-class area, seem unduly focused on middle-class people exchanging organic food, yoga lessons, music therapy, lifts for children attending a local Steiner school and car services to Gatwick and Heathrow airports. Others, especially in older de-industrialising areas, are more clearly organised by and for those marginalised by the industrial economy and a deteriorating welfare-state: the unemployed, single parents, the disabled and council house tenants.

In both such instances, they are good examples of Gorz's 'autonomous' sector. Here are people working, through necessity or otherwise, for one another and becoming increasingly self-reliant in a mutualistic way. Skills are again acquired and retained. People are, to some degree at least, making their own choices about their lifestyles and how they spend their 'money'. And, since the trading usually takes place in a restricted area, there are (excessive travel to and from international airports apart) clear environmental advantages.

Again, no-one would wish to deny the potential significance of these labour processes. In developing new skills and connections between previously unconnected people, they may prefigure, in ways we cannot yet properly see, important anti-modern and anti-capitalist developments. They represent important challenges to dominant ways of work, lifestyles and relations to nature. Furthermore, they could be state-financed, as what Lipietz (1992) calls 'a socially useful third sector'. Unemployed people could, as he suggests, be paid state money equivalent to their unemployment benefits to engage in socially and environmentally productive work of this kind.

And yet it is important to remember that all initiatives of the above kinds are arising out of societies in which real money still remains the normal means of exchange for those still in employment. Furthermore, the Lipietz strategy of paying the unemployed to look after themselves can be seen as a 'fast-track' self-help solution to the crisis of the welfare state. It can be seen as a kind of politically correct form of workfare, albeit one which the individuals themselves might actually enjoy doing.

Once more, locality or 'community' are important in all these schemes. Indeed, local trading systems necessarily depend on the small-scale and face-to-face interaction. But communities are significant primarily as means to ends. And even these ends are contradictory, resisting estrangement from the human and natural world and from the loss of skills while still offering relatively little threat to the established social order.

The aim must surely be that of making these utopias as more than just small-scale and defensive. As prototype utopias, they have, for example, the potential for demonstrating new ways of working, and in forms which do not damage the environment and at the same time challenge existing social arrangements. One example concerns food. These initiatives could prefigure alternative, and far more healthy, forms of production and consumption. And the groups to benefit could still be those who are socially and economically marginalised. It is difficult to see, however, how such emergent strategies can become established without the enabling support of outside institutions such as local, national or even cross-national governments.

CYBERCULTURE AS VIRTUAL COMMUNITY: EMANCIPATION AT LAST?

The transmission and manipulation of knowledge is now undergoing some very significant changes. If our central concern is with knowledge, its form, its use and its liberatory potential, it is clearly important that we should assess the implications of these technological developments and, as much as possible, actively use them. Although these innovations are important, there is a real danger of their being associated with yet more over-utopian thinking.

'Information superhighways' are now being constructed that will vastly increase the flow of communications (Poster 1995). The replacement of copper wire by fibre optic lines, combined with the digital encoding of sound, text and image, all mean an enormously increased potential for the transmission of information. This means it will soon be possible to send any of these types of information from any point on the network to anywhere else. The superhighway will be complemented by various types of 'cyberspace' on the Internet. Places of work, public buildings, 'electronic cafés' and in due course individual homes will all be able to partake, in an interactive fashion, in the massive sharing of information. Will this prove to be emancipatory, a way of spreading and democratising knowledge?

It is at least possible that these developments will help the lay public to promote their own knowledge and to engage in the transmission and exchange of information. This includes information about the environment, an area which seems particularly prone to superficial reporting, government secretiveness and the separation of people's daily experience from massive and disembodied abstractions (Hansen 1993, Nohrstedt 1993).

More generally, the promise said to be arising from these technologies is no less than that of human freedom, this time with the aid of 'electronic democracy'. And the threat to such democracy is seen as coming from those who would control these technologies. Let us first elaborate on this thesis with the aid of one of the most influential commentators in this field, Ithiel de Sola Pool (1984). With particular reference to the contemporary merging of publishing, broadcasting, cable television and telephone networks he argues that:

> freedom is fostered when the means of communication are dispersed, decentralized, and easily available, as are printing presses or micro-computers. Central control is more likely when the means of communication are concentrated, monopolized, and scarce, as are great networks.
>
> (p. 5)

For Pool, therefore, the promise of these developing technologies is that they allow for more knowledge to be dispersed and for the rights of free speech to be upheld. It is what Stallabrass (1995) calls 'an electronic agora'. The technologies allow pluralism and individual choice to be developed and sustained.

196

Furthermore, any government threatening these processes by, for example, controlling ownership and property rights in these broadcasting, publishing and film media is said to be very seriously impinging on these freedoms. 'In a free society, the burden of proof is for the least possible regulation of communication' (p. 246). At one time, Pool argues, the means of communication was dominated by large oligopolistic networks of common carriers and broadcasters. Under these circumstances 'regulation was a natural response' (p. 5). 'Fortunately and strangely', however,

> as electronics advances further, another reversal is now taking place, toward growing decentralization and toward fragmentation of the audience of the newest media.
>
> (p. 5)

Leaving aside the surely arguable proposition that the major corporations still very much involved in these media (the likes of the Bell Corporation, AT&T and Western Union) are indicators of a revival in competitive capitalism, there are several questions to be asked about these 'freedoms'. Citizenship and human rights backed by legislation are of course important. But, as we have seen earlier, the idea that these can be equated with human emancipation is, to say the least, far-fetched. The right of individuals to choose between an increasing number of television channels would frankly not be a principle worth going to the wall for. Rather than passively choosing between pre-made packages, the division of labour needs changing in such a way that people are given the opportunity to be involved in the creation of the product itself.

But such a proposition seems a very long way from the agenda proposed by Pool and other influential commentators calling for their use in developing human freedoms. Instead, the debate seems to revolve around 'the information-rich' versus 'the information-poor'. Again, there is certainly a problem about information as such being available to some and not available to others. And the implications certainly are that the already powerful will be those with the greatest access to information via these new technologies. But this only states half the problem. Why should there be such emphasis on *quantities* of information and with information in its own right? The problem is surely not only to do with the sheer amount of information available to the socially and politically dispossessed. It has as much if not more to do with the quality of this information, who has made it and for what purposes. Is it information, for example, about the workings of central government policy-making or the workings of capitalist economies? And how do different types of information and levels of abstraction relate to one another?

Much the same can be said of the more academic literature surrounding these emergent technologies, much of which claims to be of a 'radical' nature. The emancipatory potential of the Internet has received special attention. It is again claimed to be a 'virtual community', one replacing the supposed decline of 'real' community and enabling the thirty million citizens now on the net to become fully fledged participants in the public realm. They are therefore the means of recovering the lost public realm as outlined by Habermas (Ess 1994, Negroponte 1995). Rational discourse between citizens is restored, but with rationality in this case excluding face-to-face communication (Palmer 1995). The threat to such virtual community comes, it is argued, from those interests who would attempt to own or control this hitherto anarchic form of communication and citizenship. Rheingold (1995: 4–5) argues, for example, that:

> The technology that makes virtual communities possible has the potential to bring enormous leverage to ordinary citizens at relatively little cost – intellectual leverage, social leverage, commercial leverage, and most important, political leverage. But the technology will not in itself fulfil that potential; this latent technical power must be used intelligently and deliberately by an informed population. More people must learn about that leverage and learn to use it, while we still have the freedom to do so, if it is to live up to its potential. The odds are always good that big power and big money will find a way to control access to virtual communities.

Although the form of politics is somewhat more persuasive than that represented by Pool, the image is similar. It is one of a massive network of individuals interacting with one another but with powerful and ill-disposed interests blocking this communication. As with the 'citizen rights' discourse, it is in many ways difficult to argue against such a picture. Presumably few people would wish to stop individuals communicating, especially if they feel in some way estranged from the society and the environment in which they live. The Internet may, for example, have an important role to play in environmental politics. Electronic mailing lists and computer networks have long been linking dispersed individuals and organisations and underpinning eco-activism (Rushkoff 1994, Rheingold 1995). Again, few could mount a serious argument against these developments. They could be very significant in making connections between people previously separated by their own specialised forms of knowledge. But this is not happening. Largely arcane knowledge is exchanged. Existing divisions of labour remain intact.

At the same time, we are still dealing here with bourgeois freedoms, with the rights of supposedly equal citizens to acquire and transmit knowledge to one another.

> In this ostensibly democratic forum, a chairman of some Western conglomerate and an impoverished peasant in central Africa will both use a device, much the size of a Walkman, to communicate by satellite with a panoply of open information systems.
>
> (Stallabrass 1995: 10)

But we also have great emphasis on communication as a worthy thing *per se*. It remains a consumerist vision, with little emphasis on what all this knowledge is all about, who produced it, how different types of knowledge relate to one another and whether the simple acquisition of knowledge on its own really does very much in terms of human, and non-human, emancipation. The danger is that it offers an illusion of a unified and global understanding, but without spelling out the deep-lying causal processes affecting the human and natural world as it is experienced and observed.

We even have little information about who is actually using these technologies. The indications are that the main participants are educated white males (Davidson 1995). The eco-activists and monkey-wrenchers on e-mail and the Internet are surely doing a great job. But there remains the danger that, as citizens still largely divorced from ways in which societies actually use nature, they are involved in a series of mainly defensive manoeuvres against institutions and labour processes which continue to generate the problems in the first place. And, again, there remains the danger of acquiring and sharing information as a self-evident 'good' in its own right. Is this information the same thing as a knowledge of the underlying processes involved? Does it, on its own, really provide an adequate basis for action?

It may be argued that much of the above literature on 'cyberspace', 'the electronic village' and so on is either journalistic or the product of a politics whose sole end is to protect powerful property-owning interests. The picture becomes more cloudy when we come to more academic literature or to forms of politics claiming to support the disempowered. Indeed, in certain important ways, it repeats some of the above errors.

Developments in 'cyberia', the Internet and so on have both inspired and been interpreted by theories of postmodernity. There are several arguments here. One is that they are encouraging and enhancing a new form of culture, one which is diverse, authorless, has no clear beginning and end. In short, it is 'postmodern' (Douglas 1994, Landow 1994). Nobody can, or wants to, read the whole of the Internet. As much of this literature insists, nobody even *knows* who has read or consumed what on the emergent communications technologies. In the light of the arguments made earlier in this book, information has become, distressingly enough, just a massive resource. It is one which people may choose or sample from. But again few people seem to be asking about its real value in understanding the social and natural worlds.

The argument from much of existing more-academic literature is that these new technologies and forms of communication constitute what Poster (1995) calls 'a mode of information'. It is at this point that there is a major contradiction within the promises of virtual reality.

Contemporary economies and societies are seen as largely consisting of the production and circulation of images and symbols. (See Chapter 5 and, for a detailed discussion, see Lash and Urry 1994.) One of the most important results of this process is seen to be the reconstitution of the human subject and the formation of new types of identity and citizenship. Furthermore, these are

199

'constructions' which can be chosen by individuals themselves. As Taylor and Saarinen (1994: 6) put it:

> In cyberspace, I can change my self as easily as I change clothes. Identity becomes infinitely plastic in a play of images that knows no end. Consistency is no longer a virtue but becomes a vice; integration is imitation. With everything always shifting, everyone is no one.

For example, it is argued that the new technologies are enabling people, and women in particular, to be reconstituted as half nature and half constructed by society. This is again the famous 'cyborg' image created by Haraway and developed by later authors such as Woodward (1994). Interventions such as genetic engineering, transplants, artificial insemination and synthetic drugs are said to be leading to wholly new images and identities for human beings. As mentioned earlier in this study, there is no clear evidence that such images are shared by people other than academics. But this is not the point here. Whether they are shared or not, the emergent communications technologies are said to enable the construction and choice of new, multiple, and eventually liberating, human identities.

Thus it is argued that a new form of 'virtual community' may be under construction, but it is not necessarily the same as the old form of community which has been lost. This is because subjects in the new cyberian culture are other than the rational, autonomous individual.

> The familiar modern subject is displaced by the mode of information in favour of one that is multiplied, disseminated and decentred, continuously interpellated as an unstable identity. At the level of culture, this instability poses both dangers and challenges which, if they become part of a political movement, or are connected with the politics of feminism, ethnic/racial minorities, gay and lesbian positions, may lead to a fundamental challenge to modern social institutions and structures.
>
> (Poster 1995: 57)

So what, if anything, is wrong with this literature? First it represents at best a very partial picture. These new technologies should be welcomed. They may indeed be liberating and challenge modern social institutions and structures. On the other hand, there is an equally good chance that they may not make a very great difference at all. It is misleading to see people's developing multiple identities (or having multiple identities created for them) as a result of engaging in cyberia and the new communications technologies. At the private level people are still very much the prisoners of identities they have had most of their lives. Acting is not being.

Second, it is difficult to imagine all these promises being simultaneously realised. On the one hand we are told that we have the electronic agora connecting up isolated, alienated individuals, offering possibilities for a kind of social life through exchanging information and engaging in debate. On the other hand, these same individuals are, it seems, constantly changing their identity. Like people in 'real' reality, they play roles, and adopt alternative selves. But in the case of virtual reality there will be no physical reality to such people. There are no actual physical people there engaging in this new kind of community (Stallabrass 1995). Plus ça change . . . .

It is therefore by no means clear that such shifts signal the end of one kind of civilisation as we know it and the start of another more emancipated or democratic era. The point can be made by remembering the struggles of the Lucas Aerospace workers. Does 'the choice of another identity' on the Internet really bring about the overturning of power relations or a shift in the division of labour towards the dispossessed? Or are we not still in the sphere of civil society (the circulation of commodities and the reproduction of culture) which finishes by offering limited challenges to the division of labour and the social relations of production? Are groups of people such as the unemployed, women, children and others genuinely strengthened by the new technologies or are they being offered the illusion of power by their introduction to streams of disorganised data? Or, more optimistically, can we envisage them as consciousness-raising? Raising the issues, that is, if still at a fairly superficial level.

A thorough-going empowerment would be gained not through the outright rejection of these technologies but through their subversion. They could be used by people to make their own information and knowledge. The technologies may have been developed in and by a society constituted by massive inequalities in power and knowledge. But that does not mean they have necessarily to be used in this way. At Sussex University a group of us is using and even subverting these technologies. We are asking people, children in this case, to collect information about their natural and social environments and to make flow-charts describing what they have found. These flow-charts are being made, with the help of a professional software specialist on the research team, into compact discs which can be shown on the new multimedia hardware and, in due course, shared via the Internet with other children in other schools, localities and, in due course, countries in Europe. Thus children themselves, in conjunction with adults such as teachers and adults with specialist expertise, are combining the children's lay information and tacit skills and judgements with more abstract and global information about the environment and human society in which they are living. All this information can be combined and shared on compact discs which, unlike 'read only' pre-packaged computer games, the children have made and, in a sense, 'own'.

In such ways, using the new technologies of communication rather than being subjected to them, power could start to be handed back to those groups whose knowledge is being marginalised. The children are in effect engaged in a new kind of knowledge-making labour-process in which their own 'lay' understandings and tacit skills are linked to more abstract ideas about the environment and the impacts of modern society. They are using and challenging the ideas offered to them in textbooks while at the same time linking such ideas to what they can observe on an everyday basis. This is a different kind of division of labour to that normally experienced in modern societies. It is in effect a public space constituted by people bringing to it different knowledge and experience. Unlike economic divisions of labour and knowledge, the participants do not become economically dependent on one another through their specialisms.

We are examining whether, and how, this use of the new technologies makes a significant difference to the children's social and environmental awareness and their actions 'on the ground'. The reaction from both the children and their teachers has so far been quite favourable, though it is as yet too early to say what the outcome will be. The key is the development of the children's own capacities. The next stage is the more overtly political one of enabling children to become engaged in the management of the ecological centres which they are studying.

An innovation of this kind is therefore a contribution to more general attempts to link types of knowledge and significantly alter dominant and obfuscatory divisions of labour in the production of knowledge. It parallels attempts such as those by the Lucas Aerospace Shop Stewards, and the Microbiological Resources Centres in some developing countries, to benefit threatened social groups and at the same time enable people to carry out projects that are socially and environmentally beneficial. It is linked to those strategies in civil society in which people are learning for themselves how local ecosystems work and how local systems of money might lead to new relations between people, money and one another.

Such innovations are therefore meant to systematically enable the dispossessed to gain access to knowledge and power. They are, in the words used by the Greater London Council, 'restructuring for labour'. There is no great appeal to the state to bring about these strategies. The problems of states and state-bureaucracies as 'alienated communities' are, as we have seen, well recognised. On the other hand, state power and resources can be used to enable those reconstructing their relationships with one another and with nature 'from below'. Such mini-utopias also do not attempt to over-ride the power of the market. Nor do they try to undermine completely the social differentiation and division of labour. Rather, they again try to shift power relations as they find them. Unlike much 'green' thinking they do not abandon modernity. Rather, they see in modernity the material and social conditions for making a new start. Furthermore, these are flexible new starts, there being no grand, permanent or long-term plans being handed down by small elites. They take life as they find it, but the galvanising ideal is a profound shift of power and the division of labour. Such micro-utopias, for all their limitations, are late twentieth-century equivalents of the self-governing producers praised by Marx about one hundred and fifty years ago.

EPILOGUE
Humanising nature, naturalising humans

In recent years an important debate has emerged over the meaning of humanism in relation to ecological politics. Does stressing the specific qualities and needs of humans necessarily entail speciesism and the degradation of the environment? Or are the needs of humans compatible with a sustainable environment and the needs of other species? (Benton 1993, Soper 1995, Hayward 1995). The debate is important in a number of ways, not least that of whether, and if so precisely how, we can consider human beings to be a natural sort, one with continuities with other species. Humans, like all animals, eat, sexually reproduce and seek shelter and security. But what does that mean in terms of human practices and their demands on the environment?

Let us first briefly consider the question of human practices. Humans certainly engage in the same reproductive and life-giving activities as all other animals. But of course they engage in these activities in very specific ways, using all kinds of rituals and practices which are unique to human beings. In a very loose sense their specifically human qualities are founded on the biological needs which they share with other species. But perhaps the chief characteristic of human beings is that their behaviour is not determined by their biological needs. In this respect their powers of reflexivity, of conceptualising and constantly monitoring what they are doing, are especially important. The result is that there is a vast range of ways in which they fulfil these needs, what Marx called their 'natural being'. Or, to put it another way, the same practice can be based on very different understandings as regards serving human needs. As regards security, for example, some humans believe that the manufacture of atomic weapons is the best way of ensuring that they remain safe. Others, of course, believe just the opposite.

This brings us to the question of the relation between these needs and the environment. There are again many possible relations here. The human species' needs to survive and reproduce can take a number of forms. So far, the pursuit of human needs has indeed entailed widespread environmental degradation and the misuse of other species. These are the ways in which humans, by converting the powers of nature into the things they want, have attempted to achieve their self-preservation and the good life. But, as Soper (1995) has recently argued, there are many ways of 'flourishing'.

> In practice, as we know, the 'coat' of 'flourishing' can be cut in many differing ways, depending on who is in charge of the tailoring and what the priorities are.
>
> (p. 169)

Much current 're-thinking' now suggests, however, that these domineering ideas about and practices towards the environment are actually not the best way of fulfilling human needs. Furthermore, care for other species is not necessarily at odds with the needs of human beings. If nature really is what Marx called 'man's inorganic body' (if, that is, humans need it to develop emotionally as well as physically) then there is every *human* reason why human beings should tend to this external body. In short, there is no inherent conflict between humanism on the one hand and nature on the other. As Hayward (1995: 75) has recently put it:

> Human emancipation can ... be seen not in terms of an extension of humans' power over external nature, but rather in terms of an attempt to develop human capacities of internal development and adaptation. It may therefore be argued that if human emancipation is conceived in terms of learning to live within natural limits, rather than seeking to overcome or continually push them back, this will mean the development of self-mastery, discipline, and a responsible exercise of freedom such that distinctively humanist ends are pursued in ways which do not depend on the Promethean aim.

The central important point here is a dialectical one. Humans convert nature into the things they need but in doing so they develop their *own* nature. They develop their inborn capacities and potentials in new and wholly unanticipated ways. In this sense, as indeed Marx argued, humans 'naturalise' themselves in the process of humanising nature. They enhance their own natural being.

But of course in the real social and political world, matters are far more complex than this. In humanising nature we have indeed made great advances in terms of understanding nature and our relations to it. On the other hand, modern societies have done so through creating divisions of labour and knowledge which in many respects operate *against* an adequate understanding of ourselves and our relations to nature. Can the complex social and technical division of labour which is necessary for modern society be made compatible with a new form of ecological humanism? That has been the key question running through this book. Critical realism represents an important way of reorganising knowledge to this end. On its own, however, it offers few answers. It needs combining with improved understandings of the mechanisms operating in and between different strata in the human and non-human worlds. Emancipation lies in linking dominant forms of abstract, explicit, global and expert knowledges to subordinated concrete, tacit, local and lay understandings. The hard political and conceptual work remains to be done. But in doing this work human beings will realise new skills, capacities and potentials. In reconstructing nature, our knowledge of nature and understandings of how we relate to nature, we will have reconstructed ourselves.

BIBLIOGRAPHY

Alvater, A. (1993) *The Future of the Market. An Essay on the Regulation of Money and Nature after the Collapse of Actually Existing Socialism*, London: Verso.

Alvater, A. (1994) 'Ecological and economic modalities of time and space', in M. O'Connor (ed.) *Is Capitalism Sustainable? Political Economy and the Politics of Ecology*, New York: Guilford.

Amanor, K. (1994) *The New Frontier. Farmers' Response to Land Degradation. A West African Study*, London: Zed Books.

Arditti, R., Klein, R. and Minden, S. (eds) (1989) *Test Tube Women. What Future for Motherhood?*, London: Pandora.

Bahro, R. (1984) *From Red to Green*, London: Verso.

Bahro, R. (1986) *Building the Green Movement*, London: GMP.

Barde, J-P. and Pearce, D. (1991) *Valuing the Environment*, London: Earthscan.

Beck, U. (1992a) *Risk Society. Towards a New Modernity*, London: Sage.

Beck, U. (1992b) 'From industrial society to the risk society: questions of survival, social structure and ecological enlightenment', *Theory, Culture and Society* 9: 97–123.

Beck, U. (1992c) 'How modern is modern society', *Theory, Culture and Society* 9: 163–9.

Beck, U. (1995) *Ecological Politics in an Age of Risk*, Oxford: Polity.

Beck, U., Giddens, A. and Lash, S. (1994) *Reflexive Modernization*, Oxford: Polity.

Beckerman, W. (1995) *Small is Stupid*, London: Duckworth.

Begley, S. (1995) 'The baby myth', *Newsweek*, 4 September: 34–41.

Benor, R. (1994) 'Holistic nursing: reaching into the foundations of society', *Caduceus* 24: 10–13.

Benton, T. (1988) 'Humanism = speciesism: Marx on humans and animals', *Radical Philosophy* 50: 3–18.

Benton, T. (1989) 'Marxism and natural limits: an ecological critique and reconstruction', *New Left Review* 178: 51–86.

Benton, T. (1992) 'Animal rights and wrongs. Prologemena to a debate', *Capitalism, Nature, Socialism* 3(2): 79–82.

Benton, T. (1993) *Natural Relations. Ecology, Animal Rights and Social Justice*, London: Verso.

Benton, T. (1995) 'A green and pleasant land', *New Times*, 21 January: 6–7.

Bhaskar, R. (1978) *A Realist Theory of Science* (2nd edn), Brighton: Harvester.

Bhaskar, R. (1989) *The Possibility of Naturalism* (2nd edn), Hemel Hempstead: Harvester.

Bhaskar, R. (1994) *Dialectic. The Pulse of Freedom*, London: Verso.

Birke, L. (1994) *Feminism, Animals and Science*, Milton Keynes: Open University Press.

Boehmer-Christiansen, S. (1994a) 'A scientific agenda for climate policy?', *Nature* 372, 1st December: 400–2.

Boehmer-Christiansen, S. (1994b) 'Global climate protection policy: the limits of scientific advice', *Global Environmental Change* 4(2): 140–59.

Boehmer-Christiansen, S. (1995a) 'Britain and the International Panel on Climate Change: The impacts of scientific advice on global warming. Part II: The domestic story of the British response to climate change', *Environmental Politics* 4(2): 175–96.

Boehmer-Christansen, S. (1995b) 'Britain and the International Panel on Climate Change: The impacts of scientific advice on global warming. Part I: Integrated policy analysis and the global dimension', *Environmental Politics* 4(1): 1–18.

Bohm, D. (1980) *Wholeness and the Implicate Order*, London: Ark.

Boldt, L. (1993) *Zen and the Art of Making a Living*, New York: Arkana/Penguin.

Bond, G.C. and Gilliam, A. (1994) 'Introduction', in G.C. Bond and A. Gilliam (eds) *Social Construction of the Past*, London: Routledge, pp. 2–22.

Bookchin, M. (1970) *Post-Scarcity Anarchism*, Montreal: Black Rose.

Bookchin, M. (1980) 'Open letter to the ecology movement', in *Toward an Ecological Society*, Montreal: Black Rose.

Bookchin, M. (1990) 'Ecologizing the dialectic', in J. Clark (ed.) *Renewing the Earth. The Promise of Social Ecology*, London: Greenprint, pp. 202–19.

Bower, J. (1987) 'The scientist, the stockman and the animal', *The Ecologist* 17(6): 230–5.

Braverman, H. (1974) *Labor and Monopoly Capital. The Degradation of Work in the Twentieth Century*, New York: Monthly Press.

Breeze, N. (1989) 'Who is going to rock the petri dish? For feminists who have considered parthenogenesis when the movement is not enough', in R. Arditti, R. Klein and S. Minden (eds) *Test Tube Women. What Future for Motherhood?*, London: Pandora.

British Broadcasting Corporation (1993) 'The mouse that laid the golden egg'. Transcript of programme in the series 'Cracking the Code', transmitted by BBC2 on 14 September.

British Medical Association (1992) *Our Genetic Future. The Science and Ethics of Genetic Technology*, Oxford: Oxford University Press.

Brown, L., Kane, H. and Ayres, M. (1993) *Vital Signs. The Trends that Are Shaping our Future*, London: Earthscan.

Brown, M., Fielden, K. and Scutt, J. (1990) 'New frontiers or old recycled? New reproductive technologies as primary industry', in J. Scutt (ed.) *The Baby Machine. Reproductive Technology and the Commercialisation of Motherhood*, London: pp. 77–107.

Buckman, R. and Sabbagh, K. (1993) *Magic or Medicine? An Investigation of Healing and Helpers*, London: Macmillan.

Capra, F. (1976) *The Tao of Physics*, London: Flamingo / Harper Collins.

Capra, F. (1983) *The Turning Point. Science, Society and the Rising Culture*, London: Flamingo.

Cohen, J. and Arato, A. (1992) *Civil Society and Political Theory*, Cambridge, Mass.: MIT.

Cole, S. (1992) *Making Science. Between Nature and Society*, London: Harvard University Press.

Collier, A. (1989) *Scientific Realism and Socialist Thought*, Hemel Hempstead: Harvester.

Collier, A. (1994) *Critical Realism. An Introduction to Roy Bhaskar's Philosophy*, London: Verso.

Collins, H. (1985) *Changing Order. Replication and Induction in Scientific Practice*, London: Sage.

Collins, S. (1990) *Black Feminist Thought: Knowledge, Consciousness and the Politics of Empowerment*, London: Unwin Hyman.

Cooley, M. (1987) *Architect or Bee? The Human Price of Technology*. London: Hogarth Press.

Coontz, S. and Henderson, P. (1986) 'Property forms, political power and female labour', in S. Coontz and P. Henderson (eds) *Women's Work, Men's Property*, London: Verso, pp. 108–55.

Corea, G. (1985) *The Mother Machine*, London: The Women's Press.

Coward, R. (1989) *The Whole Truth. The Myth of Alternative Health*, London: Faber.

Cozzens, S. and Woodhouse, E. (1995) 'Science, government and the politics of Knowledge', in S. Jasanoff, G. Markle, J. Petersen, and T. Pinch (eds) *Handbook of Science and Technology Studies*, London: Sage, pp. 533–53.

Crouch, D. and Ward, C. (1988) *The Allotment. Its Landscape and Culture*, London: Faber and Faber.

Dalton, R and Kuechler, M. (1990) *Challenging the Political Order*, Oxford: Polity Press, pp. 157–61.

Darwin, C. (1950) *On the Origin of Species*, London: Watts.

Dass, R. and Bush, M. (1992) *Compassion in Action*, London: Rider.

Davidson, K. (1995) 'Liberté, Egalité, Interneté', *New Scientist*, 27 May, pp. 38–42.

Dawkins, A. (1976) *The Selfish Gene*, Oxford: Oxford University Press.

Devall, B. and Sessions, G. (1985) *Deep Ecology*, Salt Lake City: Peregrine Smith.

Dickens, P. (1992) *Society and Nature. Towards a Green Social Theory*, Hemel Hempstead: Harvester.

Dittmar, H. (1992) *The Social Psychology of Material Possessions*, Hemel Hempstead: Harvester.

Dobson, A. (1995) *Green Political Thought*, London: Unwin Hyman (2nd edn).

Donnelly, D. (1994) 'Complementary medicine at the crossroads', *The Journal of Contemporary Health* 1: 26–9.

Douglas, J. (1994) '"How do I stop this thing?" Closure and indeterminacy in interactive narratives', in G. Landow (ed.) *Hypertext Theory*, Baltimore: Johns Hopkins, pp. 159–88.

Douglas, M. (1966) *Purity and Danger*, London: Routledge & Kegan Paul.

Drexler, K (1990) *Engines of Creation*, London: Fourth Estate.

Duden, B. (1993) *Disembodying Women. Perspectives on Pregnancy and the Unborn*, Cambridge, Mass.: Harvard University Press.

Duncan, S. and Goodwin, M. (1988) *The Local State and Uneven Development*, Oxford: Polity.

Dunlap, R. and Catton, W. (1994) 'Struggling with human exemptionalism: the rise, decline and revitalization of environmental sociology', *The American Sociologist* 25: 5–30.

Eder, K. (1993) *The New Politics of Class*, London: Sage.

Elsworth, S. (1990) *A Dictionary of the Environment*, London: Paladin.

Engels, F. (1959) *The Dialectics of Nature*, Moscow: Progress.

Ereira, A. (1990) *The Heart of the World*, London: Cape.

Ernst, E, (1994) 'The thriving fringe of medicine', *The Journal of Contemporary Health*, Winter: 21.

Ess, C. (1994) 'The political computer: hypertext, democracy and Habermas', in G. Landow (ed.) *Hypertext Theory*, Baltimore: Johns Hopkins, pp. 225–67.

Etzioni, A. (1993) *The Spirit of Community. The Reinvention of American Society*, New York: Simon and Schuster.

Faber, D. and O'Connor, J. (1989) 'The struggle for nature: environmental crisis and the crisis of environmentalism in the United States', *Capitalism, Nature, Socialism* 2: 12–39.

Firestone, S. (1979) *The Dialectic of Sex. The Case for Feminist Revolution*, London: The Women's Press.

Foweraker, J. (1995) *Theorizing Social Movements*, London: Pluto.

Fowler, C. and Mooney, P. (1990) *The Threatened Gene. Food, Politics and the Loss of Genetic Diversity*, Cambridge: Lutterworth.

Franklin, S. (1988) 'Life story. The gene as a fetish object on TV', *Science as Culture* 3: 92–100.

Franklin, S. (1993) 'Postmodern procreation. Representing reproductive practice', *Science as Culture* 3, 4(17): 522–29.

Freeman, C. (1982) *The Economics of Industrial Innovation* (2nd edn), London: Pinter.

Gandy, M. (1994) *Recycling and the Politics of Urban Waste*, London: Earthscan.

Garrett, L. (1995) *The Coming Plague. Newly Emerging Diseases in a World Out of Balance*, London: Virago.

George, S. (1986) *How the Other Half Dies*, Harmondsworth, Penguin.

Geyer, R. and Schweitzer, D. (eds) (1981) *Alienation: Problems of Meaning, Theory and Method*, London: Routledge.

Giddens, A. (1990) *The Consequences of Modernity*, Oxford: Polity.

Giddens, A. (1991) *Modernity and Self-Identity. Self and Society in the Late Modern Age*, Oxford: Polity.

Giddens, A. (1994) *Beyond Left and Right,* Oxford: Polity.

Gimenez, M. (1991) 'The mode of reproduction in transition: a Marxist-feminist analysis of the effects of reproductive technologies', *Gender and Society* 5(3): 334–50.

Glasman, J. (1970) 'Genetics researcher quits science for politics', *Science* 167: 963–4.

Gleick, J. (1987) *Chaos. Making a New Science*, London: Cardinal.

Glover, D. (1994) 'Global institutions, international agreements, and environmental issues', in R. Stubbs and G. Underhill (eds) *Political Economy and the Changing Global Order*, London: Macmillan.

Goodman, D. and Redclift, M. (1991) *Refashioning Nature. Food Ecology and Culture*, London: Routledge.

Goodman, D., Sorj, B. and Wilkinson, J. (1987) *From Farming to Biotechnology. A Theory of Development*, Oxford: Blackwell.

Goodwin, B. (1994) *How the Leopard Changed its Spots. The Evolution of Complexity*, London: Weidenfeld and Nicholson.

Gorz, A. (1985) *Paths to Paradise. On the Liberation from Work*, London: Pluto.

Gorz, A. (1987) *Ecology as Politics*, London: Pluto.

Gorz, A. (1988) *Critique of Economic Reason*, London: Verso.

Gorz, A. (1994) *Capitalism, Socialism, Ecology*, London: Verso.

Gosling, P. (1994) 'Fair exchange', *Red Pepper* 6, November: pp. 28–9.

Greenwood, D. (1994) *Realism, Identity and Emotion. Reclaiming Social Psychology*, London: Sage.

Gribbin, J. (1988) *The Hole in the Sky*, London: Corgi.

Gribbin, J. (1990) *Hothouse Earth*, London: Transworld.

Gribbin, M. and Gribbin, J. (1992) *Too Hot to Handle? The Greenhouse Effect*, London: Corgi.

Grossinger, R. (1985) *Planet Medicine*, Berkeley: North Atlantic Publishing.

Grundmann, R. (1991) *Marxism and Ecology*, Oxford: Oxford University Press.

Guha, R. (1991) *The Unquiet Woods. Ecological Change and Peasant Resistance in the Himalaya*, Delhi: Oxford University Press.

Haas, P. (1992) 'Banning chlorofluorocarbons: epistemic community efforts to protect stratospheric ozone', *International Organization* 46: 187–224.

Habermas, J. (1987) *The Theory of Communicative Action*, Vol. 2, *Lifeworld and System: a Critique of Functionalist Reason*, Boston: Beacon Press.

BIBLIOGRAPHY

Habermas, J. (1989) *The Structural Transformation of the Public Sphere*, Oxford: Polity.

Hannigan, J. (1995) *Environmental Sociology: A Social Constructionist Approach*, London: Routledge.

Hansen, A. (1993) 'Introduction' to Hansen, A. (ed.) *The Mass Media and Environmental Issues*, Leicester: Leicester University Press.

Haraway, D. (1989) *Primate Visions. Gender, Race and Nature in the World of Modern Science*, New York: Routledge.

Haraway, D. (1991) *Simians, Cyborgs and Women. The Reinvention of Nature*, London: Free Association.

Haraway, D. (1992a) *Primate Visions. Gender, Race and Nature in the World of Modern Science*, London: Verso.

Haraway, D. (1992b) 'Otherworldly conversations: Terran topics, local terms', *Science as Culture* No. 14, Vol. 3, Part 1.

Harrison, C., Burgess, J. and Filius, P. (eds) (1994) 'From environmental awareness to environmental action', Available from the authors, Department of Geography, University College London, 26 Bedford Way, London WC1H 0AP.

Harvey, D. (1989) *The Condition of Postmodernity*, Oxford: Blackwell.

Harvey, D. (1992) 'Capitalism, the factory of fragmentation', *New Perspectives Quarterly*, Spring: 42–5.

Harvey, D. (1993) 'The nature of environment: the dialectics of social and environmental change', *Socialist Register*, pp. 1–51.

Hay, C. (1994) 'Environmental security and state legitimacy', in M. O'Connor (ed.) *Is Capitalism Sustainable? Political Economy and the Politics of Ecology*, New York: Guilford, pp. 217–31.

Hay, D. (1995) 'The religion of human solidarity', *Interbeing*, Spring: 20–1.

Hayek, F. (1988) *The Fatal Conceit. The Errors of Socialism*, London: Routledge.

Hayry, H. (1994) 'How to assess the consequences of genetic engineering', in J. Harris and A. Dyson (eds) *Ethics and Biotechnology*, London: Routledge.

Hayward, T. (1990) 'Ecosocialism – utopian and scientific', *Radical Philosophy* 56, Autumn: 2–14

Hayward, T. (1995) *Ecological Thought. An Introduction*, Oxford: Polity.

Hobbelink, H. (1991) *Biotechnology and the Future of World Agriculture*, London: Zed Books.

Hornstein, F. (1989) 'Children by donor insemination: a new choice for lesbians', in R. Arditti, R. Klein and S. Minden (eds) *Test Tube Women. What Future for Motherhood?*, London: Pandora.

Hurrell, A. (1995) 'International political theory and the global environment', in K. Booth and S. Smith (eds) *International Relations Theory Today*, Oxford: Polity, pp. 129–53

Ignatieff, M. (1990) *The Needs of Strangers*, London: The Hogarth Press.

Inglehart, R. (1990) 'Values, ideology and cognitive mobilization in new social movements', in R. Dalton and M. Kuechler (eds) *Challenging the Political Order. New Social and Political Movements in Western Democracies*, Oxford: Polity, pp. 43–66.

Ingold, T. (1990) 'Environment and culture in ecological anthropology', Paper to British Association for the Advancement of Science meeting (Paper available from the author, Dept. of Anthropology, University of Manchester).

Irwin, A. (1995) *Citizen Science. A Study of People, Expertise and Sustainable Development*, London: Routledge.

Jackson, C. (1993a) 'Doing what comes naturally? Women and environment in development', *World Development* 21(12): 1947–63.

Jackson, C. (1993b) 'Environmentalisms and gender interests in the Third World', *Development and Change* 24: 649–77.

Jackson, C. (1994) 'Radical environmental myths: a gender perspective', *New Left Review* 210: 124–40.

Juma, C. (1989) *The Gene Hunters. Biotechnology and the Scramble for Seeds*, London: Zed Books.

Kauffman, S. (1994) *The Origins of Order. Self-Organisation and Selection in Evolution*, Oxford: Oxford University Press.

Keenan, L. (1994) 'The nurse as healer', *Caduceus* 24: 23–5

Keulartz, J., Kwa, C. and Radder, H. (1985) 'Scientific and social problems and perspectives of alternative medicine: analysis of a Dutch controversy', *Radical Philosophy* 41, Autumn: 2–9.

Kiley-Worthington, M. (1993) *Food First Farming. Theory and Practice*, London: Souvenir Press.

Kimbrell, A. (1995) 'The body enclosed: the commodification of human "parts"', *The Ecologist* 21(4): 134–41.

Klein, R. (1989) 'Doing it ourselves: self insemination', in R. Arditti, R. Klein and S. Minden (eds). *Test Tube Women. What Future for Motherhood?*, London: Pandora

Kloppenburg, J. (1988) *First the Seed. The Political Economy of Plant Biotechnology, 1492–2000*, Cambridge: Cambridge University Press.

Kollek, R. (1995) 'The limits of experiential knowledge: a feminist perspective on the ecological risks of genetic engineering', Chapter 6 of V. Shiva and I. Moser (eds) *Social Construction of the Past*, London: Routledge.

Koval, R. (1990) 'The commercialisation of reproductive technology', in J. Scutt (ed.) *The Baby Machine. Reproductive Technology and the Commercialisation of Motherhood*, London: Greenprint.

Kropotkin, P. (1985) *Fields, Factories and Workshops Tomorrow* (with introduction and commentary by C. Ward), London: Freedom Press. (Originally published 1899.)

Kumar, K. (1993) 'Civil society: an inquiry into the usefulness of an historical term', *British Journal of Sociology* 44(3): 375–95.

Landow, G. (1994) 'What's a critic to do? Critical theory in the age of hypertext', in G. Landow (ed.) *Hypertext Theory*, Baltimore: Johns Hopkins, pp. 1–50.

Lang, R. (1994) *Lets Work. Rebuilding the Local Economy*, Bristol: Grover.

Lang, T. and Baker, L. (1993) 'The rise and fall of domestic cooking: turning European children into passive consumers', Paper for XIII International Home Economics and Consumer Studies Research Conference, 'The European Consumer', 8–10 September, Leeds, UK.

Lash, S. (1994) 'Reflexivity and its doubles: structure, aesthetics, community', Chapter 3 of Beck, U., Giddens, A. and Lash, S. *Reflexive Modernization. Politics, Tradition and Aesthetics in the Modern Social Order*, Oxford: Polity.

Lash, S. and Urry, J. (1987) *The End of Organized Capitalism*, Oxford: Polity.

Lash, S. and Urry, J. (1994) *Economies of Signs and Space*, London: Sage.

Lawrence, G. (1989) 'Genetic engineering and Australian agriculture: agenda for corporate control', *Journal of Australian Political Economy* 25: 1–16.

Lean, G. (1995) 'Global warming is leading to climatic upheaval, say scientists', *The Independent on Sunday*, 15 October, p. 5.

Lee, K. (1989) *Social Philosophy and Ecological Scarcity*, London: Routledge.

Leff, E. (1992) 'A second contradiction of capitalism?' *Capitalism, Nature, Socialism* 3(4) (Issue 12): 109–16.

Levidow, L. (1994a) 'Risk controversy: de/politicizing uncertainty', Paper to 3rd Annual Conference of the Interdisciplinary Network on the Environment and Society, Warwick University, UK, September 1994.

Levidow, L. (1994b) 'Scientizing security: agricultural biotechnology as clean surgical strike', available from the author, 48 Fortress Road, London NW5.

Levins, R. and Lewontin, R. (1985) *The Dialectical Biologist,* Cambridge, Mass.: Harvard University Press.

Lewontin, R. (1982) 'Organism and environment', in H. Plotkin (ed.) *Learning, Development and Culture,* Chichester: Wiley.

Lewontin, R. (1993) *The Doctrine of DNA*, Harmondsworth: Penguin.

Lindlahr, H. (1975) *Philosophy of Natural Therapeutics*, Maidstone, Kent: Maidstone Osteopathic Clinic.

Lipietz, A. (1992) *Towards a New Economic Order. Postfordism, Ecology and Democracy,* Oxford: Polity.

Luhmann, N. (1989) *Ecological Communication*, Oxford: Polity.

Lyman, R. (1991) 'Barbarism and religion', in L. DeMause (ed.) *The History of Childhood. The Untold Story of Child Abuse*, London: Bellew.

McFadden, T. (1990) 'Surrogate motherhood – refusing to relinquish the child', in J. Scutt (ed.) *The Baby Machine. Reproductive Technology and the Commercialisation of Motherhood*, London: Green Print.

McKenzie, D. and Spinardi, G. (1995) 'Tacit knowledge, weapons design and the uninvention of nuclear weapons', *American Journal of Sociology*, 101(July): 44–99.

MacNaghten, P. and Urry, J. (1995) 'Towards a sociology of nature', *Sociology* 29(2): 203–20.

Manicas, P. (1987) *A History and Philosophy of the Social Sciences*, Oxford: Blackwell.

Mannion, A. (1991) *Global Environmental Change*, Harlow: Longman.

Manor, K. (1994) *The New Frontier. Farmers' Response to Land Degradation. A West African Study*, London: Zed Books.

Martell, L. (1992) 'Towards an ecological sociology', Mimeo from the author, School of Social Sciences, University of Sussex.

Martell, L. (1994) *Ecology and Society*, Oxford: Polity.

Martin, E. (1993) *The Woman in the Body. A Cultural Analysis of Reproduction*, Milton Keynes: Open University Press.

Martinez Allier, J. (1987) *Ecological Economics. Energy, Environment and Society*, Oxford: Blackwell.

Martinez Allier, J. (1993) 'The loss of agricultural biodiversity: an example of "the second contradiction" ', *Capitalism, Nature, Socialism* 4(3), Issue 15, pp. 89–98.

Marx, K. (1969) *Theories of Surplus Value*, London: Lawrence and Wishart.

Marx, K. (1973) *Grundrisse. Introduction to the Critique of Political Economy*, Harmondsworth: Pelican.

Marx, K. (1975) *Early Writings* (L. Colletti (ed.)), Harmondsworth: Penguin.

Marx, K. (1981) *Capital,* Vol. 3, Harmondsworth: Penguin.

Marx, K. and Engels, F. (1969) 'The German ideology', in L. Feuer (ed.) *Marx and Engels. Basic Writings on Politics and Philosophy*, London: Fontana, pp. 287–302.

Matthews, D. (1995) 'Commons versus open access. The collapse of Canada's east coast fishery', *The Ecologist* 25(2/3): 86–96.

Melucci, A. (1989) *Nomads of the Present*, London: Radius.

Melucci, A. (1992) 'Liberation or meaning? Social movements, culture and democracy', in J. Pieterse (ed.) *Emancipations, Modern and Postmodern*, London: Sage.

Merchant, C. (1980) *The Death of Nature: Women, Ecology and the Scientific Revolution*, San Francisco: Harper and Row.

Mies, M. (1986a) *Patriarchy and Accumulation on a World Scale. Women in the International Division of Labour*, London: Zed Books.

Mies, M. (1986b) 'Why do we need all this?', *Women's Studies International Forum* 8(6): 553–60.

Mies, M. and Shiva, V. (1993) *Ecofeminism*, London: Zed Books.

Miliband, R. (1989) *Divided Societies. Class Struggle in Contemporary Capitalism*, Oxford: Clarendon Press.

Mingione, E. (1985) 'Social reproduction of the surplus labour force: the case of Southern Italy', in N. Redclift and E. Mingione (eds) *Beyond Employment*, Oxford: Blackwell, pp. 14–54.

Mingione, E. (1988) 'Work and informal activities in urban southern Italy', in R. Pahl (ed.) *On Work. Historical, Comparative and Theoretical Approaches*, Oxford: Blackwell, pp. 548–78.

Mitter, S. (1994) 'What women demand of technology', *New Left Review* 205(May/June): 1004.

Mol, A. (1995) *The Refinement of Production. Ecological Modernization; Theory and the Chemical Industry*, The Hague: CIP-Data Koninklijke Biblioteek.

Mole, P. (1992) *Acupuncture. Energy Balancing for Body, Mind and Spirit*, Shaftesbury: Health Essentials.

Money, M. (1994) 'Shamanism and health', *The Journal of Contemporary Health*, pp. 40–3.

Murphy, J. (1989) 'Egg farming and women's future', in R. Arditti, R. Klein and S. Minden (eds) *Test Tube Women. What Future for Motherhood?*, London: Pandora.

Murphy, R. (1994) *Rationality and Nature. A Sociological Enquiry into a Changing Relationship*, Oxford: Westview Press.

Naess, A. (1989) *Ecology, Community and Lifestyle*, Cambridge: Cambridge University Press.

Negroponte, N. (1995) *Being Digital. The Road Map for Survival on the Information Highway*, London: Hodder & Stoughton.

New, C. (1995a) 'Sociology and the case for realism', Mimeo from author, Faculty of Education and the Human Sciences, Bath College of Higher Education, Newton Park, Newton St. Loe, Bath, UK.

New, C. (1995b) 'Man bad, woman good? Dissolving the dualisms', Mimeo from the author, Bath College of Higher Education, Newton Park, Newton St. Loe, Bath, UK.

Nohrstedt, S. (1993) 'Communicative action in the risk society: public relations strategies, the media and nuclear power', in Hansen, A. (ed.) *The Mass Media and Environmental Issues*, Leicester: Leicester University Press.

North, R. (1995) *Life on a Modern Planet. A Manifesto for Progress*, Manchester: Manchester University Press.

Noske, B. (1989) *Humans and Other Animals. Beyond the Boundaries of Anthropology*, London: Pluto.

O'Brien, T. (1995a) 'Genetic engineering. The ultimate exploitation', *Agscene* (Quarterly Magazine of Compassion in World Farming), 118: 10–11.

O'Brien, T. (1995b) *Gene Transfer and the Welfare of Farm Animals*, Petersfield: Compassion in World Farming.

O'Connor, J. (1988) 'Capitalism, nature, socialism. A theoretical introduction', *Capitalism, Nature, Socialism* 1: 11–38.

O'Connor, J. (1989) 'Political economy of ecology of socialism and capitalism', *Capitalism, Nature, Socialism*, 3: 93–106.

O'Connor, M. (ed.) (1994) *Is Capitalism Sustainable? Political Economy and the Politics of Ecology*, New York: Guilford.

Odum, E. (1989) *Ecology and Our Endangered Life-Support Systems*, Sunderland: Sinauer.

Offe, C. (1987) 'Changing boundaries of institutional politics: social movements since the 1960s', in C. Maier (ed.) *Changing Boundaries of the Political*, Cambridge: Cambridge University Press.

O'Neill, J. (1993) *Ecology, Policy and Politics. Human Well-Being and the Natural World*, London: Routledge.

213

O'Riordan, T. (1981) *Environmentalism*, London: Pion.
Outhwaite, W. (1994) *Habermas. A Critical Introduction*, Oxford: Polity.
Pahl, R. (1984) *Divisions of Labour*, Oxford: Blackwell.
Palmer, M. (1995) 'Interpersonal communication and virtual reality: mediating interpersonal relationships', in F. Biocca and M. Levy (eds) *Communication in the Age of Virtual Reality*, Hillsdale, NJ: Erlbaum, pp. 277–99.
Parkin, F. (1979) *Marxism and Class Theory. A Bourgeois Critique*, London: Tavistock.
Pearce, D., Markandya, A. and Barbier, E. (1989) *Blueprint for a Green Economy*, London: Earthscan.
Pearce, F. (1995) 'Breaking up is hard to do', *New Scientist*, 24 June: 14–15.
Pearson, M. (1995) 'The age of miracles?', *The Independent*, 18 March.
Pepper, D. (1993) *Eco-Socialism. From Deep Ecology to Social Justice*, London: Routledge.
Perlas, N. (1994) *Overcoming Illusions about Biotechnology*, London: Zed Books and Third World Network.
Perlas, N. (1995) 'The seven dimensions of sustainable agriculture', Chapter 15 of V. Shiva and I. Moser (eds) *Biopolitics. A Feminist and Ecological Reader on Biotechnology*, London: Zed Books.
Pieterse, J. (1992) 'Emancipations, modern and postmodern', in *Development and Change* 23(3): 5–41.
Plant, C and Plant, J. (1991) *Green Business. Hope or Hoax?*, Bideford: Green Books.
Plant, S. (1992) *The Most Radical Gesture. The Situationist International in a Postmodern Age*, London: Routledge.
Platt, J. (1993) 'Networks of scientism', available from the author, Graduate Research Centre in the Social Sciences, Arts E, University of Sussex, Falmer, Brighton, UK.
Platt, J. (1994) 'Scientistic theory and scientistic practice', paper given to XIII World Congress of Sociology, Bielefeld; available from the author.
Plumwood, V. (1993) *Feminism and the Mastery of Nature*, London: Routledge.
Polanyi, M. (1958) *Personal Knowledge*, London: Routledge.
Polanyi, M. (1967) *The Tacit Dimension*, New York: Anchor.
Pool, I. de Sola (1984) *Technologies of Freedom*, Cambridge, Mass.: Harvard University Press.
Poster, M. (1995) *The Second Media Age*, Oxford: Polity.
Preston, R. (1994) *The Hot Zone*, London: Doubleday.
RAFI (Rural Advancement Fund International) (1989) 'Biotechnology and medicinal plants', RAFI, PO Box 1029, Pittsboro, North Carolina.
Ramos, A. (1994) 'From Eden to limbo: the construction of indigenism in Brazil', in G.C. Bond and A. Gilliam (eds) *Social Construction of the Past*, London: Routledge, pp. 74–88.
Rattansi, A. (1982) *Marx and the Division of Labour*, London: Macmillan.
Ravaioli, C. (1993) 'On the second contradiction of capitalism', *Capitalism, Nature, Socialism*, 4, 3, Issue 15, pp. 98–104.
Recio, A. (1992) 'A flawed and incomplete model', *Capitalism, Nature, Socialism*, 3, 4, Issue 12, pp. 117–19.
Red-Green Study Group (1995) *What on Earth is to Be Done?*, Manchester: Red-Green Study Group.
Regan, T. (1990) 'Introduction' to P. Clarke and A. Linzey (eds) *Political Theory and Animal Rights*, London: Pluto, pp. xiii–xxii.
Regan, T. and Singer, P. (eds) (1976) *Animal Rights and Human Obligations*, Englewood Cliffs, NJ: Prentice-Hall.
Rheingold, H. (1995) *The Virtual Community. Finding Connection in a Computerized World*, London: Minerva.

Ridley, M. (1995) *Down to Earth: a Contrarian View of Environmental Problems*, Studies on the Environment 3, London: Institute of Economic Affairs.

Rose, S., Lewontin, R. and Kamin, L. (1984) *Not in Our Genes*, Harmondsworth, Pelican.

Rowland, R. (1992) *Living Laboratories. Women and Reproductive Technology*, London: Lime Tree.

Rucht, D. (1990) 'The strategies and action repertoires of new movements', in R. Dalton and M. Kuechler (eds) *Challenging the Political Order*, Oxford: Polity Press.

Rueschemeyer, D. (1986) *Power and the Division of Labour*, Oxford, Polity.

Rushkoff, D. (1994) *Cyberia. Life in the Trenches of Hyperspace*, London: Flamingo.

Rustin, M. (1986) 'Lessons of the London Industrial Strategy', *New Left Review* 155: 75–84.

Ryan, S. (1995) 'Look what's cooking', *Sunday Times*, 14 May.

Savage, M., Barlow, J., Dickens, P. and Fielding, T. (1992) *Bureaucracy, Property and Culture. Middle-Class Formation in Contemporary Britain*, London: Routledge.

Sayer, A. (1992) *Method in Social Science. A Realist Approach* (2nd edn), London: Routledge.

Sayer, A. (1995) *Radical Political Economy. A Critique*, Oxford: Blackwell.

Sayer, A. and Walker, R (1992) *The New Social Economy. Reworking the Division of Labor*, Oxford: Blackwell.

Schacht, R. (1971) *Alienation*, London: Allen and Unwin.

Schaff, A. (1980) *Alienation as a Social Phenomenon*, Oxford: Pergamon.

Schechter, D. (1994) *Radical Theories. Paths Beyond Marxism and Social Democracy*, Manchester: Manchester University Press.

Schmidt, A. (1971) *The Concept of Nature in Marx*, London: New Left Books.

Schmitt, R. (1983) *Alienation and Class*, Cambridge: Schenkman.

Scott, A. (1992) 'Political culture and social movements', in J. Allen, P. Braham and P. Lewis (eds) *Political and Economic Forms of Modernity*, Oxford: Polity.

SEEDS (1993) *Green Plan Final Report*, Strategy Study 34, South East Economic Development Strategy, Stevenage, UK.

Seligman, A. (1992) *The Idea of Civil Society*, New York: Free Press.

Seyfang, G. (1994) 'The local exchange trading system: political economy and social audit', Thesis presented in part-fulfilment of the degree of Master of Science, School of Environmental Sciences, University of East Anglia, Norwich, UK.

Shiva, V. (1988) *Staying Alive: Women, Ecology and Development*, London: Zed Books.

Shiva, V. (1991) 'Biodiversity, biotechnology and profits', in V. Shiva, H. Anderson, A. Schücking, L. Gray, Lohmann and D. Cooper (eds) *Biodiversity. Social and Ecological Perspectives*, London: Zed Books.

Shiva, V. (1995) 'Biotechnological development and the conservation of biodiversity', Chapter 12 of V. Shiva and I. Moser (eds) *Biopolitics. A Feminist and Ecological Reader on Biotechnology*, London: Zed Books and Third World Network.

Singer, P. (1990) 'All animals are equal', in P. Clarke and A. Linzey (eds) *Political Theory and Animal Rights*, London: Pluto.

Smith, A. (1970) *The Wealth of Nations*, Harmondsworth: Pelican.

Sohn-Rethel, A. (1975) 'Science as alienated consciousness', *Radical Science* 2/3: 65–101.

Sohn-Rethel, A. (1978) *Intellectual and Manual Labour*, London: Macmillan.

Soper, K. (1995) *What Is Nature? Culture, Politics and the Non-human*, Oxford: Blackwell.

Spallone, P. (1989) *Beyond Conception. The New Politics of Reproduction*, London: Macmillan.

Stabile, C. (1994) *Feminism and the Technological Fix*, Manchester: Manchester University Press.

Stallabrass, J. (1995) 'Empowering technology: the exploration of cyberspace', *New Left Review* 211: 3–32.

Stammers, N. (1993) 'Human rights and power', *Political Studies* 41: 70–82.

Stammers, N. (1995) 'New social movements and civil society – learning the lessons from Eastern Europe', In a selection of papers from the conference 'Alternative Futures and Popular Protest', Vol. II, Manchester: Manchester Metropolitan University.

Swabe, J. (1994) 'The socialisation of nature', Paper to University of Sussex 'Isle of Thorns' conference, November 1994. Available from the author, Amsterdam School for Social Science Research.

Sydie, R.A. (1987) *Natural Women, Cultured Men. A Feminist Perspective on Sociological Theory*, Milton Keynes: Open University Press.

Szerszynski, B. (1993) *Uncommon Ground. Moral Discourse, Foundationalism and the Environmental Movement*, Submitted by the author to Lancaster University as a thesis for the degree of Doctor of Philosophy in Sociology.

Szerszynski, B. (1996). 'On knowing what to do: environmentalism and the modern problematic', in S. Lash, B. Szerszynski and B. Wynne (eds) *Risk, Environment and Modernity: Towards a New Ecology*, London: Sage.

Tamas, P (1992) 'Neoclassical development models and environmental regulation: new dilemmas in Eastern Europe', Paper to symposium on current developments in environmental sociology, SISWO, 1018 Amsterdam, Netherlands.

Taylor, M. and Saarinen, E. (1994) *Imagologies. Media Philosophy*, London: Routledge.

Tester, K. (1991) *Animals and Society. The Humanity of Animal Rights*, Routledge: London.

Thompson, E. (1979) *The Secret State*, State Research Pamphlet No.1, London: Independent Research Publications.

Touraine, A. (1981) *The Voice and the Eye. An Analysis of Social Movements*, Cambridge: Cambridge University Press.

Touraine, A. (1995) *Critique of Modernity*, Oxford: Blackwell.

Tucker, K. (1991) 'How new are the new social movements?', *Theory, Culture and Society* 8: 75–98.

Urry, J. (1981) *The Anatomy of Capitalist Societies. The Economy, Civil Society and the State*, London: Macmillan.

Vandana, S. (1993) 'Women's indigenous knowledge and biodiversity', Chapter 11 of M. Mies and S. Shiva *Ecofeminism*, London: Zed Books.

Waddington, C. (1961) *The Nature of Life*, London: Allen and Unwin.

Wainwright, H. (1994) *Arguments for a New Left. Answering the Free Market Right*, London: Blackwell.

Wainwright, H. and Elliot, D. (1982) *The Lucas Plan. A New Trade Unionism in the Making?* London: Allison and Busby.

Ward, C. (1985) *When We Build Again*, London: Pluto.

Webster, J. (1990) 'Animal welfare and genetic engineering', Chapter 4 of P. Wheale and R. McNally *The BioRevolution. Cornucopia or Pandora's Box?*, London: Pluto.

Wesson, R. (1991) *Beyond Natural Selection*, Cambridge, Mass.: MIT.

Wheale, P. and McNally, R. (1988) *Genetic Engineering. Catastrophe or Utopia?*, Hemel Hempstead: Harvester.

Williams, R. (1973) *The Country and the City*, London: Chatto and Windus.

Wilson, A. (1994) *The Culture of Nature. North American Landscape from Disney to the Exxon Valdez*, Oxford: Blackwell.

Wilson, E.O. (1975) *Sociobiology: the New Synthesis*, Cambridge, Mass.: Harvard University Press.

Wilson, E.O. (1992) *The Diversity of Life*, Harmondsworth: Penguin.

Woods, A. and Grant, T. (1995) *Reason in Revolt. Marxist Philosophy and Modern Science*, London: Welred.

Woodward, K. (1994) 'From virtual cyborgs to biological time bombs: technocriticism and the material body', in G. Bender and T. Druckery *Culture on the Brink. Ideologies of Technology*, Seattle: Bay Press, pp. 47–64.

World Commission on Environment and Development (1987) *Our Common Future* ('The Brundtland Report'), Oxford: Oxford University Press.

Wynne, B. (1989) 'Sheepfarming after Chernobyl. A case study in communicating scientific information', *Environment* 31(2).

Wynne, B. (1991) 'Knowledges in context', *Science, Technology and Human Values*, 16(1): 111–21.

Yearley, S. (1995) 'The environmental challenge to science studies', in S. Jasanoff, G. Markle, J. Petersen, and T. Pinch (eds) *Handbook of Science and Technology Studies*, London: Sage.

Yoxen, E. (1986) *The Gene Business. Who Should Control Biotechnology?* London: Free Association.

Zohar, D. and Marshall, I. (1993) *The Quantum Society*, London: Bloomsbury.

Zvosec, C. (1984) 'Environmental deterioration in Eastern Europe', *World Affairs* 147(2): 97–127.

INDEX

Drexler, K. 128
Duden, B. 117
Duncan, S. 169, 177
Dunlap, R. 39–40, 73, 77
Durkheim, E. 10, 132

Earth First! 178
Earth Summit, Rio de Janeiro (1992) 87–9
ecofeminism 65–8, 78–9, 159
ecology 35–6; deep 38–9, 188
Economic and Philosophical Manuscripts 155
Eder, K. 176
Einstein, A. 35
Eisenberg 116, 161
Elliott, D. 192
Elsworth, S. 21–2, 25
emancipation: Bookchin's approach 188;
    commodities 139; Gorz on 183–4; Marx
    on 18, 66; virtual community 196–202;
    ways towards 15, 205
Engels, F.: class politics 176; Darwinism 75;
    on division of labour 50; on political
    strategy 28; on science 19–20, 31; on
    society and nature 18–21, 33, 40–1
entropy 34, 140
environment, sociology of 39–44
environmental: crisis 3, 29; economics
    142–4; movement 3, 27–8, 134–5, 187–8
Ereira, A. 1–2
Ernst, E. 161
Espinas, A.V. 75
Ess, C. 198
Etzioni, A. 133, 135
European Union 125
evolution, theory of 75–6

Faber, D. 30
factory farming 11, 60 (Figure 2.2), 61, 63–5,
    166
family, patriarchal 188
farming *see* agriculture, animals, cattle,
    factory farming, genetic engineering, pigs,
    sheep
feminism 5, 71, 110, 117, 125–7; *see also*
    ecofeminism
fertility 26, 76, 108–11, 117–19, 125–8
Firestone, S. 127
fish 72–3
food production 13, 146–7
forests 24, 66–7, 90
Fourier, C. 36
Foweraker, J. 171
Fowler, C. 125

Fox, W. 38
France 163
Frankfurt School 155
Franklin, S. 138
free-market economics 27–8
'free rider problem' 3
Freeman, C. 46
French Revolution 165
Freud, S. 155
Friends of the Earth 178
Fromm, E. 155

Gaia 159
Gandhi, M. 157, 160
Gandy, M. 145
Garrett, L. 26
gender 67–8, 78–80, 88–91, 108–9
genetic engineering: animals 113–14, 121–3;
    consequences 13–14; 'essence' of man 54;
    mass production 44; plant breeding
    115–16, 120–1, 124; relationship of
    humans and animals 62; reproductive
    technologies 76, 108, 129
George, S. 13
German Ideology, The 50
German Social Democrat Party 186
Germany 46
Geyer, R. 56
Giddens, A. 96–7, 100–1; (1990) 86, 170;
    (1991) 2, 86, 170; (1994) 41–3
Gilliam, A. 79
Gimenez, M. 111, 118
Glasman, J. 105
Gleick, J. 19–20
global warming 22–4, 26, 169–70
globalisation 86, 170, 172, 190
Glover, D. 169
Goddess 159
Goldsmith, E. 149
Goodman, D. 112–14, 116
Goodwin, B. 31, 37–8, 80–2, 122
Goodwin, M. 169, 177
Gorz, A. 27, 182–7, 191, 194–5
Gosling, P. 194
Gouldner, A. 134
Gramsci, A. 135
Grant, T. 19
Greater London Council (GLC) 192, 193, 202
Greece, ancient 141
green movement: consumerism 14, 144, 145,
    161; deep ecology 38–9, 188; philosophy
    108; politics 15, 27, 153–4, 160, 170–1,

INDEX

South East Economic Development Strategy
(SEEDS) 193
Soviet Union 21, 132, 166
Spallone, P. 108
specialisation, work 5
'species being' and 'natural being' 57, 114,
155, 173, 183, 203
Spencer, H. 47, 75
Spinardi, G. 163
Stabile, C. 151
Stallabrass, J. 196, 198, 201
Stammers, N. 132, 171, 179
state: as alienated community 164–6;
environmental knowledge and 168–70;
knowledge and the 166–8; power 15, 177;
role in green utopia 185, 188–9
Sussex University 201; see also Mass-
Observation Archive
Sydie, R.A. 77, 108
systems theory 52–3
Szerszynski, B. 4, 95, 100

Tahiti 164
Tamas, P. 50
Taylor, M. 200
Taylorism 63
Tester, K. 72, 73
Thatcher, M. 193
thermodynamics, laws of 34–6
Thompson, E. 165
Touraine, A. 172–4
tourism 140
trade unions 16, 172, 183, 185
tradition 157–8
'Tragedy of the Commons' thesis 3–4
Trotsky, L. 176
Tucker, K. 179
turkeys 122

unemployment 195
United Kingdom see Britain

United Nations Conference on Environment
and Development 87–9
United States of America (USA) 23, 46, 47,
134, 161
Urry, J.: (1981) 135–6; Lash and (1987) 177;
Lash and (1994) 138, 199; MacNaghten
and (1995) 20–1, 47, 82, 140
utopianism: green 15, 17, 181, 182–9, 202;
socialist 36–7

Vaneigem, R. 142
Vienna/Montreal agreements 169

Waddington, C. 121
Wainwright, H. 48, 174, 192
Walker, R. see Sayer
Ward, C. 146–7
Weber, M. 40, 45
Webster, J. 114
Wesson, R. 80–1, 122
Western Union 197
Wheale, P. 114
Williams, R. 15, 148–50, 152–3
Wilson, A. 150
Wilson, E.O. 24, 27–8, 49, 81
Woman on the Edge of Time 127
women's movement 177; see also ecofeminism,
feminism, gender, reproductive
technology
Woodhouse, E. 45
Woods, A. 19
Woodward, K. 200
worker consciousness 172
World Commission on Environment and
Development 27
Wynne, B. 167–8

Yoxen, E. 103, 108, 120<SP_IND.
Zohar, D. 36–7
Zvosec, C. 50

224

80 must be some correspondence?
83 material processes distinguished from disco...
95 landscape reminding them who they are
96 not skeptical about serene
131 "environmental problems" can be attributed to
   division of labour
132 campaign against "community"
134 public opinion
141 green theory as alienated knowledge of
   fetishized nature
145 green consumption